Natural Resource Policymaking
in Developing Countries

Natural Resource Policymaking

in Developing Countries

Environment, Economic Growth, and Income Distribution

William Ascher and Robert Healy

Duke University Press · *Durham and London 1990*

© 1990 Duke University Press
All rights reserved
Printed in the United States of America
on acid-free paper ∞
Library of Congress Cataloging-in-Publication Data
appear on the last page of this book.

To

Beckie Ascher (1909-89)

For

Matthew Healy (1981-   )

Contents

Any book about policymaking is necessarily a book about dealing with complexity. Policymaking, whether in natural resources or other areas, has been analyzed by scholars in terms of efficiency in the allocation of scarce resources, the dynamics of contending interest groups, and the psychology and needs of individual decisionmakers. Yet actual policymaking is a yeasty blend of all these considerations—further complicated by the fact that many policies are not the result of a single decision, but of an incremental process with many turning points and many sources of influence.

Natural resource policymaking, however, seems to be subject to its own special complexity. For one thing, we expect most natural resources to be available to society over long periods of time, as underlined by the ever-present references in laws, speeches, and position papers to "duties to future generations." This long time frame means that it is particularly difficult to evaluate whether natural resource policies have actually been successful. It is easy to make extravagant claims of future disaster, and equally easy to shrug off the possibility of future difficulties. Another source of complexity is the fact that natural resource management frequently involves biological as well as socioeconomic factors. This is particularly true in the case of renewable resources such as forests and of environmental systems such as watersheds or wildlife habitats. Policymakers often have difficulty incorporating biological information in their decisions, or even understanding what information is relevant.

Additional elements of complexity are added when one considers natural resource policy in developing countries. In most developing countries natural resources are owned by a bewildering variety of individuals and institutions, including government agencies, state corporations, villages, and tribes. Frequently the distribution of property rights among these entities is either unclear or in active dispute. In many cases, natural resources are open access commons, available without charge to the first to take them—and hence subject to chronic overexploitation. In a large part of the world, natural resources are also a mainstay of the poor, particularly the rural poor, who rely on them for food and fuel, and who often bear the brunt of land degradation and floods when resources are mismanaged. A final complexity, just coming to the surface, is the increased involvement of nongovernmental groups (NGOS), both indigenous and foreign, in resource policy debates. Representing the poor, environmental concerns, or both, these groups increasingly participate in resource decisionmaking on behalf of those affected by negative externalities of resource use and of future generations of users.

This book is an attempt to use systematic analysis to confront and, we hope, to dissect the complexities of natural resource policymaking in developing countries. We approach the problem from two starting points. First, we integrate natural resource policymaking into the framework of economic development theory, a task made easier by the recent explosion of theoretical work on ''sustainable development.'' This provides some useful insights into how resources are related to the traditional developmental goals of income growth and poverty alleviation. Second, we use a framework, originally developed by Harold Lasswell and elaborated upon by other policy scientists, to analyze the phases of policymaking. The phase framework proves to be particularly useful in identifying points where mistakes in policymaking are chronically made.

The greater portion of this book consists of applying our theoretical frameworks to cases of actual resource policymaking in several developing countries. Case studies include examinations of the Green Revolution in agriculture, the replacement of natural forests by plantations of fast-growing exotic trees, the harnessing of water resources by large dams, the resettlement of large populations into jungle ''frontiers,'' and agricultural irrigation projects. Although the case studies do not cover all possible resource policies, they represent a reasonably good variety of resources where environmentalists—and an increasing number of development planners—have claimed that bad policy choices are chronically made.

The emphasis on the case studies is on how decisions are made on *new* uses of natural resources—new ways to increase agricultural or forest productivity, new sources of hydroelectric power or irrigation water, and the occupation of new spatial frontiers. We believe that decisions on the transformation of resources provide particularly good examples of how complex decisionmaking systems work, and on how various parties at interest respond to those decisions. In many cases, we find that these transformations prove to be "bad" decisions, leading not only to environmental degradation but sometimes to financial disaster. Yet when most of the cases are examined closely, decisions that are bad for the interests of some parts of society are good for other parts. This distributional complexity cuts across nearly all of the cases. Indeed, in many cases (for example, the aborted dams and plantation project) the economic failure of decisions is a direct result of reactions by those who feel injured—or at least not sufficiently benefited—by the decision.

Our study is the result of a collaboration between two scholars—one a political scientist, the other an economist—and a group of experienced development practitioners. Much of the material was initially prepared for, and discussed in, the 1987–88 and 1988–89 sessions of the Program in International Development Policy, a program that brings senior officials from government and the private sector in developing countries to Duke University for year-long training and research on problems of economic development. Other cases were prepared by the Senior and Graduate Seminar in Natural Resource Policymaking of Duke University's Institute of Policy Sciences. The seminar drew on students in Public Policy Studies as well as participants from the Duke School of Forestry and Environmental Studies.

Acknowledgments

The Fellows of the Program in International Development Policy for 1987–89 provided invaluable case development and stimulating discussions of the analytical framework:

Mohamed Amr—Egypt (government of Egypt)
Arunoday Bhattacharjya—India (government of India)
Doreen Crompton—United Kingdom (World Bank)
Huang Fangyi—China (Center of International Studies)
Brayn Khunguni—Malawi (government of Malawi)
Krishna Kant Sharma—India (government of India)
Alangudy Srinivasan—India (Jaiprakash Industries)

Duke University graduate and undergraduate students similarly contributed essential case materials and helped to sharpen the analysis of natural resource policymaking as participants in the Graduate and Senior Seminar on Natural Resource Policymaking:

Kiran Asher (India)
Merrill Buice
Kristen Clements
Suzanne Duryea
Christin Eaton
Charles Ganote
Christopher McLinn
Herman Pye III

Moira Quinlan
Mohammad Rafiq (Pakistan)
Bindu Sharma (India)
Yasuhisa Tanaka (Japan)

While this book could not have been written without the contributions of these participants, it is important to note that the chapters based on the case studies were written, interpreted, and structured by the authors, such that any errors in interpretation or fact are the responsibility of the authors rather than the PIDP Fellows or the participants in the Graduate and Senior Seminar on Natural Resource Policymaking.

Special thanks are also due to Prof. Garry Brewer, Yale School of Forestry and Environmental Studies; Mr. R. Max Peterson, retired head of the U.S. Forest Service; and Dr. Visvanathan Rajagopalan, Vice President for Sectoral Policy of the World Bank, for their presentations to the seminars.

William Ascher
Robert Healy

1
Introduction

Each year the forest recedes a little farther up the hillsides, and each year more soil washes away. The locale may be the Himalayan foothills of Nepal, the uplands of Honduras, or the islands of Luzon or Mindanao in the Philippines. The process at work is by now a familiar one, the subject of both scholarly studies and innumerable media accounts.[1] Impoverished peasant cultivators, impelled by physical scarcity of land or by institutional barriers that keep them from more easily cultivable land, are trying to make a living by bringing new land into production.

The land they are clearing is marginal, in several senses of the word. It rarely yields a bounteous crop, and its meager production tends to decline over time as topsoil and nutrients are lost. Cultivation on the slopes is inconvenient, sometimes even dangerous, to the farmers. The loss of forest cover reduces wood supply, diminishes wildlife numbers and diversity, and can ultimately change the area's microclimate. Perhaps worst of all are the effects downstream—higher floods, silted hydroelectric reservoirs, clogged irrigation works. The poor farmers are at once mortgaging their own future and imposing substantial economic costs on others.

The details of this process of resource misuse, environmental degradation, and impoverishment obviously vary greatly from place to place, due to physical, social, and institutional factors.[2] But common to a diversity of specific situations are links that tie together resource use, environmental quality, and economic development, and that tie the resource-use system to inequalities in the distribution of income and resource ownership. The links may be relatively simple, as in the case of the peasant farmers too poor to conserve resources for tomorrow and with no incentive to mitigate the externalities they impose on others. Or they may be very complex—as we find when we demonstrate how achievement of higher incomes by the rich can increase environmentally destructive behavior by the poor. Many of the links in some way involve rural land use, whether for agriculture or forestry. These links and their relationship to public policy make up the subject of this book. But we suspect that similar mechanisms could be discovered in urban and industrial development, energy supply and consumption, and national choices involving trade, technology, and sectoral subsidies.

Some of the ground we cover will be familiar; it is difficult for any well-informed person to be unaware of the Third World's resource and environmental crisis, whether it takes the form of deforestation, soil erosion, or rampant pollution. In the course of this book, we will document the extent of this crisis and set forth the many ways in which it manifests itself. But our purpose goes well beyond that.

First, we want to integrate recent thinking about resources and environment into the mainstream of development theory. Over the years society has learned many lessons about how to promote development and researchers and practitioners have created an enormous body of hard-won knowledge. It would be most unfortunate if resources and environment, which in the real world have such complex links with the overall development process, are not clearly placed within this larger theoretical context. This leads us very directly to looking at the distribution of income. Since the early 1970s, income distribution—particularly the share of income going to the very poor—has become an explicit focus of development policy. Encouraged in great part by the World Bank's emphasis on the alleviation of ''absolute poverty,'' concern for distribution has affected the allocation of development budgets at both national and international levels. Distribution has also become an important focus of the theoretical and empirical literature on development. This literature has indicated that income distribution is not only an *effect* of development but is in many cases a *determinant* of both levels and patterns of development.

We will argue in this book that distribution is central to resource and environmental management as well. For example, the distribution of income determines how individual decisionmakers compare future consumption to current consumption and thereby helps determine the rate at which they will consume resource capital. The distribution of ownership rights to income-producing assets, such as cropland and forests, is crucial not only to the determination of absolute and relative incomes but also to how these assets are managed. The distribution of management authority among individuals, governments, and community institutions is critical to resource allocation. In many cases, the effective lack of management authority leads to a "tragedy of the commons" in which forest, soil, or wildlife resources are used at unsustainable rates and thereby destroyed. When we consider the many links between resources/environment and development, distribution regularly appears as a key mediating factor. Therefore, in relating resources and environment to development theory it appears worthwhile to look with particular care at the theory of income and asset distribution.

Second, we want to emphasize the role of public policy, reflecting our conviction that development can be promoted or retarded by public institutions. These institutions subsidize certain activities or products and tax others, ration access to physical resources or to markets, regulate private business, and engage in investment and production through state-owned enterprises. Surely public policies must have a great deal to do with why resource-rich countries fail to develop, while other nations take fuller advantage of much more modest endowments. We will argue in this book that the policies that matter are not merely resource and environmental policies, but a much broader policy set, including policies on income distribution and asset ownership.

We adopt the analytic approach of the *policy sciences* to explain why current styles of resource-based development so often produce little economic growth and negative environmental and distributional consequences. The policy sciences approach emphasizes the policy *process,* rather than outcomes alone.[3] There have been a number of recent studies of political and institutional factors in resource management, both in the United States and other developed countries and, increasingly, in the Third World.[4] Our study is the first, however, to apply a formal policy process framework to resource management in developing countries.

Reflecting both the policy sciences approach and our own somewhat practical bent, our object is not to outline a set of ideal policies and leave others to worry about the realities of implementation. The policy sciences approach gives equal attention to policy formulation and to policy implementation. In the Third World, implementation difficulties are often particularly prevalent, and in many instances one might identify a serious "implementation gap." The implementation gap is the complex of obstacles that makes it extremely hard for the institutional system to obtain results even after a problem has been correctly diagnosed and a sensible policy has been framed. It includes such familiar pitfalls as political rivalry, regional and ethnic jealousy, bureaucratic ineptitude, and outright corruption. We believe that institutions matter—and so do the human beings who run them. Therefore our attempts at policy analysis will include a heavy dose of institutional analysis and concern for how policies actually are implemented.

The Theory of Economic Development

Early post-wwii thinking about economic development emphasized growth in per capita income as the primary objective of development efforts. Early development theorists were not oblivious to world poverty but generally believed that it could best be alleviated within a setting of sustained overall income growth. Basing their expectation largely on the experience of Western industrial countries during the nineteenth century, development theorists anticipated that the operation of labor markets would ensure that the benefits of increasing per capita GNP would automatically "trickle down" to the poor. Even if trickle-down failed to occur or took place only slowly, it was thought, economic growth would enable governments to provide services to the poor.

As development theory evolved, there was a series of emphases on specific ways to achieve income growth—physical capital, human capital, food self-sufficiency, basic needs, appropriate technology, export promotion, and high technology.[5] During the 1970s, in part due to the ceaseless emphasis on the subject by World Bank President Robert S. MacNamara, new attention was paid to equitable distribution of income as a parallel and in many ways coequal goal of development (MacNamara 1973; Chenery 1974). Distinctions were made between the relatively poor, defined as those receiving less than a specified level (often one-third) of national per capita income, and the absolutely poor, often defined on the basis of inadequacy of nutritional intake. Through the 1970s, the World Bank increasingly directed both concessional and market-rate lending to the poorer countries and to types of development projects, such as rural development, that were intended to benefit low-income populations (World Bank 1983). This emphasis on poverty alleviation was also adopted by other development institutions, including the U.S. Agency for International Development (USAID).

During the 1980s, attention has turned to natural resources and the environment. It is argued that abuse of these endowments is not only harmful in its own right, but can ultimately constrain income growth. Forests, watersheds, grasslands, and fisheries provide important flows of economically valuable services, particularly vital in countries with large rural populations. One observer has called these renewable resources "the often-forgotten underpinnings of much economic activity" (Eckholm 1986, 7).

Sustainable Development

The slogan "sustainable development" has been coined to bring attention to the role of resources and environment in economic development. As a slogan and a symbol, sustainable development has taken on many connotations and implications. From our perspective, however, it is useful to begin by defining the term analytically, and only then sketch out its history as a slogan.

Sustainable development can be defined most generally as the development path that maximizes the net long-term benefits to mankind. Thus sustainable development is not merely the maximum exploitation of a particular resource for an indefinite period of time (or "maximum sustainable yield," to use the forestry term). That strategy would not necessarily yield the greatest benefit; it does not permit drawing on the natural resource endowment (or converting that endowment) in order to increase reproducible capital or employment opportunities that might, in some circumstances, produce greater long-term benefits. The idea of a sustainable yield forever is not even theoretically meaningful for exhaustible resources. Thinking about sustainable development requires thinking about the possibilities of reconstituting the resource base; about shifting from reliance on one resource to another; about converting part of the natural resource base into other forms of wealth and capital. In short, thinking about sustainable development requires thinking comprehensively and, when it comes to resource management, acting comprehensively. Thus the idea of sustainable development is an inherently complicating element in determining a natural resource exploitation strategy; such a strategy must go beyond the natural resource base to analyze the pace and purposes of using the capital generated from the natural resource endowment.

Therefore it is rather curious that it was largely the environmentalists who invoked sustainable development to argue that while resource abuse can severely limit development, wise use of resources and safeguarding the free services provided by environmental systems can actually spur the overall development process. From their perspective, sustainable development legitimizes conservation by casting it as the guardian of long-term growth potential. It is for this reason that the idea of sustainable development has been embraced by the worldwide environmental movement, which is manifested through thousands of nongovernmental environmental organizations (NGOs in United Nations parlance) in both developed and developing countries.

Yet sustainable development has also been widely adopted in rhetoric and often in practice by a variety of development institutions. For them, the concept legitimizes development, by a) defining the ultimate objective as a net long-term benefit for mankind (and not in terms of preserving particular natural systems for the sake of such preservation); and b) emphasizing that development, a reasonable degree of conservation, and careful husbanding of natural resources are all compatible. Sustainable development thinking is influencing both environmental policy and development policy.

The concept of sustainable development arose virtually simultaneously with the increase in public interest in the Third World's environment. At the United Nations Conference on the Human Environment, held in Stockholm in 1972, it was widely believed that there would be a split between the developed nations, seen as willing to accept somewhat slower economic growth in exchange for environmental protection, and the developing countries, expected to want growth at any price. But the split was effectively contained by Western environmentalists' endorsement of the need for Third World economic development and continual reference to the argument that continued development was necessary to finance environmental protection.[6] Barbara Ward and Rene Dubos, in preparing the book associated with the conference, devoted three of fifteen chapters to the developing regions, with much of the text devoted to problems of development as well as traditional environmental concerns. "It is not difficult . . .," they wrote, "to understand the driving dedication of governments in developing countries to get their peoples out of a trap of poverty more locked and complicated than any experienced in earlier times" (Ward and Dubos 1972: 147).

A milestone in the creation of both the concept of sustainable development and the environmental NGOs' commitment to the concept was the 1980 publication of the World Conservation Strategy (International Union for the Conservation of Nature and Natural Resources 1980). The Strategy was a product of the International Union for the Conservation of Nature and

Natural Resources (IUCN), a prestigious international scientific organization based in Switzerland; the World Wildlife Fund, an important environmental NGO; and the United Nations Environment Programme.

The authors of the Strategy argued that "humanity's relationship with the biosphere . . . will continue to deteriorate until a new international economic order is achieved . . . and sustainable modes of development become the rule rather than the exception" (IUCN 1980, 1). The Strategy then asserted that among the prerequisites for sustainable development is the conservation of living resources, a process involving three specific objectives:

(a) to maintain essential ecological processes and life-support systems;
(b) to preserve genetic diversity (the range of genetic material found in the world's living organisms);
(c) to ensure the sustainable utilization of species and ecosystems.

The first two of these objectives are preservation-oriented; they express limits on development strategies. Even with respect to these, however, the Strategy tended to describe benefits in human-centered, sometimes even economic, terms. For example, it pointed out the role of ecosystems in cleansing pollution and recycling nutrients, and the importance of preserving gene pools to improve strains of cultivated crops. Ignoring the preservation objectives, the Strategy contended, could threaten "human survival and development" and "the security of the many industries that use living resources" (IUCN 1980, 1).

The last objective, however, was what really put environmental considerations (and the environmental NGOs) into the center of the economic development debate for the first time. The Strategy began its discussion of sustainable use not with an admonition to limit development but with an endorsement of the need to develop in order to be able to conserve: "Probably the most serious conservation problem faced by developing countries is the lack of rural development." This was followed by a quite startling offer: "This section [of the Strategy document] recommends means of helping rural communities to conserve, as the essential basis of the development they so sorely need." As conceived in the Strategy, environmental and resource considerations were not merely *constraints* on development, but *sources* of development.

After its initial publication, the Strategy was reprinted in several countries and translated into several languages. Its release was followed by the preparation of a large number of "national conservation strategies" that represented attempts to apply its principle of development through conservation to a wide variety of specific situations. At least twelve national conservation strategies have been prepared to date, representing countries as diverse as Great Britain, Nepal, Australia, and Zambia. An additional thirty-nine are reported to be in preparation (World Resources Institute 1988; for example, see Johnson 1983; Government of Australia 1984; Bass 1987). The prominence of sustainable development in a number of reports issued by environmental organizations in developing countries indicates the eclipse of the presumption that the Third World cannot afford to worry about the environment and natural resource abuse.

This new interest in sustainable development was accompanied by an increasing sophistication among scientists, government environmental officials, and NGO activists in understanding the scope of interactions between environment and development. For the first time, significant attention was paid to industrial and urban pollution in developing countries, as well as the more traditional issues of soil erosion, water supply, and wildlife. In 1984, the International Chamber of Commerce and the United Nations Environment Programme sponsored a World Industry Conference on Environmental Management, with representation from both the business and environmental communities. The industrial accidents that occurred in Mexico City; Cubatao, Brazil; and Bhopal, India that year underlined the new set of environmental issues that were arising as developing countries around the world developed substantial industrial sectors and huge urban population concentrations.

In 1987, the World Commission on Environment and Development, established by the United Nations and chaired by Norwegian Prime Minister Gro Harlem Brundtland, issued a report calling for "global sustainable development" (World Commission on Environment and Development 1987, 343). Like the World Conservation Strategy, the Brundtland Commission asserted that environmental protection and economic growth were compatible, even mutually supporting, objectives. "The Commission's overall assessment," the report contended, "is that the international economy must speed up world growth while respecting the environmental constraints" (World Commission on Environment and Development 1987, 89).

Sustainable development has quite recently attained considerable respectability in the international development community. The World Bank, pressured by U.S. environmental groups and counseled by the Brundtland Commission to make "a fundamental commitment to sustainable development,'' has increased its environmental analysis staff and is preparing an environmental issues paper for each of the countries in which it operates (World Bank 1988). Bank President Barber Conable has noted that in 1988 one-third of all Bank projects contained specific environmental components (Conable 1989). International aid agencies and private groups promoting Third World development have endorsed sustainable development, and focus increasingly on identifying projects—such as afforestation and water-shed rehabilitation—that are specifically intended for environmental improvement. The head of the Overseas Development Council recently endorsed the "current rethinking" that "environmental preservation does not have to be seen as a trade-off for the elimination of poverty in the Third World. Instead, integration of these twin issues will be central to the global agenda in the 1990s" (Sewell 1989). The president of the American Agricultural Economics Association recently noted that sustainable development is a concept "that is increasingly guiding environmental policy and, to a lesser extent, agricultural, economic and development policy." She notes that sustainable development challenges the agricultural economics profession "[to reconsider] questions that neoclassical economists have tended to neglect" (Batie 1989).

The focus of many advocates of sustainable development goes beyond "systems of nature." Such people and organizations—both in developed countries and in the Third World—tend to have deep sympathy with the alleviation of absolute poverty; a tendency to favor small-scale, locally controlled development projects and the coevolution of appropriate social structures (Norgaard 1981); and an understanding that sustained increases in per capita income are necessary for social progress and even for long-term environmental protection. A statement released by a group of NGOs in conjunction with the 1989 World Bank Group annual meeting in Washington, D.C., clearly expresses this multiple agenda. The groups noted that the current global state of affairs, which "threatens the well-being of not just people, but all life" reflects not only the "lack of proper maintenance of life-giving ecological systems" but also "lack of equal distribution of the world's resources—both among and within nations . . ." The statement expressed concern with the "nature of the economic development process that is directly responsible for a deepening poverty, severe environmental degradation, the further marginalization of women, children, indigenous people, and other vulnerable groups, and, in many instances the deterioration of basic political, economic, cultural, and social rights" (Anonymous 1989).

"Sustainable development" is in many ways a catchphrase whose breadth makes it susceptible to many definitions and which can be appropriated by quite diverse groups. Nevertheless, a substantial proportion of the identification with the concept comes from individuals and groups concerned not just with environment but with human economic progress, poverty alleviation, and the empowerment of excluded groups. Reflecting this multifaceted concern, we propose to define sustainable development as a process of development that achieves the following goals:

(a) high per capita consumption sustainable for an indefinite period, which implies, among other things, an optimal rate of use of natural resources over time;
(b) distributional equity;
(c) environmental protection, including protection of biological diversity and the continued functioning of complex natural systems;
(d) participation of all sectors of society in decisionmaking.

Thus the fundamental problem for sustainable development, as we define it, is: How do we achieve economic growth with equity and participation while wisely using natural resources and preserving the environment?

Our hypothesis is that the individual components of the sustainable development agenda are interrelated, and that all depend on having appropriate public policies. The new attention paid to environment and resources will be most effective, even in terms of achieving high per capita consumption, if we simultaneously try to improve distributional equity and promote participation. Our "bias for hope" (to use Albert Hirschman's phrase) is not only that better resource and environmental management can promote income growth, but that appropriate policies can allow us to move toward all our goals simultaneously. Rather than trade-offs, we are blessed with complementarities.

Policy Process Weaknesses in Responding to the Need for Sustainability

When natural resource policies have tried to cope with the need for sustainability, government and policy performance have often been very poor. While it has been argued that the very origin of government was based on the need to control natural resources—whether the waters of the Nile or the Tigris-Euphrates or the carefully terraced agriculture of highland Peru—it seems abundantly clear that conventional governmental structures are not adept at transforming natural resource use in sustainable ways. We believe that this inadequacy stems from several weaknesses inherent in the conventional policymaking process (see table 1).

If sustainability means paying attention to future as well as present benefits of resource exploitation, then the well-known phenomenon of the politician's short-term time horizon becomes a central problem. Intergenerational concerns are difficult to address because future generations cannot be directly represented. Future generations are, in a sense, the "new colonials"; decisions that governments make today determine the resources available to those who come after (Bock 1967). The problem goes far beyond politicians and politics: the conventional governmental apparatus also lacks a built-in incentive to focus on long-term sustainability. The traditional government agency that oversees highway or bridge construction, or allocates financial resources to agriculture, has little institutional interest in the sustainability of any given resource-using venture. Long before a given venture proves to be unsustainable, that agency has gone on

Table 1   Characteristics of the Conventional Governmental Policymaking Process and Requisites for Pursuing Sustainable Development

Typical characteristics of policymaking	Sustainable development needs not well served by those characteristics
Short time horizons	Emphasis on *long-term* net benefits
Lack of long-term project-specific accountability	Incentives to focus on *long-term sustainability*
	Incentives to incur only moderate risks
Functional fragmentation	Analytic comprehensiveness to assess *net* benefits
	Coordination to balance activities to maximize *net* benefits and ensure sustainability
Weakness of development planning	Emphasis on *long-term* net benefits
	Analytic comprehensiveness to assess *net* benefits
Centralization	Adaptiveness
	Micro-level knowledge to ensure sustainability
	Coevolution of local social systems
	Participation

to administering other projects, setting other policies, or spending other monies. If the ministries of public works and agriculture will survive regardless of whether a given cultivation strategy, resettlement venture, dam, irrigation system, or plantation is ultimately successful or unsuccessful, then there is little connection between sustainability and the incentive structure facing that ministry.

The development planning function—the single most future-oriented and potentially comprehensive analytic function in government—has been notoriously weak in developing countries. To be sure, we must acknowledge the absurdity of expecting development planning to produce definitive, binding five-year plans that need no midstream modifications. But we must also judge the more realistic and modest potentials of planning— namely focusing greater attention on future impacts and requiring that technical analysis be applied whenever significant policies are being formulated—as being largely unfulfilled when it comes to natural resource policymaking.

Sustainable development's emphasis on *net* long-term benefits also reveals why conventional governmental structures often fare poorly. The sum total of direct costs and benefits of natural resource use plus the less direct externalities cuts across the functionally specific mandates of the standard governmental agency. Whether in *calculating* the net benefit (a formidable analytic challenge) or *administering* programs and projects so as to find the balance that yields the greatest net benefit, the fragmentation of government into functionally specific entities typically pits one agency against another in the rivalry of "bureaucratic politics." This rivalry is completely divorced from the goal of seeking the proper balance of resource use, resource conservation, employment, population distribution, and other factors that would have to be struck for the greatest net benefits to be pursued.

The natural resource transformations explored in this volume are necessarily bolder than the usual maintenance efforts of government to continue to regulate resource uses, maintain order, deliver the mail, and so on. Boldness is often commendable—"nothing ventured, nothing gained"— but the key question is whether those who decide that society ought to undertake a given risk are themselves subject to, or at least accountable for, that risk. Yet the governments of most developing countries are typically highly centralized, such that the decisions on natural resource use are largely made by people who are subjected to neither the direct costs and benefits nor the externalities of the projects they launch. Thus mechanisms are typically lacking to "internalize" the risks of such projects to those who make the decisions. Many initiatives to transform the natural resource endowment or its uses reflect an inordinate "Pollyanna optimism." They are often also presented as benefiting everyone, and producing indirect costs for no one ("Pollyanna optimality"). Therefore projects that are excessively risky to ecosystems and people remote from the capital often go unchecked by officials who bear little risk or accountability. Indeed, the more remote the site of the project, the less political risk and accountability faced by the centralized government.

The divorce of project- or program-specific risks from the risks faced by political leaders often leads to the following pattern. A flamboyant endowment-transforming initiative is launched because of its political attractiveness. As the initiative unfolds, serious flaws are revealed, especially in unanticipated consequences that escaped notice by the cursory and fragmented analytic effort undertaken prior to launching the project or program. However, the initiative is maintained because of the political risk to the leaders if it were ignominiously abandoned or even modified. This pattern denies resource management of the necessary *adaptiveness* that sustainability requires.

Centralization also means that natural resource policymakers, typically far removed from the ecosystems under their control, lack intimate knowledge of the constitution and operation of these ecosystems. Insofar as sustainability depends on how people and resources mesh on the "micro-level," decisions made at the center are prone to the error of endorsing plans that appear to be sustainable on paper but fail in the field.

Finally, centralization is often at odds with the coevolution of social systems to cope with changing situations. Organizing takes time, energy, and resources, and therefore in poor countries typically occurs only when it is justified by the organization's capacity to control outcomes. When centralized government dominates over decisionmaking—and especially when it controls financing—local organizing tends to languish, and thus the communities in direct contact with the resource endowment may fail to develop their own capacity to sustain their uses of the natural resources (for example, to deal with common property in a disciplined and equitable manner).

These typical shortcomings of government policymaking should not be cause for despair. Indeed, it is heartening that many failed natural resource initiatives can be traced to faulty policymaking procedures and structures *that can be remedied*. While the conventional approaches to natural resource policymaking may have serious weaknesses, there are unconventional structures and procedures that offer considerable hope. Throughout this volume, we encounter such approaches: river valley authorities designed such that policymakers have a stronger institutional interest in the long-term sustainability of the valley's ecosystem; successful community organizing to counteract overcentralization; constructive debates between critics and advocates of development projects that permit learning from past mistakes and better accommodation of environmental and equity concerns. We have not one but two levels to approach improving natural resource policy: the substantive content of the policies themselves and the policymaking process through which these policies are developed and applied. This book examines both levels and the connections between them.

The Structure of the Book

The book has three major parts. First, a theoretical framework is elaborated that demonstrates the interrelationships among economic production, natural resources, the environment, and the distribution of income and wealth. The framework allows us to trace the complex impacts which change in one of these elements has on all the others, emphasizing impact sequences that start with deliberate attempts by policymakers to raise the level of economic production. This "impact framework" is introduced in chapter 2.

The second part of the book applies the impact framework to major development efforts that entail transforming resource endowments and uses: the modernization of agriculture and forestry (chapter 3), population resettlement schemes (chapter 4), large dams (chapter 5), and irrigation projects (chapter 6). Each chapter contains many examples taken from the literature and from case studies specially prepared for this book. The cases presented here are only a subset of the enormous number of possible examples which could be used to explore the implications of our analytic framework. They cover several important sectors, and come from a number of important developing countries, including India, Sri Lanka, Indonesia, Brazil, and Mexico. We are confident that equally persuasive cases could be found in energy, fisheries, and other resource sectors.

The third part of the book analyzes current and potential roles of public policy. Chapter 7 analyzes the process of resources policymaking from the point at which problems reach the policy agenda (initiation stage) through successive stages of policy analysis and consideration of alternatives (estimation stage), authoritative selection, implementation and, eventually, policy evaluation and termination. We observe that each stage of the policy process seems to be associated with characteristic pitfalls, mistakes that are made again and again, in very different sectors and in many parts of the world.

Chapter 8 analyzes possibilities for policy reform intended to address the pitfalls identified in chapter 7. Using the policy process framework, it evaluates the usefulness of such frequently suggested reforms as comprehensive planning, decentralized administration, citizen participation, and greater use of market incentives. The chapter offers concrete suggestions for improving administrative structures and the policies they formulate and implement.

In a seminal book on development theory first published in 1953, Ragnar Nurkse observed that "in discussions of the problem of economic development, a phrase that crops up frequently is 'the vicious circle of poverty.' . . . It implies a circular constellation of forces tending to act and react upon one another in such a way as to keep a poor country in a state of poverty" (Nurkse 1953, 4). Nurkse further observed that "fortunately, the circle is not unbreakable. And once it is broken at any point, the very fact that the relation is circular tends to make for cumulative advance. We should perhaps hesitate to call the circle vicious; it can become beneficent" (Nurkse 1953, 11).

One has only to consider the most obvious examples of resource misuse or environmental degradation to realize the aptness of the "vicious circle" metaphor. Consider, for example, the tragic story of desertification in the African Sahel. Population growth and the sinking of tubewells in desert oases led nomadic pastoralists to build up flocks of sheep and goats. As the ratio of animals to biomass increased, the ability of the grasses and shrubs to reproduce themselves began to fall. Yet grazing pressure continued because the marginal return to an additional sheep or goat was still positive, though sharply declining. The damage to vegetation became severe, even irreversible. Animals and people began to starve.

The same sort of circular process of degradation is taking place worldwide among farmers practicing swidden or slash-and-burn agriculture. Traditionally, swidden cultivation has involved clearing small plots of forestland, perhaps two to three hectares at a time, burning to release nutrients locked up in vegetation, cultivating row crops for a few years until the soil's fertility has been exhausted, and then abandoning the land to recover in a long "forest fallow" period. Studies (for example, UNESCO 1983) have shown that the swidden system may well be the most economically efficient way for a sparse population to obtain income from a tropical forest. But as the ratio of people to land has increased, swidden cycles have steadily shortened; for example, in India, a survey of the extensive literature reveals the generalization that the swidden cycle has been reduced to three to six years, compared with twenty to thirty in the past (UNESCO 1983, 1: 47). The shortening of the cycle greatly reduces the land's ability to regenerate, either in terms of soil nutrients or in terms of the quality of the forest that can grow up. This can have a serious impact on the income prospects of the cultivator. For example, in Peru one researcher observing the shortening of forest fallow periods predicted that "[a]griculture without chemical fertilizers will then not be possible for many decades" (Smith 1987, 34–35). As in the case of desertification, the more the poor try to maintain their present level of income, the more they foreclose income opportunities in the future.

These two examples, though very important on a world scale, show only some of the simplest of the many vicious circles uniting resources, distribution, and development. Moreover, because they have the rural poor at their center, they might be taken to imply that the peasant cultivator is in some way to blame for their creation. Nothing could be farther from the truth. We believe that even these simple circles are bound up in a very complex web involving income shares of the rich and their attendant investment and consumption behavior, national and regional development policies, the nature and distribution of property rights, and the way in which large-scale development projects are designed and financed. The observable resource-degrading behavior by the poor is in most cases symptomatic of a larger system gone awry.

In this chapter, we will use the circle metaphor to show the complex interrelationships among four key aspects of sociophysical production: economic production, the distribution of income, natural resources, and the environment (see figure 1). Each aspect deserves some elaboration.

Economic production is the level, source, and composition of the goods and services produced by the economy at any point in time. It includes the sectoral makeup of the economy (for example, the portion of GDP originating in agriculture), the degree to which production is export or national

Figure 1   Aspects of Sociophysical Development

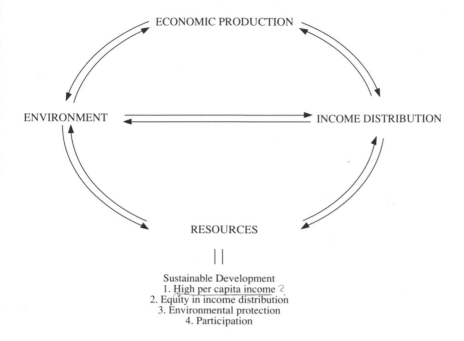

Sustainable Development
1. High per capita income 2
2. Equity in income distribution
3. Environmental protection
4. Participation

market oriented, the scale of enterprises, the division of production among state and private enterprises, and the degree to which production is capital or labor intensive.

Income distribution includes the functional distribution (i.e., how much to labor and to capital), the size distribution among recipients of different income levels (including the incidence of absolute poverty, however defined), the distribution of in-kind income such as government services or the enjoyment of environmental quality, and the regional distribution. As used in our analysis, this aspect includes such distribution-related attributes as savings and investment propensities associated with various income classes, and the ability of various groups to improve their education and health ("human capital formation").

Natural resources include a wide variety of tangible natural endowments, including land, water, timber, and minerals. Resources may be renewable (timber) or nonrenewable (fossil fuels). Resources generally require some form of human manipulation (for example, harvesting timber, mining ores, or channeling water) before they become economically useful. Among the salient aspects of natural resource use are the processes of exploration, exploitation, processing, use, and disposal of residuals.

Environment refers to the natural systems that provide the background or surroundings for human activity. Environmental systems encompass a broad range of geophysical and ecological systems, including meteorological systems, forest ecosystems, and watersheds. They are assessed in terms of environmental qualities, such as air and water purity, visual amenity, biological diversity, and the capacity of watersheds to control floods and erosion. The environment provides some useful services without human manipulation—for example, scenery, flood control, carbon absorption through photosynthesis, and wildlife habitat. However, other benefits provided by environmental systems do require human action—for example, the timber and water that we have already defined as natural resources.[1]

Figure 1 shows each of the four aspects connected together by arrows representing bidirectional relationships. Obviously, some of these relationships will be stronger than others. Let us consider some of the most important simple relationships, then go on to more complex circles involving three or four aspects and complicated two-way linkages and feedback loops.

Some Simple Relationships

First, consider what might appear to be the most obvious of vicious circles, one which links national economic production to natural resources. A country attempts to increase production by exploiting its resources—a tropical timber resource, for example. But, as has happened so many times around the world, the resource is used inefficiently. In many tropical timber-harvesting operations, for example, less than 10 percent of the available woody material is taken from the forest. As a result of this rapid and partial exploitation, the timber is soon depleted and the country is no better off than before. If one considers environmental benefits that had been provided by the uncut forest, such as watershed services and wildlife habitat, the country is arguably worse off.

Burns (1986) refers to this sort of exploitation as "treadmill deforestation," which he distinguishes from the sort of "runway deforestation" that leads to a Rostovian takeoff into sustained economic growth. In the treadmill variety, forests are exploited without contributing to development; in runway deforestation, forest capital is converted to some other, more productive form.

Looked at from the perspective of capital formation, many instances of apparent waste in the historical development of natural resources turn out to be economically rational. For example, the cutting and burning of the great forests of the eastern U.S. and of central Europe during the course of settlement "wasted" great quantities of wood, yet paved the way to agricultural land use and greater national development. One can also find developmental value in the depletion of England's forests for smelting charcoal, the depletion of the iron ores of the Mesabi Range, and the exploitation of the petroleum reserves of Venezuela.

Why is the current exploitation of the Third World's natural resources resulting in so little long-term development? The answer appears to lie in three aspects of resource management. First, in many cases no person or institution takes responsibility for managing the resource. Timber, water, fish, game, and other valuable resources are frequently available as "open access commons." In some circumstances this situation gives the users an incentive to appropriate as much as possible for themselves without regard for other users or for long-term sustainability (Hardin 1968).

Second, government has frequently claimed responsibility for managing resources without having clear management goals or adequate implementation capacity. This contrasts with the historical resource management situation in many developed countries, where relatively effective government institutions stepped in to stop the ravaging of open access commons.

Third, management of Third World natural resources is hampered by poorly functioning price systems. Optimal exploitation of resources requires that market prices adjust rapidly to depletion in order to signal emerging scarcity. This allows users of scarce resources to respond to slowly rising prices by economizing on their consumption, finding substitutes, or discovering new sources of the same resources. Price responsiveness also allows resource users to make well-informed decisions as to how rapidly they ought to allow the resource to be depleted. Yet these conditions occur only rarely in most developing countries, which are marked by prices largely determined by administrative fiat and an often desperate rush to exploit natural resources to counteract economic stagnation and indebtedness.

The vicious circle relating development and natural resources is paralleled by a second relationship—that between development and the environment. Consider this scenario: attempts to increase production create a wide range of environmental externalities, including reduction in biological diversity, soil erosion, watershed damage, depletion of common property fisheries, even such urban environmental problems as crowding, noise, and automobile emissions. These impacts ultimately lead to lower long-run productivity in the economy because of the loss of environmental system services (for example, watershed services) or because direct economic costs are created (for example, emissions of lead from urban automobiles cause serious human health effects.)

A third simple set of linkages are those that link economic production and income distribution. It is quite clear that the nature and level of economic production influence income distribution—functional distribution, regional distribution, and size distribution. However, income distribution also affects production. On the supply side, a high level of income inequality inhibits the formation of human capital, as those on the lower end of the distribution suffer from malnutrition, inadequate health care, and the inability to take advantage of educational opportunities.[2] On the demand side, high income inequality prevents the emergence of a mass market for inexpensive locally made consumer goods. The more sophisticated consumption requirements of the rich are more likely to be served either by imports or by locally made goods with a high proportion of imported components.

The vicious circle that builds on the links between economic production and income distribution looks like this. As development proceeds, income inequality increases. The relatively low income share going to the majority of the population means that they will neither be effective mass consumers nor a very healthy or productive labor force. This may at best result in stagnation and import dependence, at worst in class mistrust or even violence.

More Complex Vicious Circles

Having explored these simple relationships and feedbacks, it is possible to describe much more complex interactions, ones which more truly merit the term "vicious circle." Consider the following scenario: attempts to increase economic production result in major inequalities in income distribution, if only temporarily. For example, a policy of rapid industrialization may be financed by forced capital transfers from agriculture through taxes or unfavorable terms of trade. This raises income for urban entrepreneurs and a small class of urban industrial workers, but reduces both relative and absolute incomes for the rest of society. An impoverished peasantry is forced to consume the available natural resources at a very high rate. For example, a growing rural population with no alternative income source is impelled to exploit swidden cultivation at rates so high that the forest recovery cycles are extremely short or nonexistent. This reduces forest product availability in both the short and the long run, causes soil erosion, and contributes to flooding and siltation downstream.

The continued damage to underlying environmental systems causes peasant incomes to fall still farther, resulting in low savings rates and ever more desperate attempts to use resources to produce current income. Government attempts to deal with the resource and environmental crisis are hindered by the low tax base and the indifference of the richer segments of the population, who do not make their living from agriculture and who can maintain food consumption through imports. In the long run, the inability of peasants to purchase modern sector goods sets a limit on overall national demand, while the increased costs connected with resource and environmental degradation reduces what can be supplied. Overall economic performance is likely to decline.

Another complex circle involves choices in agricultural investment. In an effort to increase foreign exchange earnings, a country decides to increase the production of high-value export crops (for example, cotton production in El Salvador in the 1960–75 period).[3] This creates new entrepreneurial opportunities which neither the traditional landowning class nor the rural peasantry are fully prepared to exploit. As a result, urban middle- and upper-class individuals with access to capital and technology begin to enter cash crop production. Using both legal and extralegal means, they cancel long-standing peasant land rental arrangements and use rights, creating a mobile, ill-paid seasonal labor force. The higher return to cash crops removes land from food production, raising prices of locally consumed staples. Displaced farmers or share-tenants move to marginal areas, where they clear forests or cultivate erosion-prone slopes. Meanwhile, the new cash crop producers are employing environmentally problematic technologies, such as aerial spraying of pesticides and water diversion schemes. Ultimately, the resulting income inequality causes the product demand and human capital formation effects described previously, while the breakdown of traditional economic ties between landowner and peasant sets the stage for revolutionary struggle.

The Mediating Factors

It should be obvious by now that the links between the four aspects which compose our analytic system are not any sort of fixed technical relationship such as one might find in an input-output table. Rather they are the product of a number of submechanisms, many of them the product of specific institutional arrangements or prior policy choices. We will call these "mediating factors." At least eight of these may be identified:

1) *The effect of income distribution on population,* which in turn affects resource consumption, environment, and the investment required to maintain a given per capita consumption level. Murdoch (1980) has persuasively described the mechanism involved: the poorer the parents, the more likely that they will regard children as economic assets (sources of current income, protectors in old age) rather than as economic burdens. Moreover, poverty leads to lower educational levels, lower female labor force participation, and higher child mortality—all of which tend to increase the rate of population growth (high child mortality tends to lead to higher gross birthrates as families try to ensure that a given number of children survive). Murdoch argues that "the solution to the population problem is to increase the level of economic well-being of the vast majority of families. Aggregate economic growth may not cause this [e.g., Brazil, Mexico], but economic development with broad participation will. . . . The economic well-being of the poor can also be increased with very little aggregate economic growth if the available benefits are spread evenly across the population" (Murdoch 1980, 82). It is this somewhat complex mechanism that gives us hope that the Malthusian dilemma of population growth and subsequent resource depletion can be avoided, not through abstaining from economic development but through more equitable development.

2) *The effect of income distribution on human capital formation.* Poverty, as mentioned above, leads to a less educated, less healthy labor force, reducing the long-term potential for increases in production. Low educational levels may also affect resources and environment, by making it more difficult for extension programs to disseminate information about environmental values or resource-conserving production techniques. In general, the entire poverty–ill health–low education constellation may incline people to fatalism and a short time horizon, making them less interested in conservation or in reducing environmental damage.

3) *The effect of resource access on resource use and on the environment.* Access to resources may occur through ownership or through participation

in communal or governmental decisionmaking. Economists have long argued that resources for which clear ownership is established are better managed that those held as commons or for which ownership is uncertain. More recent work by scholars from several disciplines (U.S. National Research Council 1986; Ostrom 1988; Gardner, Ostrom, and Walker 1989) has uncovered numerous instances of public resources that are managed in sustainable, and often equitable, fashion through effective communal institutions. The clarity and defensibility of property rights, rather than the identity of the owner, seem to be the key factors. Clarity of property rights depends on having good records of property ownership and widespread consensus on who possesses use rights; defensibility depends on having effective courts and police to protect property rights uniformly rather than protecting the privileges of the wealthy. The situation for environmental systems is generally even worse than for resources, because environmental systems tend to be biologically complex, and because it is frequently difficult to exclude users even when they are clearly doing damage.

In many Third World countries, government is the primary resource owner. Although some government-owned resources are well managed— for example, petroleum deposits in Kuwait—many are depleted either too rapidly or too slowly. Corruption and inefficiency often keep governments from realizing maximum return from resource exploitation and from efficiently reinvesting revenues for the long-run benefit of the nation. Perhaps the worst case is the all-too-common situation in which government extends theoretical control over a resource, disrupting past communal management arrangements without obtaining effective managerial control. Bromley and Chapagain (1984) have documented how this occurred with village forests in Nepal.

4) *The effect of resource access on income distribution.* In rural societies in developing countries, access to land, water, and timber is an extremely important determinant of the distribution of family income. Income may be received through resource rents (and occasionally dividends), through wage incomes derived from applying one's own labor to resources, from personal consumption of resource products (such as firewood), and from various kinds of services provided by environmental systems, such as flood control. Rose, Stevens, and Davis (1988) provide detailed guidance on modeling the distribution of money resource incomes using input-output techniques. Access to resources also influences savings rates by determining who has funds to save and helps determine the distribution of investment opportunities. Those with secure access to resources tend to be blessed with

greater investment opportunity and more funds to invest than do their brethren without such access.

5) *The pricing of natural resources.* Pricing can include subsidies, rates of payment for government-owned resources, existence of monopoly or oligopoly in resource markets, and trade policy. Subsidies may exist for resource production (for example, low tax rates on minerals relative to other commodities) or for resource consumption (for example, subsidized fertilizer). These subsidies can lead to overproduction or overconsumption and are often very unequally distributed. Poor price policies can also lead to pervasive corruption, which misallocates resources and misdirects entrepreneurship.

6) *Technology.* Specific technologies often imply certain linkages among the four aspects in figure 1. Technologies may embody a certain scale of production, a specific factor mix (for example, capital intensity or profitability of child labor), a level of management sophistication, a use of resources (for example, energy intensity), and particular environmental externalities. For example, the technology of aerial spraying of pesticides implies certain links with the environment, natural resources, and income distribution that are very different from the alternative pest control technology of crop diversification and the planting of crops that trap or repel pests. Agricultural mechanization has very different linkages from those of an agriculture dependent on draft animals. So-called "appropriate technologies" may be specifically directed to improve income distribution, to minimize environmental externalities, or to make use of specific resources.

7) *Placement.* This refers to where people and resources are located spatially. For example, resource use and environmental externalities may be greatly affected by whether poor populations live in the hills, on the plains, or in the forest. In many countries, there has been conscious government policy to move people to areas where resources are more abundant. In some cases (for example, Indonesia and Brazil) this has led to both further impoverishment of the migrants and significant environmental damage. Poor populations may also be involuntarily located where resources are scarce. This frequently occurs when people are displaced by war—for example, the Ethiopian refugees in the Sudan and Somalia—or by famine. In South Africa, government-instigated relocation of millions of urban blacks to agriculturally inhospitable "homelands" has created large numbers of desperately poor people and new pressures on resources and the environment (Iliffe 1987, 260–77).

8) *"Rent-seeking" behavior,* the process through which people try to

obtain various economic benefits through the political system. Individuals and groups use political influence to obtain subsidized prices, to obtain ownership rights to various resources, or to secure employment.[4] This is the essence of politics and is unavoidable. It has the useful attribute of allowing political allocation to reduce some of the obvious inequities caused by the pursuit of economic efficiency. However, rent-seeking can also create serious distortions in resource allocation, particularly when the favored group is able to obtain some commodity (for example, food or timber cutting rights) at prices far below the true market value. This leads to overuse of scarce resources and can seriously retard economic growth. Unchecked rent-seeking can also have a corrosive effect on the political system itself, as each group eyes suspiciously any project likely to benefit its rivals. Rent-seeking by individuals can easily become corruption, which also tends to erode trust in the system itself.

Some Virtuous Circles

The linkages which we have described need not result in vicious circles of resource misuse, environmental degradation, income inequality, and stagnating economic production. As Nurkse (1953) observed, the existence of these linkages and feedbacks holds out the promise of beneficial effects as well as negative ones. These include the redistribution of income to the poor, which improves health status and savings potential; improvements in the productive capacity of renewable natural resources, which increases future income streams; and the rehabilitation of natural systems, which increases their output of useful services. A clear task for policymakers is to increase the proportion of these positive movements through the system. McCord (1986) uses the term "virtuous cycle," to describe such positive flows—we rather like the term's Confucian overtones.

What might constitute a virtuous circle involving our four aspects of sociophysical development? Consider the following: a country institutes policies that promote agricultural development in such a way that benefits are relatively equally distributed among rural people. This creates rural savings that can be mobilized for further development, either rural or urban. Higher rural incomes increase human capital through improved health, better nutrition, and a greater ability to allow children to become educated rather than going to work immediately. Population growth slows as child survival increases and parents are better able to seek security through asset accumulation rather than a large family. Peasant time horizons become extended as immediate needs are not so pressing. Higher incomes produce a market for simple modern-sector goods—bicycles, radios, clothing. Social cohesion and cooperation increase as it becomes apparent that economic growth benefits the vast majority of people.

Resource management also improves as rural people obtain the capital needed to intensify production rather than extend it to marginal land. Better education and longer time horizons also help. With pressure on marginal lands reduced, natural systems are better able to repair themselves. As resources and environmental systems are better managed, there are additional positive feedbacks on overall production and on the income status of the poor.

This scenario of a potential virtuous circle is an appealing one, but perhaps overly rosy. Certainly, not all of the feedbacks will be positive, even if the initial impetus (higher, more equally distributed rural income) is so. Higher incomes can be used to introduce new, environmentally unsound technologies. Peasants may be able to afford pesticides that can be used to poison fish, saving them the time and trouble of mending and casting nets; they may buy more firewood harvested in an unsustainable way or purchase more guns to be used in poaching. Greater demand for modern consumer goods can increase the overall economy's demand for energy; greater housing consumption can increase urbanization of agricultural land. The fact that higher incomes—even when equally distributed—do not lead directly to a more environmentally sound economy can be easily seen by referring to the experience of the U.S. and other developed countries. Rich farmers produce erosion as well as poor ones.

This example, and several others that can be adduced, point to a rather obvious lesson. Virtuous circles are possible and can replace vicious ones. But a positive starting point is only that—it does not guarantee that all the feedbacks will occur in a positive direction. The right policy structure—with particular attention to the various mediating factors we have described—is needed to increase the number of positive loops. Neither vicious circles nor virtuous ones are inevitable.

The nature of these desired policies is readily apparent from our description of the mediating factors. They include policies to direct income toward the poor; policies that encourage investment in renewable resources, such as trees and soil fertility; policies that improve the management of common property resources; and policies that reduce the production of negative environmental externalities. The difficult question, however, is not "What are such policies?'' but *"How* can appropriate policies be formulated and implemented in societies seeking rapid economic development?''

The succeeding four chapters of this volume attempt to answer this question by analyzing how policies affecting natural resources are made and implemented in several key areas of development promotion: agricultural modernization, plantation forestry, hydroelectric dams, population resettlement projects, and irrigation schemes. The experiences we analyze reveal many key policy errors, many of them made again and again by different policymakers in different parts of the world. The last two chapters examine these errors as part of the policymaking process, demonstrating that each stage of policymaking is accompanied by characteristic pitfalls. It is the very regularity of these errors that gives us hope that bad policies are not inevitable, and that appropriate reforms, *not just of policy but of the policy process,* can turn vicious circles into virtuous ones.

3

Agricultural Modernization

Some of the most profound social and economic changes experienced in developing nations since the end of World War II have been associated with attempts to modernize agriculture. Agricultural development has been particularly important as a goal of national development policy since about 1960, when many countries learned that forced industrialization and neglect of the farm sector were creating a major bottleneck for the growth of the national economy.

Successful agricultural modernization has increased real per capita incomes in a number of countries by increasing export revenues, increasing domestic food supplies, or both. At the same time, failures in agriculture have resulted in low or negative national income growth, particularly in sub-Saharan Africa since 1970.

Success or failure in agriculture has also affected the distribution of income. The poor spend a high percentage of their total income on food and are the members of society most likely to be malnourished. Increases in food prices that may be an inconvenience to high- and middle-income citizens can be disastrous for the poor. Many countries have adopted food price controls or food price subsidies aimed at redistributing purchasing power to the poor—particularly to the urban poor. Urban working-class and even middle-class groups are sometimes also recipients of food subsidies, either as a deliberate result of policy or because they take advantage of programs aimed at the poor (Streeten 1987). Agriculture also influences

Case materials for this chapter were initially prepared by Kiran Asher, Christin Eaton, Brayn Khunguni, Herman Pye III, and Krishna Sharma.

income distribution on the production side. In many developing countries agriculture is the principal source of employment for a large proportion of the population—in some countries even for a majority. Agricultural earnings are particularly important to the poorest members of society, who, despite urbanization, tend in most countries to be found in disproportionate numbers in rural areas.

Finally, agriculture is an important resource-using sector, occupying major portions of the national land area and accounting for most of the consumptive use of water. Agriculture is also the origin of many environmental externalities, among them sedimentation, species extinction, deforestation, and pesticide pollution. Some of these are associated with traditional agricultural practices; others occur or are exacerbated when agriculture is modernized.

Agricultural policies thus seem very likely to affect the full range of subjects we wish to investigate: income production, distribution, natural resources, and the environment. Agricultural policy represents a particularly rich case because it frequently has multiple goals—for example:

(a) supplying food for rural and urban people
(b) creating savings that can be tapped for industrialization
(c) providing rural jobs and incomes
(d) generating foreign exchange through exports or import substitution
(e) creating demand for manufactured goods through backward or forward linkages
(f) maintaining political goodwill of farmers
(g) protecting the environment and husbanding land and water resources
(h) securing national food self-sufficiency (or self-determination)

In their search for agricultural development, countries have tried a great number of policies. Some policies concentrate on only one of the above goals—export promotion, for example—while others attempt to pursue several goals simultaneously. Although there are abundant possibilities for multiple-goal strategies, much of the tension in agricultural policymaking is the result of the inherent incompatibility of certain goals. For example, even developed countries have found that providing cheap food for urban dwellers makes farmers unhappy and reduces their incentive to produce, while high prices for farmers cause high urban food prices and reductions in export possibilities.

A common denominator for most Third World agricultural policies has been the "modernization paradigm," the idea that traditional peasant agriculture should be replaced by a more scientific, market-oriented, specialized agriculture (Schultz 1964). This view, which dominated agricultural policy during the 1960s and still has wide support today, has come under serious attack for a number of reasons—that it neglects the poor, that it creates dependency on national and multinational corporations supplying inputs and markets, that it leads to resource degradation and environmental damage, and that it has not even been a viable way to permanently raise farmers' incomes (see George 1977; Pearse 1980; Glaeser 1987).

This chapter will analyze the effects and side effects of two important approaches to agricultural modernization—the worldwide Green Revolution based on genetically improved seed varieties, and the spread of nontraditional agricultural export products. The Green Revolution will be exemplified by the case of corn and wheat production in Mexico between 1960 and 1980; nontraditional exports will be exemplified by the case of cattle raising in Central America during approximately the same period. This will be followed by an analysis of attempts to modernize forestry through introduction of plantation species, a process in many ways analogous in both technology and effects to the Green Revolution in agriculture. A subsequent chapter will analyze a related agricultural development, the use of irrigation.

The Green Revolution

Among the most important developments in Third World agriculture has been the Green Revolution based on the utilization of improved varieties of wheat, corn (maize), and rice. First introduced in the mid-1960s, they have been rapidly adopted throughout the developing world, particularly in Asia and Latin America. Dalrymple (1985) estimates that Green Revolution varieties of wheat and rice were planted on 123 million hectares in major developing countries in 1982–83. That amounted to a little more than half the total acreage planted with wheat and rice in those countries. The rapidity with which the new varieties have spread around the developing world is remarkable. In South and Southeast Asia alone, the acreage planted in high-yield varieties rose from 26,000 in 1965–66 to 61 million in 1982–83. The Green Revolution has been credited with saving millions from famine and changing several Third World countries from grain importers to occasional exporters. It has also been accused of changing the rural income distribution in ways unfavorable to the poor, increasing the number of landless and unemployed peasants, exacerbating regional disparities, reducing the genetic diversity of plant cultivars, fostering dependence on multinational corporations, and harming the environment through chemical pollution.

Origins

The beginning of the Green Revolution can be traced to a meeting in Washington, D.C., on February 3, 1941, between officials of the Rockefeller Foundation and Henry A. Wallace, Vice President of the United States (Stakman, Bradfield, and Mangelsdorf 1967). The Foundation, long active in promoting public health in Mexico, had become increasingly convinced that greater food production was necessary if the Mexican people were to receive adequate nutrition. Wallace's advice was sought because he was an expert on agriculture, having served as the editor of *Wallace's Farmer* and as a developer, popularizer, and vendor of several strains of high-yielding hybrid corn. He had also just returned from a month-long visit to Mexico, where he had taken a keen interest in the problems of Mexican agriculture. Wallace advised the Rockefeller Foundation that raising the per-acre yields of corn and beans, Mexico's staple crops, "would have an effect on the national life of Mexico greater than almost anything that could be done" (Stakman, Bradfield, and Mangelsdorf 1967, 22).

A Rockefeller-funded research station was set up in central Mexico in 1943. It conducted research on a number of crops, including potatoes, vegetables, and soybeans, but it achieved its greatest success with corn and wheat. In 1962, through joint efforts by the Rockefeller Foundation and the Ford Foundation, an international rice research program was begun in the Philippines, extending the research effort to Asia's most widely cultivated crop.

The Rockefeller Foundation's scientists approached their tasks with a single-minded determination. According to one account of the Mexico program, "The basic objective of increasing food supplies as quickly and directly as possible by means of the genetic and cultural improvement of the most important food and feed crops was always paramount. Intellectual and financial resources were not frittered away in distracting side operations, however alluring they might have been" (Stakman, Bradfield, and Mangelsdorf 1967, x).

The same sentiment is echoed by Norman Borlaug, who was to win the Nobel Peace Prize for his work with the plant-breeding program in Mexico: "Research from the outset was production-oriented and restricted to that which was relevant to increasing wheat production. Researchers in pursuit of irrelevant academic butterflies were discouraged, both because of the acute shortage of scientific manpower and because of the need to have data and materials available as soon as possible for use in the production program'' (Nobelstiftelsen 1971, 237).

Among the "academic butterflies" not pursued were studies of the potential economic and sociological impacts of the biological advances the scientists were making. Although economists on the Rockefeller Foundation's Board of Trustees and Board of Consultants for Agriculture had earlier advocated that the project add an agricultural economist to its staff, it was not until 1957 that the first full-time agricultural economist was appointed (Stakman, Bradfield, and Mangelsdorf 1967, 211–12). By that time, the basic direction of the research had long since been set—it was directed toward improving the yield and pest-resistance characteristics of basic grain cultivars through genetic improvement.

A major focus of the yield-improvement research was to make grain plants more responsive to the application of fertilizer. This had been quite successful with corn in the U.S. and was a major reason for dramatic postwar yield increases for that crop. One major problem for the plant breeders was overcoming their wheat and rice plants' tendency to "lodge" or fall over before maturity when their stem growth had been overstimulated by fertilizer; this destroys most of the grain. A significant achievement in plant breeding overcame the lodging tendency by crossing high-yielding but lodging-prone plants with short-stemmed (dwarf) plants with low grain yield. The resulting hybrids could tolerate very high rates of fertilization, producing yields several times as high as the general Mexican or Philippine average.

Increased fertilization and higher-yielding hybrids were only part of the technological package that came to be termed the "Green Revolution." Another ingredient was insect and weed control. Green Revolution varieties were not necessarily more susceptible to pests—indeed breeding for disease resistance was an early program emphasis—but the higher yield meant that more intensive efforts to control pests could be economically justified. Pest-reduction techniques might include more intensive hand cultivation but, following developed country practice, they might involve application of chemical insecticides, fungicides, and herbicides.

Another ingredient was water. Heavily fertilized plants required more water to take full advantage of the added nutrients. Moreover, the greater potential value of the crop meant that there would be a higher return to reducing drought losses. The result was that in many parts of the world the potential for the Green Revolution was greatest on land that was already irrigated or that could be brought under irrigation.

Implementation

As the Green Revolution technologies were diffused to farmers around the world, the idea of a "package of technologies" became almost universally popular. The new seeds—whose high yield made them of great interest to farmers and to national governments—were seen as the way to introduce rapid modernization into a sector that seemed otherwise slow to change. Farmers who received the new seeds would also be provided with irrigation, pest-control technologies, transportation facilities, and the help of agricultural extensionists and educators. This made economic sense—the marginal return to pest control and irrigation was presumed to be higher where yield potential was highest. But it also made strategic sense for national and international development institutions. Resources could be concentrated in a single big push toward modernization, rather than in the frustrating process of incremental change.[1]

Also important to the introduction of the Green Revolution technologies was the concept of the "early adopter." Although the myth that Third World peasants were irrationally slow to accept change was being slowly discarded by development economists, it was widely believed that some farmers were more willing to change than others. This was thought to be particularly true when the change—the package of inputs—was large rather than incremental. Agricultural development agencies believed that making the package available to innovative farmers in economically promising and socially progressive regions would cause a demonstration effect that would induce farmers nationwide to clamor for the new technologies.

The rapid diffusion of the new grain varieties and the impressive increases in national grain output in many nations led experts and the popular press alike to enthuse about what was soon called the "Green Revolution." It was not until the late 1970s, when the new seeds had reached about half of their present acreage, that large numbers of studies began to reveal some unpleasant distributional and environmental side effects. It was discovered, as Susan George put it, that "no technological innovation consists merely in technology" (George 1977, 115).

Among the earliest socioeconomic studies of the Green Revolution were those undertaken in 1970–74 by the UN Research Institute for Social

Development (UNRISD). These studies revealed that the delivery of the technological package to the early adopters had a strong tendency to favor the rich peasant over the poor one, the educated over the uneducated, the landed over the landless, and the politically well-connected over the powerless. Andrew Pearse, who was one of the principal UNRISD researchers, writes of the "talents effect," named after

> the Biblical parable in which it is recounted that one servant receives money to the value of ten talents from his master and is able to invest and prosper, while the very insecurity of his humbler fellow restrains him from utilizing the single talent entrusted to him, which is wrathfully reappropriated by the master, and given to the successful investor (Pearse 1980, 5).

The Green Revolution's critics did not claim that the new technologies were more suitable agronomically to large-scale farms rather than small ones, but they contended that a high level of purchased inputs was required. The irrigation, the pesticides, the fertilizers, and the seeds themselves meant that the new technological package was particularly well suited to those who had access to capital and who were able to comfortably take on the risk of borrowing. This gave a decided early advantage to the wealthier members of the community. Sometimes the new technologies were distributed through a government allocation system, favoring the politically well-connected, who were often also the rich. Least favored of all were the landless, who could benefit from the new seeds only if new jobs were created tending the plants or harvesting and processing them; of course, they could also benefit from lower prices for the food they consumed.

It was also widely recognized, even among the Green Revolution's most ardent defenders, that there were inequalities connected to the particular crops whose seeds were improved. Wheat, whose production rose, is most often consumed by urban populations and elite groups; lentils and cassava, for which new cultivars were not made available, are in many areas the staples of the poor. Africa seemed entirely bypassed by the new grain varieties, partly because the African farmers and consumers were not accustomed to the crops and partly because the cultivars were not adapted to African conditions.

Subsequent studies have offered a more complex picture of the distributional impact of the Green Revolution. Ruttan (1977) pointed out that while the rich and landed may have received the greater proportion of the benefits, even the poor and landless were often made better off in *absolute* terms.

Ruttan contended that while landowners' gains may have been relatively greater than those of tenants and laborers, the latter enjoyed a higher demand for labor and increases in their real wage. Ruttan also observed that despite the initial adoption by the larger farmers, "what the available data do seem to imply is that within a relatively few years after introduction, lags in adoption rates due to size or tenure have typically disappeared" (Ruttan 1977, 16). He found, however, that the Green Revolution varieties were associated with widening income and wage differentials among regions, favoring those regions with suitable climates or available infrastructures.

Hossain (1988) found similar results in Bangladesh. The new varieties were adopted by both large and small farmers and doubled production per hectare. The use of the new seeds, however, proved more profitable for the larger farmers. The landless benefited indirectly because of the higher demand for labor. Hossain observed that "diffusion of the new technology thus increases income for all groups of farmers, but also increases the inequality in the distribution of agricultural income among farm households." In spite of this *relative* inequality, Hossain also found that poor families in villages where farming was technologically advanced were better off than poor families where the new technology had not been adopted.

Scott (1985), in a study of a Malaysian village deeply affected by the introduction of new rice varieties and an associated irrigation scheme, found significant improvements—in the total income of the community, in nutrition, and, at least initially, in labor demand. "Even smallholding tenants," he reported, "with a single relong (.71 acre) can now grow enough rice to at least feed a family, although they may be desperately short of cash. It is a rare peasant these days who does not eat rice twice a day." Scott also found, however, that the greater returns to land pushed land prices up beyond the reach of the small cultivator. The proportion of land in the class of holdings of the smallest size declined, while that in medium and large holdings increased. Perhaps most striking was a sharp drop in the proportion of land cultivated by pure tenants—farmers who rent land and own none of their own. At the same time there were increases in the numbers of owner-operators and renter-operators. "The evidence suggests," said Scott, "that we are witnessing the not-so-gradual liquidation of [the region's] pure tenant class." Scott also noted a shift from share tenancy to cash rents, a shift in leasing practice that tended to price the poorest tenants out of the rental market.[2]

Perhaps the greatest impacts on the poor in the area studied by Scott were those associated with the mechanization of agriculture. This occurred several years after the new seeds had been widely adopted. Although the greater output made possible by the new seeds had created new jobs for landless laborers, these were wiped out when mechanized harvesters were introduced. Mechanization also made field consolidation more profitable and reduced the desirability of renting small plots to landless tenants. Overall, Scott found that during the first eight years after the Green Revolution came to the area studied, real incomes rose substantially for all classes of farmers, including the poor, but that in the subsequent five years, with mechanization and lower profit margins on rice, large farmers benefited far more than small farmers, and small tenants were actually worse off than initially.

The environmental impacts of the Green Revolution were recognized somewhat more slowly than the distributional impacts. The pesticide component of the technological package began to be questioned in terms of impacts on the applicator, on the food consumer, and on wildlife populations (Weir 1981; Bull 1982). It should be noted, however, that the most dangerous pesticides—both in potency and in quantity and frequency applied—are those associated with export crops such as cotton and vegetables rather than with the Green Revolution grains. There was also concern that the introduction of the high-yield seed varieties was leading to the creation of large-scale monocultures of genetically uniform crops vulnerable to catastrophic disease outbreaks. The new varieties also tended toward the extinction of traditional local grain cultivars. Ironically, the genetic variability in the native varieties might have been useful in future crop breeding. In some cases, the profitability of the Green Revolution crops encouraged the expansion of agriculture onto wetlands and other environmentally problematic areas, although it can equally be said that the higher yield per acre significantly reduced the amount of land needed to produce a given amount of grain. The Green Revolution also encouraged the expansion of irrigation, whose environmental side effects will be detailed in chapter 6 below.

Somewhat neglected in the debate over the distribution of the production impacts of the Green Revolution have been its impacts on consumption. In theory, increases in domestic grain supply should particularly help the poor, who spend a relatively high proportion of their income on food; however, several complicating factors intervened. First, food prices may be subsidized or regulated so that higher production will save the government money without affecting the market price. Second, because many of the poor are farmers and hence both producers and consumers of food, price reductions due to greater output may reduce small farmer income, even as they reduce the urban and rural cost of living.

Ruttan (1977) cited one Colombian study that found that the benefits of increased rice production were differentially enjoyed by the poorest people, with the lowest income quartile—which received only 4 percent of household income—receiving 28 percent of the consumer benefits.

The Scientists' Response

As researchers began to receive word of both the success and the side effects of the Green Revolution, they began to react. On one hand, the Rockefeller scientists received great acclaim, including the award of the 1970 Nobel Peace Prize to the leader of the wheat research team. This reinforced their commitment to the Green Revolution approach—to abruptly change direction would be inconsistent with much of their careers—but the scientists did acknowledge that there were problems. The problems were approached, unsurprisingly, as technical problems, to be addressed by further work with the plants. For example, the failure of Green Revolution varieties to prosper under dryland conditions was addressed by breeding drought-resistant plants, and the lack of success of the Green Revolution in Africa was addressed by doing research on staple African food crops.

The attempt to respond to the Green Revolution's problems by broadening the scope of institutional research is best evidenced by the creation in 1971 of the Consultative Group for International Agricultural Research (CGIAR), which became an umbrella for the wheat and rice research groups and for two other tropical agricultural research institutes (CGIAR 1980; Oasa 1987). Almost immediately, CGIAR began to create new institutions that broadened research both geographically and in terms of type of crop. For example, an institute was created to study farming systems for the semiarid tropics, and new emphasis was placed on agricultural research in Africa. In 1974 an institution was created specifically to preserve plant genetic resources by collecting and storing seeds. The criticism that social science had been neglected was addressed by bringing into CGIAR the already-created International Food Policy Research Institute.

Oasa (1985) noted a change over time in CGIAR's philosophy from the "major breakthrough mentality" that characterized the early wheat, maize, and rice work to the expectation that "future science-based technological advances for agriculture would be cumulative and incremental." Oasa also found that, starting around 1976, CGIAR scientists began to make a major effort to develop technologies suitable to the small, resource-poor farmer. One example of this is the emphasis on "farming systems" approaches, which look not just at a single crop but at the entire set of opportunities and constraints of the farm household. Another is integrated pest management, which tries to reduce farmer costs and environmental damage by reducing insect predation on crops with minimum use of chemicals.

There is little doubt that the agricultural research establishment has reacted to criticism of the distributional and environmental shortcomings of the Green Revolution. CGIAR (1980) asserts that it "has become increasingly mindful that the high-yielding varieties that have dramatically increased total yields have not yet materially helped the great majority of resource-poor farmers. The group has accordingly placed increased emphasis on the development by the international centers of new technologies suited to the farmer who lacks access to good soil, purchased inputs, irrigation, and other resources." Critics such as Oasa (1987) and Glaeser (1987) note these changes but severely fault the research system for failing to address more directly the institutional structures and built-in inequalities that undermine even the most careful attempts to improve the lot of the poor. They assert that research operating within such structures cannot be neutral and that it cannot avoid actively reinforcing the unequal system's own viability.

The Green Revolution in Mexico

Because the Rockefeller Foundation's wheat and corn improvement work was done in Mexico, that country was the first beneficiary of the new varieties. The new technology represented a potential godsend to a country whose internal food supply was struggling to keep up with extremely rapid population growth.

It is more than a little ironic that the early plant-breeding success in Mexico occurred with wheat and not with corn. Corn has been Mexico's traditional staple food and it is the principal sustenance of its poorest classes, both rural and urban. It is grown in virtually all parts of Mexico, but is particularly important in the central uplands where most of Mexico's small farmers are found. In 1950 corn occupied 4.3 million hectares of farmland (Barkin and Suarez 1985).

Wheat has been a crop of moderate, though rising, importance in Mexico. It is associated with the urbanization process and the replacement of corn tortillas with wheaten bread. Sanderson (1986) notes that some wheat in Mexico goes into "internationally recognizable confections and snack foods, such as Doni Donas, Ding Dongs, Twinkies, and, of course, the redoubtable veteran Pan Bimbo . . . [while] in other production perhaps less susceptible to obvious criticisms of taste and food value— pasta, crackers, wheat tortillas, wheat flour itself—wheat products have become one of the more obvious elements in the Mexican government's 'cheap food' policy for urban workers." Wheat is also associated with urban Mexico's increasing demand for meat, because it is fed directly to livestock and used to compound the popular "balanced" commercial livestock feeds. Wheat occupied 0.64 million hectares in 1950.

Improved varieties, particularly of wheat, began to be released in quantity to Mexican farmers toward the end of the 1940s (Hewitt de Alcantara 1976). There were successive waves of releases, each more productive than the last. Yields per hectare for wheat rose approximately fivefold between 1945 and 1980 (Barkin and Suarez 1985), with the greatest increases coming during the early 1960s when the new varieties were in wide use. Corn yields roughly tripled during the same period.

The availability of improved wheat varieties in Mexico coincided with a tremendous increase in irrigated farmland, mainly in northern Mexico. Irrigated land nationwide doubled between 1940 and 1970, with particularly large increases in large new irrigation districts in the arid north. This expansion involved substantial investment by the Mexican government as well as loans from the World Bank and other international agencies. Demonstrating the Mexican government's commitment to irrigation is the fact that during the term of President Camacho (1940–46) irrigation works accounted for 97 percent of all public investment in the farm sector (Yates 1981).

Mexico's irrigation districts proved to be fertile ground for the Green Revolution's wheat varieties and the technological package of fertilizers and pesticides. Whereas in 1950 federal irrigation districts accounted for 23 percent of national wheat area, by 1965 they accounted for 64 percent (Sanderson 1986). Producers in the northwestern part of Mexico, where most of the irrigated land was located, even created very successful associations for the propagation and distribution of wheat seeds (Barkin 1987).

Although the total acreage devoted to wheat rose in the early stages of Mexico's Green Revolution, peak acreage was achieved around 1960. Production subsequently continued to rise because of productivity gains, but acreage in wheat stagnated, then declined. This was due to two causes. The first was the government price ceilings intended to hold down consumer prices, which made production of wheat and other basic grains relatively unattractive, despite higher yields. This policy was abruptly reversed in 1980 under Mexico's SAM (Sistema Alimentario Mexicano), a program encouraging domestic food self-sufficiency through production incentives. The second factor limiting wheat production was the growing opportunity in the irrigated areas to produce other, more profitable, crops, including export-oriented winter vegetables, feed for livestock, grapes, and barley for Mexico's expanding beer industry.

Given the irrigation dependence of wheat and the concentration of irrigated acreage in a relatively small part of the country, there was never much chance that Mexico's poor farmers would benefit from the improved seeds. The government apparently did make some efforts to redirect credit to small peasant producers and peasant cooperatives within the irrigated region (Sanderson 1986). The nature of the industry, however, preordained that benefits would be far from equally distributed. The benefits to the poor were expected to come on the consumer side with greater domestic production keeping prices down. This did occur to a great extent, although the benefits accrued to the wheat-eating urban middle and working class rather than to the maize-eating rural poor.

The government's lack of attention to producer incentives eventually led to a situation in which wheat production no longer could keep pace with population growth—by 1971 Mexico was a major importer of wheat from the U.S. Not until the foreign exchange crisis of the early 1980s did these incentives change. When producer prices were raised, Mexican wheat production again shot up.

Mexico's production of maize, both a major product of the rural poor and one of their staple foodstuffs, had much more potential to be affected by genetically improved seeds. Unfortunately, for a variety of biological reasons, the scientists' experimentation with corn did not produce results as rapidly as their work with wheat. Even when improved corn cultivars did become available, they took considerable time to become widely used.

One problem was that, unlike wheat, the corn seeds were hybrids that could not replicate themselves. Thus farmers needed new seeds yearly. The Mexican government set up a central seed-production program, but its lack of resources meant that there was a chronic shortage of seeds. As late as 1971, it was calculated that the government was providing only 9 percent of the national need for corn seeds (Hewitt de Alcantara 1976). Another problem was that corn was a far more widely cultivated crop than wheat (7.5 million hectares in 1970 against less than 1 million for wheat). Use of hybrid corn seeds caught on rapidly and profitably in irrigated areas, but these made up only a tiny fraction of the total area planted in corn in Mexico. The vast majority of Mexico's corn acreage was nonirrigated and cultivated by peasants who faced serious obstacles—among them credit, risk-bearing ability, crop storage, and information—in adopting the new agricultural technology.

A government study done in 1975 found that only 2 percent of Mexico's corn acreage was irrigated, mechanized, and grown with a high level of inputs (Barkin and Suarez 1985). Although this land produced yields more than three times the national average, it accounted for only 6 percent of Mexico's corn production. More typical was the 28 percent of Mexico's corn acreage cultivated under rain-fed conditions, unmechanized, and with low input use. This land had a yield less than half the national average and produced only 14 percent of Mexico's corn. The most important segment of corn production (25 percent of area, 36 percent of production) came from farmers who cultivated rain-fed corn with a high level of inputs. Barkin and Suarez (1985, 87) sum up the impacts of technological development on Mexico's corn production: "Scientific research, performed over many years, favored other crops and left aside the cultivation of corn. Despite the stimulus to certain lines of hybrid maize in irrigated areas, in the rainfed regions these forces are isolated and of little national impact."

How one judges the success or failure of hybrid corn and hybrid wheat in Mexico depends to a large extent on the breadth of one's expectations. If one looks simply at national food production, both corn and wheat appear to be short-term successes. During the 1940s Mexico was self-sufficient in corn and a significant net importer of wheat. By the mid-1960s, despite rapid population growth, Mexico was able in good years to export fairly substantial amounts of both wheat and corn. In 1972, however, Mexico began a decade of very heavy importation of both wheat and corn, and declining national production. It would be easy to attribute this to a petering out of the Green Revolution, but in fact it was heavily influenced by the availability of foreign exchange due to rising oil imports, access to low-cost U.S. grain supplies, and the fact that Mexico's irrigated areas were increasingly devoted to high-value export crops, such as vegetables, and to sorghum and other livestock feedstuffs.

If one looks at the *distribution* of benefits, one finds that consumers gained from the increased food supply, but that much of the benefit accrued to urban consumers. Sanderson (1986) points out that because most Mexican wheat is eaten by the middle and upper classes and by the urban industrial work force: ''In effect, the vast federal irrigation system devoted to wheat production has become a life support system for the industrializing Mexican economy and its population.'' The Mexican government's turn during the 1970s toward serving urban food needs through imports rather than through domestic wheat and corn production indicates, however, that Mexico did have more than one option in this matter.

Owners of Mexico's irrigated land, mostly in the northern states, clearly gained the most from the country's agricultural modernization. Not only did they obtain highly productive irrigated land, technical advice, and subsidized credit, they were uniquely situated to take advantage of the Green Revolution's seeds because they had available the rest of the needed inputs. Even where there were bottlenecks, as in the government's failure to provide sufficient seeds, the large-scale irrigators simply created alternative seed supply institutions of their own (Barkin 1987). Many of the beneficiaries of the Green Revolution in irrigated areas were not traditional landowners but new, technologically sophisticated entrepreneurs. The new development also created a migrant labor force, which, while ill-paid by U.S. standards, was relatively well-off in comparison with the rest of Mexican farm labor.

Mexico's peasants were ill-suited to take advantage of the Green Revolution. Not only did they lack irrigation, they suffered chronic shortages of seeds, fertilizers, credit, and extension help. It does not appear that they lost ground, except in a relative sense, but the majority seems to have been simply bypassed. A major difference between Mexico and other countries is the importance in Mexico of the *ejido* system, a form of communal landholding that limits the alienation of land. Because of this system, wealthier peasants were not prone, as they were in India and Pakistan, to adopt the new production technologies and squeeze their neighbors out of the land purchase or rental market.

Yates (1981) does perhaps the best job of capturing the complexity of the distribution of benefits from Mexico's agricultural modernization experience:

It has been said that the opening up of new lands and the building of irrigation works intensified the income differences in the Mexican countryside just as some writers have accused the [G]reen [R]evolution of accentuating the contrast between haves and have-nots in India and Pakistan. A more objective description of what was happening between 1940 and 1965 in Mexico would identify three distinct processes occurring simultaneously: first, a descent of formerly large landowners from the top to a middle-income group; secondly, an ascent of many poor people, especially the migrants, from the bottom to various middle-income groups; and thirdly, a continuation in poverty by those who remained living in the hostile and marginal agricultural areas.

Analyzing the Green Revolution

Given the fact that the food produced through Green Revolution technologies has been vital to keeping a number of countries, particularly in Asia, from crushing food deficits, it is hard to count the effort unsuccessful. Yet the serious side effects that have been produced lead us to wonder whether—and how—they might have been avoided. One approach to an analysis is to identify major points at which the Green Revolution's future direction has been set, either by conscious decision or because it has encountered institutional or other obstacles.

In many ways, the Green Revolution's long-term direction was set when it was first conceived. The effort was based on a missionary-like enthusiasm for the "modernization paradigm" of agricultural development. As the Rockefeller Foundation scientists who participated in the earliest data-gathering mission to Mexico wrote, "From the ox to the tractor, from back-breaking peasant farming to the intelligent business of farming is a long and happy step; but the Survey Commission had witnessed that step in various areas of the United States. And they had faith that Mexico could take the same kind of step in an even shorter time" (Stakman, Bradfield, and Mangelsdorf 1967, 24). The extremely successful U.S. experience with hybrid corn reinforced the idea that the then-rapidly modernizing U.S. agriculture had much to teach the developing world.

The Green Revolution was from the very start a plant-breeder's revolution. The initial group of scientists sent to Mexico were experts on plant genetics, soils, and plant pathology. They therefore gave primary emphasis to breeding high-yield, pest-resistant plants. It is likely that both the direction of research and its eventual impact would have been quite different if the team had had a greater proportion of animal scientists (a Mexican animal improvement program was started much later) or of extensionists or experts in agricultural economics and policy.

The initial direction of plant breeding was reinforced by its relatively rapid success in improving wheat varieties. This reinforced scientists' faith that they were pursuing the right path and kept them from investigating alternative approaches. Work on rice begun in 1962 in the Philippines and inspired by the progress in Mexico with wheat also yielded rapid results. Although vegetables, beans, and other plants were the subject of early research in Mexico, they were apparently de-emphasized as the successes with basic grains grew.

As Green Revolution varieties were diffused around the world, they encountered institutional structures that shaped their impacts. These institutions, which included landownership structure, access to capital, favoritism in distribution of inputs and technical assistance, and government irrigation policies, have tended to bias toward the higher-income farmer the benefits of a technology which is arguably (see Ruttan 1977) scale-neutral.

The model which we outlined in chapter 2 may be used to identify three basic forms of disagreement between Green Revolution admirers and Green Revolution critics. The first concerns the levels of impacts flowing between the model's various components—for a known increase in grain output, how great have been the environmental costs? How have the gains been distributed, both between rural producers and urban consumers and between different classes of producers? Have increasing relative inequalities occurred within a context of absolute improvement for virtually all?

The second disagreement concerns the nature of the secondary adjustment process. Given that at least some impacts are negative, does the system provide for corrective feedbacks? This could be done automatically (for example, by capturing part of income gains through progressive taxation or by allowing fertilizer bottlenecks to be corrected by greater private investment in new plants), but it usually requires deliberate policy change. In the case of the Green Revolution, there was a redirection of the research effort by the scientific groups producing the initial technologies. The disagreement in this case is in part over whether that redirection will be adequate to solve the problem.

The third disagreement is about where policy change should originate. The Green Revolution scientists, having been made aware of the side effects of their technologies, addressed them in ways that some observers see as self-serving and partial. Yet it may also be argued that the scientists were making the maximum possible adjustment given their area of jurisdiction. As Ladejinsky (1969) put it:

When all is said and done, it is not the fault of the new technology that the credit service doesn't serve those for whom it was originally intended; that the extension service is not living up to expectations; that the *panchayats* are essentially political rather than development bodies; that security of tenure is a luxury of the few; that rentals are exorbitant; that ceilings on land are merely notional; that for the greater part tenurial legislation is deliberately miscarried, or wage scales are hardly sufficient to keep soul and body together.

Finally, the abundant literature documenting the unequal distributive impact of the Green Revolution on farmers has tended to divert attention away from its favorable impacts on the supply of basic foodstuffs. The food supply benefits appear to be widely shared, though two exceptions might be pointed out. First, given the fact that the production advantage accrued, at least initially, to the larger farmers, an increased supply of food and lower food prices could be expected to benefit the urban poor more than the rural poor. The urban poor would receive full benefit of the lower food prices, while the rural poor would gain in their role as food consumers but lose in their role as food producers. This disparity would be increased to the extent that government distribution of foodstuffs might reach the urban poor but not those in rural areas. Second, the great success of Green Revolution wheat varieties affected a crop that in many countries is not a traditional staple but is rather associated with urbanization and dietary "upgrading." The improvements in rice and maize, however, did result in greater supplies of foodstuffs widely consumed by both the urban and rural poor.

Nontraditional Agricultural Exports

A second strategy by which many, indeed most, developing countries have tried to achieve agricultural development is through encouraging nontraditional agricultural exports. We will use this term in two senses: first, many countries have used modern production methods to make profitable the export of staple crops long grown in small quantities for local consumption. Cotton and beef are among the best examples. Second, countries have tried to develop high-value products such as spices, cut flowers, vegetables, and aquacultural products destined almost entirely for export to specific markets in the developed world. The modernization and increased export orientation of staple crops was a major strategy of the period between 1950 and 1975, while the development of high-value products is a major strategy of the present time.

Former U.S. Secretary of Agriculture Orville Freeman, in a recent article advocating greater development of cash crops and export crops, invoked the economic doctrine of comparative advantage. If a developing country can produce tobacco or coffee at a lower relative cost than it can produce corn or wheat, Freeman argued, it should allocate its production resources toward the production of the cash/export crop and import the foodstuff: "The income generated by the sale of these export crops would enable it to purchase far greater amounts of wheat and corn than could be produced domestically with the same inputs" (Freeman 1989).

A recent report by a research group in India asserted optimistically that "with the fast expanding world market for agricultural commodities, we have the opportunity to enhance our production and exports. While there are some essential commodities like foodgrains which can be exported only after meeting the domestic requirements there are a large number of tropical nontraditional agricultural commodities the production of which can be increased exclusively for exports as these are not sensitive mass consumption items" (Economic and Scientific Research Foundation 1986).

A major difference between the agricultural modernization associated with the Green Revolution and that associated with nontraditional agricultural exports is the latter's avowedly commercial orientation. Rather than providing a secure livelihood for the masses—the initial hope of the Green Revolution—export agriculture is expected to produce foreign exchange revenues and entrepreneurial opportunities, with the benefits filtering to the population at large only indirectly.

Cattle Raising in Central America

The Central American cattle industry is an excellent example of the social and environmental transformation that can occur when a new export opportunity arises. Cattle raising for domestic beef and dairy consumption had long been traditional in Central America. The industry was associated with large landowners, who often regarded ranching as a way of life as much as a way to make money, and with small farmers, who regarded their animals as a sideline to crop production and a convenient store of value. In both cases, productivity was very low and most of the beef was sold on local markets, where limited purchasing power kept down demand.

In the late 1950s this long-standing situation began to rapidly change because of a new export opportunity. Meat from Central American cattle was transported to the U.S. in refrigerated ships to serve the burgeoning market for hamburger and similar low-cost beef products. Central America's annual beef export revenues rose from $9 million in 1961 to over $100 million in the early 1970s, and reached $290 million in 1979 (Williams 1986). Nearly all of this meat went to the U.S. The number of cattle grew apace: from about 4 million in 1960 to 10 million in 1978.

The growth in Central American beef exports reflected the conjunction of a growing U.S. demand with an eagerness within Central America for a new source of export revenues. This enthusiasm was felt not only by local and transnational entrepreneurs, but also by Central American governments and by international aid and development agencies such as USAID, the Inter-American Development Bank, and the World Bank. Cattle exports would help the region diversify its exports away from coffee and bananas, whose price instability had produced periodic booms and busts. The foreign exchange generated by beef exports would also help Central America pay for the ambitious industrialization effort that was in its early stages by 1960.

Williams (1986) and Brockett (1988) have documented how a combination of public action and private investment positioned Central America to take advantage of the new opportunity to export beef. More than two dozen new slaughterhouses were constructed, with facilities that allowed them to meet U.S. health standards. A network of farm-to-market roads was constructed, allowing cattle to be brought to market by truck rather than herded there as in the past. A sophisticated system of transporting refrigerated containers allowed beef to move undamaged from the slaughterhouse to U.S. ports. New cattle breeds were introduced and animal health was greatly improved. The improved cattle gained weight faster, produced more offspring, and had a far higher survival rate than the scrawny *criollo* cattle traditional in the region.

Central America's beef export boom appears upon first inspection to be an entirely market-driven phenomenon—a profitable new demand bringing about an entrepreneurial response and inducing technological change in a tradition-bound industry. However, governments have played a key role in at least two ways. First, access to the U.S. market is not open to all competitors but is subject to a strict quota system designed to insulate U.S. cattle raisers from low-cost foreign competition. This keeps U.S. prices higher than they otherwise would be but severely limits those who can take advantage of the prices. Although the largest quotas have been enjoyed by Australia and New Zealand, Central America—with its nearby location and presumed strategic importance to the U.S.—garnered a share that rose steadily from about 5 percent in the early 1960s to 15 percent in 1979

(Williams 1986). Access to the lucrative U.S. market became a means by which the U.S. could reward friendly governments, and by which national governments could reward favored producers, usually packing plants.

A second way in which government policy was central in the beef industry expansion was through the provision and allocation of credit. Roads, slaughterhouses, and port facilities required large amounts of capital, a great deal of which was supplied by international loans. There was also considerable direct foreign investment, particularly by multinational food processing forms. Credit was also supplied to individual farmers for herd expansion and for pasture development. The magnitude of the new credit is staggering, especially since cattle never accounted for more than about 10 percent of the region's total agricultural output. In Costa Rica, for example, cattle received more credit in 1972 than the rest of agriculture combined and the following year the industry received 31.4 percent of all national banking system credit (Brockett 1988). Although credit was clearly necessary for the beef industry's development, the favorable terms on loans (often with interest rates that were negative when adjusted for inflation) meant that they were sought after even for projects whose economic foundations were shaky. As with the U.S. import quotas, below-market credit became sought after by various producers. Those with political influence tended to garner the greatest share. Moreover, when economic crises threatened national economies in the early 1980s, cattle producers quickly organized themselves to protect their subsidies (Annis 1987).

With this background it is useful to analyze the winners and losers in Central America's beef export boom. Perhaps the most obvious winners were the large landowners, particularly along Central America's Pacific coast. Many of these owners had long been in the cattle business, at low levels of productivity made tolerable only by the fact that they owned vast areas of pastureland. Eventually many of these owners were bought out by entrepreneurs, often professionals or businessmen from the capital who found cattle raising a convenient weekend occupation. However, the fact that cattle raising was not as capital- or knowledge-intensive as other forms of nontraditional agriculture (for example, vegetables) meant that traditional landowning elites were well positioned to enjoy its benefits.

Another group of major beneficiaries were those who were able to secure U.S. import quotas and build slaughterhouses and transport systems. Because the quotas were limited in number, one might surmise that much of the excess profit in the cattle business went to quota holders rather than to landowners. It is not surprising in this circumstance that a major owner of Nicaraguan packing plants was the dictator Anastasio Somoza Debayle (Williams 1986). The rise of the cattle industry also led to opportunities in related sectors: the transport of cattle, the manufacture of boxes, and the sale to ranchers of feed supplements, insecticides, and pharmaceuticals. Many suppliers were subsidiaries of foreign companies and much of the material came ultimately from abroad.

As landowners began to reorganize the cattle industry, they often found it profitable not only to put more cattle on existing pasture but also to bring new land into pasture. In some cases this land was part of estate holdings that had been rented at low rates to local sharecroppers. Rentals were raised and converted to cash rents, which many peasants could not afford. In a significant number of cases landowners displaced peasants by law or by violence, not only from the estates but also from land where titles were communally held or simply unclear. Much of the civil unrest that has plagued Central America over the last three decades stems directly from this displacement process and the resistance it engendered.

Displaced peasants, as well as an otherwise growing population, sought their own place in the cattle industry by clearing marginal land—slopes or former jungle. Land tenure laws frequently abetted the process, by allowing persons "improving" unclaimed land to establish use rights and eventually to gain title. Land improvement was most easily demonstrated by clearing the land and then keeping it open with grazing cattle. A substantial number of peasants throughout Central America began to engage in what might be termed "shifting land clearing": occupying unclaimed land (often including government forest reserves), clearing it for pasture, and reselling it to larger landowners.

A final beneficiary of the new opportunities in the cattle business was the military. Civil strife between landowners and displaced peasants created a demand for more military activity and increased military participation in governments. But the military saw more direct opportunities as well. The extension of roads into unsettled parts of the country could be justified on the basis of military expediency but it also opened up vast new tracts of land. Frequently military officers were rewarded for their services with large estates, much of it used for cattle. This process is most clearly evident in Guatemala's Petén region, where military-owned ranches and other enterprises control much of the land.

Some of the losers from Central America's beef export boom have already been mentioned: the peasants displaced from large estates and those who were pushed off of land they had previously occupied. Another group, surprisingly, was domestic consumers. Although productivity in the cattle industry increased greatly, supplies of beef to the domestic market did not increase. In most of Central America per capita beef consumption actually fell during the period of most rapid cattle industry expansion. Milk also became scarcer as the old dual-purpose cattle breeds were replaced by cattle bred only for beef. Another group of losers is very large but difficult to identify: the many people and institutions which might otherwise have received the funds used by governments to subsidize cattle producers. Monies spent on direct subsidies or below-market loans might have been used for education, health care, or expansion of other economic sectors. They might even have been used for other types of export agriculture, perhaps in sectors that would create more jobs or support small farmers. Because much of the capital that went into the cattle industry was borrowed, a share of Central America's current crushing debt burden must be assigned to that sector.

Probably the largest loser from cattle expansion has been the environment. Much of the new land devoted to cattle came from former forests; forests were also cleared by peasants displaced by cattle raising from their agricultural jobs on large estates. Brockett (1988, 91) calls export cattle raising "probably the major cause of [forest] denudation since 1960."

Deforestation and the expansion of settlements have led to significant declines in Central America's once-abundant wildlife population. They have also caused major damage to soil and watersheds. According to one analyst much of the production on pastures cleared from tropical forest is not sustainable over time:

> Unless there are very few animals per hectare, grass-stands are weakened; the physical, chemical, and bacterial character of the topsoil changes; and production of vegetation (and cattle) falls. [The farmer] can temporarily counter the declining fertility through repeated burnings of the forest cover—which causes the above-the-soil biological nutrients to return to the ground—but repeated burnings destroy the microorganisms necessary for biochemical decomposition and soil aeration, and eventually the soil is left susceptible to erosion (Annis 1987).

The cattle-related damage to soil has off-site impacts as well. As slopes are left unprotected, uncontrolled erosion produces downstream flooding and siltation. Particularly susceptible to damage are hydroelectric reservoirs, which supply a significant amount of Central America's electric power and provide a domestic substitute for imported oil. Siltation from degraded slopes can severely reduce reservoir life, resulting in significant reduction in the economic return to expensive projects.

Soil degradation due to cattle is particularly problematic because the marginal costs of continuing to graze a piece of degraded land are close to zero. Cattle will be kept on the land as long as there is *any* positive return, in contrast to crop agriculture, in which fixed costs of planting cause degraded land to be abandoned before all productivity is lost.

Since 1979 the Central American beef industry has experienced a long period of severe economic difficulty. The U.S. market has been shrinking, in great part because of a decline in per capita beef consumption. At the same time domestic subsidies, including credit, which provided a largely unappreciated stimulus to the industry, have been reduced. The industry has increasingly turned to other foreign customers and to the domestic market.

The rise and decline of the cattle industry provides good evidence of the complexity and variety of impacts from a seemingly simple change in the economic opportunity set. The opportunity to profitably export beef to the U.S. led to some obvious market adjustments: new packing plants, improved cattle health, more land in pasture. But it also led to a great deal of rent-seeking behavior, as powerful members of society jockeyed to obtain import quotas, infrastructure advantages, subsidized credit, and access to unoccupied land. Meanwhile, some parts of society were made worse off—notably the displaced peasants—and, as so often happens, the environment was damaged, both by the cattle producers and by those who were displaced by them.

Plantation Forestry

A number of developing countries have attempted to modernize their forestry sectors, although they have not approached the subject with nearly the same urgency evident with grain or livestock. For most developing countries—and in much of the developed world as well—forestry is a mining operation. Trees which have taken scores, even hundreds, of years to develop to maturity are harvested without any provision for subsequent regeneration. Sometimes a usable secondary forest does regenerate, but timber harvest is too often simply the prelude to agricultural land clearing and abandonment, periodic fire, and creation of low-quality pasture land.

In many parts of the world, the depletion of natural forests has led to concern about supplies of fuelwood, building materials, and raw materials for pulp mills. An increasingly popular alternative to tackling the knotty biological and social problems of sustainably managing natural forests has been to grow wood in plantations (Whitmore 1981; Evans 1982; Zobel 1987). Plantations offer several advantages over natural stands: uniformity of product (almost invariably only a single species is planted); uniform spacing to take full advantage of light and water; the opportunity to control competition from unwanted species; and the possibility of increasing productivity through genetic improvement. Advocates of forest plantations argue that they have a role in environmental protection as well. Because they can produce much more wood per hectare than can be grown in natural forests, it is argued that much of a country's fiber can be grown on a small percentage of its land area. These "replacement forests" could free natural forests for low-intensity uses, including parks (Zobel 1987). Although many native species can be grown under plantation conditions, in practice about 90 percent of plantations worldwide are of two types: pines and eucalyptus.

Many plantations in both developing and developed countries are large-scale enterprises owned and operated by vertically integrated forest products companies. This is true of the pine plantations that stretch across the southeastern U.S., the eucalyptus plantations in South Africa, and the extensive plantations in South America owned by companies such as Carton de Colombia and Brazil's Aracruz Florestal. Many, perhaps most, company plantations are planted on large tracts of abandoned pasture land or in savannah environments. In these cases, they neither compete with local people for agricultural land nor directly displace natural forests.[3] Their environmental impact may be positive or negative. Often, as in the Andes foothills, they help reclaim degraded land. However, plantations are sometimes put in place on natural grassland environments, whose subtle ecological values are rarely appreciated. Although these areas are seen by the companies and by governments as "useless" lands, they in fact harbor a rich fauna.

The type of forest plantations that will concern us here are those which displace other types of activities. In some cases, this means the deliberate replacement of natural forest with plantations; in others it involves the conversion of agricultural or actively used pastureland to plantations.

Anderson and Huber (1988) offer a vivid account of the attempt to create industrial pine plantations in India's Bastar district in Madhya Pradesh. Bastar, the size of Belgium, is the largest forested district in India. More than two-thirds of its population is made up of "tribals," many of whom depend on foraging in the natural forest for a large portion of their livelihood, including supplemental food, building materials, and marketable products such as honey, leaves for bidi cigarettes, fruits, and the oil-bearing seeds of the sal tree. Others rely on the forest as an ever-replenishing source of land for swidden agriculture.

Starting in the nineteenth century, British colonial authorities sought to restrict the forest rights of the tribals, a tendency continued by the Indian government. In 1975 the World Bank was asked by Indian state and central government authorities to consider a loan for construction of a large pulp mill to be supplied by extensive plantations of Caribbean pine. It involved, according to Anderson and Huber, "turning a complex forest into a genetically simplified plantation" (1988, 5). The project would contribute to regional development, supply a growing India with paper, and reduce the burden of imported paper on the foreign trade deficit. It would also, its proponents claimed grandiosely, create more than a million "job opportunities" (1988, 63).

After more than five years of study, the project was rejected by the Indian government in 1981. Its demise may be attributed in part to changing international pulp markets and alternative investment opportunities. But Anderson and Huber believe that "a major, if not the prime, reason for the cancellation of the Bastar forestry project was the threat of tribal resistance and retaliation" (1988, 111). Local tribals were not only markedly unenthusiastic about working in the plantations; there were also incidents in which large groups of armed tribals physically prevented logging companies from harvesting the natural forests. Although the World Bank and Indian authorities did extensive feasibility studies of the mill and the plantation, only after project planning was well underway did they do sociological studies of the impact of the proposed plantation on the tribals' access to traditional forest products. Nor were environmental issues introduced early in the process—the project was later to face criticism from Indian environmentalists.

"The status of the tribal people," write Anderson and Huber, "was extremely ambiguous. In one sense, they were continuously present—at the side of the road when jeeps whizzed by, at the weekly markets and timber auctions, and working in the forestry project itself. In another sense, they were largely absent—whether because they were uncommunicative themselves, or were ignored by others, or both. Their voice was everywhere muffled, except when they took a daring and dramatic step" (1988, 125).

By excluding the group most affected by the proposed plantation, the planners lost their opportunity to mold the project in a way that might have captured the tribals' support.

The importance of participation can even be ignored and disguised in programs hiding behind seemingly progressive labels. For example, many projects were initiated in India in the name of "social forestry" in the 1970s. Shiva, Sharatchandra, and Bandyopadhyay (1982, 158) define "social forestry" as "the strategy . . . to regenerate forest resources through the participation of the community in the protection and management of forests," but they then complicate the term by noting that "social forestry has as its primary aim the development of firewood resources, since the shortage of domestic energy . . . is expected to pose the most difficult problem in the coming years." This confusion of ends (fuelwood supply) and means (community participation) has been responsible for what many Indian observers consider a perverse approach to social forestry—the provision of fuelwood supplies through plantations of exotic species on village lands and small private holdings. Social forestry has also involved farmer-owned plantations that sell their output to large industrial firms, particularly pulp mills.

A favored species for both sorts of plantations is eucalyptus, which grows rapidly, tolerates droughts, and makes good quality charcoal. Eucalyptus leaves are unpalatable to grazing animals, however, and few understory plants survive in a eucalyptus plantation. Local people who formerly grazed animals in secondary forests or village commons find this use excluded in the new plantations. Another popular species in India is the chir pine. It produces salable wood, but local farmers cannot use this species for plows, as they had the oaks that formerly occupied the land.

Much of the controversy over social forestry plantations in India has revolved around their distributional impacts. "Whose interests are best served by the current social forestry policy as applied in practice?" asks Roy (1986, 1) rhetorically. "From the data that is available, it is clear that the two most significant beneficiaries are the paper factories and the Forest Department. The former get the raw material they need . . . and the latter obtain the revenue demanded by their political masters. . . . Subsidiary beneficiaries are the rural elites and the owners of medium-sized plots. There is almost nothing in the present policy for the most needy, including the tribal and hill dwelling peoples."

There has also been great controversy over the impact of plantations on the environment. Many Indian environmentalists are critical of government social forestry schemes, questioning the choice of tree species, the use of monocultures, and the distribution of benefits (Centre for Science and Environment 1984). Negative impacts on biodiversity are frequently mentioned. Monocultures of pines and eucalypts are distinctly inhospitable to many tropical forest animals, particularly the many frugivores supported by mature native trees. The extensive road networks associated with plantations also make it easier to hunt those animals which do survive.

A critique of India's social forestry program by Shiva, Sharatchandra, and Bandyopadhyay (1982) almost exactly reproduces the earlier criticism by others of the Green Revolution. They attribute the failure of social forestry to satisfy the basic needs of the rural population to the assumption "that just growing more trees will satisfy basic needs: no distinction is made between what trees are grown or who grows them—even though the evidence suggests that the tree species which get planted determine to a large extent which groups accrue the benefits."

Examined closely, the distributional issues in plantation forestry are very similar to those of the Green Revolution. A new, profitable investment opportunity tends to be seized by those who have land, those who have access to capital, those who can most easily obtain government subsidies, and those who can afford to bear the risks of a new enterprise. The poor— particularly the landless—do not benefit except insofar as additional planting or harvesting labor is employed. Some people may even be worse off than before because the marginal land formerly rented to them for cropping is now more profitably used for trees. In plantation forestry, as in the Green Revolution, an unequal distribution of benefits can obtain *even if production costs and opportunities are scale-neutral*. Plantation forestry promoted under the banner of social forestry tends to raise the expectation that all members of the community will be better off, much as the Green Revolution raised the expectation that increased food supply would be the economic salvation of the poor. When these expectations are not fulfilled, even when the technology itself is widely adopted, the innovation can easily be depicted as a complete failure.

Consider, for example, the following two statements about eucalyptus plantations in India. The Centre for Science and Environment (1984) observes critically that "[e]ucalyptus is in great demand from the pulp and rayon industry. Mills in Karnataka are prepared to make advance payments every year to growers until the tree is ready for harvesting in 6-8 years. The prices offered are high; one acre of eucalyptus, when ready for felling, can fetch up to Rs. 40,000 [$2,800]. As a result, many farmers, particularly in

Karnataka, have started growing eucalyptus instead of food crops.'' Sharma (1987) describes an almost identical situation in Haryana state much more enthusiastically: "In Haryana, farm forestry has been a very lucrative proposition. People can expect to get about twice the price out of their land with the trees, in about eight years' time. The most common species planted is the eucalyptus. . . . Even the small farmer, by planting some trees, can benefit." Sharma notes that "most of the farmers taking advantage of this opportunity are large landowners, who have become quite wealthy from it," but he argues that farmers tend to grow eucalyptus trees on the perimeter of their farms, so that food crops are not displaced. Moreover, "even if a farmer had only ten hectares, he could grow the eucalyptus along the border." These two statements seem to differ not only on the facts they present—does eucalyptus displace or complement food crops?—but also on their perception of the goal of forestry improvement— is it to make *most* people or *all* people better off?

A similar situation can be found in the Philippines, where the Paper Industry Corporation of the Philippines (picop) began in 1968 to try to assure a continuing supply of pulpwood to a mill (formerly based on natural forests) by encouraging nearby landowners to cultivate a fast-growing plantation species (Hyman 1983; Caufield 1985). Four thousand farmers participated in the program, which covered almost 75,000 acres. "The scheme," writes Caufield, "is credited with increasing picop's supply of wood, reclaiming degraded land with an ecologically appropriate crop, and providing poor farmers with a good living on their own land so that they do not encroach on the [picop] concession." But Caufield then concedes that the average tree farm is twenty-five acres, that landless people are not eligible to participate, and that the average income of those taking part in the plantation scheme is three times the Philippine national average (Caufield 1985, 179).

False optimism about the universality of distributional benefits could often have been avoided, we believe, if the forest planners had consulted early on with the local people affected. They would almost certainly have been avoided if *all* of the intended beneficiaries of social forestry or other forest-based rural development schemes had been given real power over the policies adopted on their behalf.

A leading advocate of plantation forestry argues that the biological problems—some of them imaginary—visualized by local people could also have been avoided if they had been involved in planning. In India, for example, there is a widespread belief that eucalyptus plantations draw down water tables, causing drought for neighboring farmers. This is almost certainly untrue, but the currency given it indicates a deep-seated mistrust of the plantations. Zobel (1987) writes that "[t]he political problems associated with exotic forestry really begin before the establishment of plantations. The political oversight of not involving the local people results in a lack of understanding of the true biological situation." Zobel also notes the need for consistency over time in forest policies, attributing poorly planned and sometimes economically disastrous plantations to "the 'on-again, off-again' forestry programs sponsored within a country by one government and then ignored by the succeeding government" (Zobel 1987, 385). This certainly appears true of forest policy in India, which has alternately ignored fuelwood and emphasized it, and has at times promoted industrial plantations while at other times advocated production by small farmers. These policy shifts are summarized in Shingi, Patel, and Wadwalkar (1986).

4

Moving the People to the Resources:

Resettlement Schemes

The most dramatic efforts to provide greater access to jobs and income are the resettlement programs through which populations are literally moved to areas of presumably greater resources. Of all the programs that attempt to provide populations with greater resource access,[1] large-scale human resettlement programs present the broadest range of issues and uncertainties. Yet, like the construction of large dams, they are often highly appealing politically and symbolically, representing seemingly bold and decisive actions. This chapter reviews three resettlement projects in India, Indonesia, and Brazil. We examine their purposes, evaluate their planning and implementation, and analyze why some objectives were attained and others were not.

Some resettlement programs are impelled by the need to relocate people displaced by other government projects, such as dams. While these programs are certainly relevant to natural resource policy, we shall defer their treatment until we look at the issue of hydroelectric projects because they are not primarily stimulated by the concern for poverty alleviation. In this chapter we focus on resettlement projects intended to make direct inroads on the poverty of land-poor people in overpopulated areas. These schemes aim for promoting equity insofar as they involve the provision of assets and government spending to move poor people. This equity appeal holds even if the nonpoor also benefit from the improved amenities brought about by relieving overpopulation.

Case materials for this chapter were initially prepared by Kristin Clements, Stephen Ganote, Mohammad Rafiq, Bindu Sharma, and Alangudy Srinivasan.

The Major Issues in Resettlement

Large-scale resettlement programs represent very distinctive implications for growth, equity, environmental protection, and participation. Resettlement projects are obviously land-use policies. They assign land to specific families, typically specify how that land is to be used (for example, some proportion of forest can be cleared but the rest must be maintained), and require the construction of roads and other facilities that directly change the landscape. Yet resettlement projects also have incidental impacts on land use as the roads provide access for other people to use the land. Time after time the roads used to make land available to officially sponsored settlers have been used by unofficial settlers, who frequently squat on reserved land, land not yet surveyed, or even tracts given to official settlers. The infrastructure designed to make official settlement sustainable also serve as "growth poles" that attract other settlement and production. These attractions also change the demand for land in other parts of the country. Thus one of the most difficult complexities of resettlement programs is the inevitability of massive incidental impacts on how the land will be used.

The environmental impact of any large resettlement program is likely to be difficult to predict in any of its specifics, and yet it is rather easy to predict that there will be major impacts. Changing population density—the essence of resettlement—inevitably changes the pressure on natural resources. With settlers transplanted from one ecosystem to another, there can hardly be a presumption that their previous practices of cultivation and resource exploitation will serve in the new environment. In light of the inevitability that resettlement will affect the environment, it is hard to imagine that considerations of environmental risk do not cross the minds of policymakers who make resettlement decisions. Yet the environmental impacts, perhaps because they can be so great, are difficult to anticipate systematically. It is also probable that these environmental impacts will be condemned by the defenders of the wilderness and species diversity; thus attending to the environmental issue can be risky for the policymakers who are strongly in favor of large and rapid resettlement programs. Finally, the areas into which migrants are typically sent may be viewed as "wasteland" by policymakers who view the value of land only in terms of its human carrying capacity.

The participation issue in resettlement schemes has several facets. The participation of the populations residing in the resettlement area is particularly problematic. By the very nature of the areas involved—sparsely populated and underdeveloped—the preexisting population is likely to be outside the usual participatory channels. In some cases—such as Brazil and Indonesia—the original inhabitants belong to cultural groups that remain linguistically and technologically isolated. Communicating with them is often hindered by remoteness and poor infrastructure. When the infrastructure comes, changes often occur too rapidly for the participation of indigenous groups to be incorporated.

Furthermore, even if the original population has the opportunity to express its views, there will typically be the presumption that this population—whose territory is the target of encroachment—is so likely to oppose the resettlement scheme that allowing them to participate can only bring trouble to the program. In fact, their opposition is not inevitable, insofar as the provision of infrastructure to the area *may* benefit them as well as the newcomers. Yet an overture to promote their participation could very well be seen as asking for trouble.

The participation of the people who are to be resettled is complicated by the fact that their input prior to resettlement would be based on virtually no familiarity with the conditions of the resettlement area. In addition, once the populations have been resettled, there may be great difficulties in getting the settlers, often from different locales, to constitute a community. There is also the problem that settlers are often competing among themselves for choice parcels of land.

The Dandakaranya Project

While the influx of Hindu refugees from West Pakistan stopped within a few years of the partition of India in 1947, the stream of refugees from East Bengal (now Bangladesh) continued unabated for many years. Of the four million who had fled East Bengal, three million were settled in West Bengal and about 700,000 in Assam, Tripura, and Manipur; the rest were still in camps in West Bengal. The Indian states that had already absorbed a large number of refugees were not eager to receive those remaining in the camps. Most of these people were farmers strongly motivated to establish permanent landholdings to resume their agricultural pursuits. The central government of India responded in 1958 with the Dandakaranya resettlement project, targeted to be the largest project of its kind for postindependence India. The project received wide publicity all over India.

The Dandakaranya area—comprising the districts of Korapur and Kalahandi in the southeastern state of Orissa, and the Bastar district in the adjoining state of Madhya Pradesh—was selected for the settlement of

35,000 families. It was a sparsely populated malarial area with more than 40 percent of its land covered by thick forest. The area was inhabited mostly by "tribals"—the official euphemism for culturally and economically isolated populations—and was economically backward. It was argued that the resettlement would accelerate the development of the area. Land clearing would provide agricultural land for the tribals as well as the refugees, although the tribals were typically nomadic.

The development program included reclamation of land and its distribution among the displaced, who would be provided with agricultural implements and supplies. Malaria eradication, road construction, and improvement of communication (nearly nonexistent at the time), and other basic services were also planned. Unlike the Indonesian *transmigrasi* program, however, the Dandakaranya planners did not envision sending balanced communities covering all required occupations; the vast majority of the settlers were Bengali farmers, and only 3 percent of the settlers were nonagriculturalists (Gupta 1965, 15).

A special agency called the Dandakaranya Development Authority, under the Ministry of Rehabilitation, was established by the central government to handle this mammoth project. The Food and Agriculture Ministry commissioned some soil analyses, though it did so only after the project had been launched and with apparently little impact in light of the pessimistic findings of these analyses. The Dandakaranya Development Authority was essentially in full control, and Authority officials in the resettlement areas (though not native to those areas) had unusually high levels of managerial discretion, to the point where S. K. Gupta, chairman of the Authority for ten months during 1964, later complained that:

> under the peculiar administrative arrangement of the Dandakaranya Development Authority most matters were dealt with at a lower level and hardly reached the Chairman unless they were regarded as matters of high policy or unless the Chairman specially called for information. There were no annual reports nor any collected body of statistical information covering all aspects of the project and its working up to date (Gupta 1965, 15).

Gupta also complained about "the illogical distribution of powers and functions at the top level, the inflated staff and the large establishment bill, the inefficiency of some technical staff, the enormous TA [technical assistance] bills and the excessive amount of unnecessary traveling . . ." He pointed out that the Dandakaranya Authority appropriated some of the best agricultural land for its own workshops, tractor parking lots, and offices (Gupta 1965, 94–96).

The Dandakaranya program faced innumerable difficulties from the beginning. Delays in obtaining and preparing land put the Authority in the predicament of either reneging on promises or relocating families before the infrastructure was in place. Trying to put the best face on it, the Authority established the Dandakaranya Development Corps, a work group to be comprised of settlers. The idea was dropped after the settlers proved to be both resistant to and untrained in infrastructure construction. From then on and until the late 1960s Dandakaranya depended on heavy machinery for road construction and land clearing, resulting in the highest costs per acre of any of the comparable colonization schemes (Farmer 1974, 156). Yet as late as 1967 the road system had only 191 miles of main roads, 297 miles of link roads, and 144 miles of roads connecting tribal settlements (India, Ministry of Rehabilitation, 1967).

The state governments of Orissa and Madhya Pradesh were at best lukewarm toward the program. After all, their land was being transferred to outsiders and the potential for additional pressures on the state treasuries grew proportionately. The state governments delayed the release of the lands (Farmer 1974, 156) even while the central government was promising rapid settlement; this was one reason why the Authority felt compelled to deliver settlers to the sites before the lands and the infrastructure had been properly prepared. When the states released the first installments of 100,000 acres of land, they were found to be hardly accessible. The four strips of land were separated by long distances. Moreover, they were basically unsuitable for cultivation. Local farmers had already cultivated virtually all the fertile valley areas enriched by silt and moisture (Gupta 1965, 16). The remaining lands required heavy and extensive contouring against erosion, highly labor-intensive cultivation to remove stumps and weeds, and more regular rainfall than the climate offered.

Even though the preparations of land and infrastructure were inadequate, the Authority started transporting the refugees to reception centers established in the command area. The idea was to use the refugees themselves to prepare the land and the road system. By providing them with this paid employment, it was believed that the refugees could overcome the demoralization of living on the dole and be prepared psychologically to settle productively in Dandakaranya.

Yet the refugees found the environment very hostile. With their background of cultivation in the fertile, rain-fed alluvial soil of East Bengal, the harsh, dry land of Dandakaranya presented a stark contrast. Many quickly concluded that the project was futile. Even the transitional period in the work centers was demoralizing. The farmers, especially the peasant proprietors, would not normally take up nonagricultural manual work outside their villages. Wage labor was extremely distasteful. Moreover, by the time resettlement was to take place, the Authority had spent much of its financial resources on the infrastructure of its top-heavy bureaucracy and on underutilized heavy construction machinery, rather than for the allotments that were supposed to go to the resettling families.

Rather than settle in Dandakaranya with inadequate land, infrastructure, and financial resources, many refugees returned to West Bengal. The 1966–67 report of the Ministry of Rehabilitation reported that only 10,051 of 13,389 families remained at their homesteads; thus a quarter of the refugees returned. Even worse, the returnees undoubtedly informed prospective settlers of the harsh conditions, with the result that the pace of resettlement was held back by settlers' reluctance as well as by the slowness of the project procedures. By 1967, some 300 million rupees had been spent on the project; since approximately 250 million rupees were spent before 1965, the bulk of its impact should have been realized by 1967. At the prevailing exchange rate,[2] the 1967 cumulative figure was equivalent to about $3,000 per family for all families moved, and almost $4,000 for each family that remained. Worst of all, even sympathetic evaluations in the mid–1960s had to point out that nearly half or more of the resettled families could not produce the minimum yield necessary to support themselves.[3]

Many of the difficulties with the Dandakaranya project could be attributed to the lack of preparation or clear purpose on the part of the central government and its officials. There was certainly a lack of appreciation of the complexity of resettling people into an unfamiliar ecosystem with major differences in climate, soil, crops, and water supply. The seemingly clever approach of relying on the settlers themselves to build roads and irrigation earthworks disregarded their deeply ingrained attitudes toward nonagricultural work. When it came to cultivating the fields themselves, the new settlers found that the seemingly generous allotment of six to seven acres, designed to offset the relatively low yield per acre, required more manpower during the cultivating season than was available. Ironically, the lack of surplus labor and the inability to bring seasonal labor into these inaccessible areas further depressed production.

The reluctance of the state governments to provide better land—and better situated land—was also a major factor. To the degree that a state government can only be assumed to defend the interests of its original population, this reluctance is certainly understandable; thus the question turns to the inability or unwillingness of the central government to demand greater cooperation from Orissa and Madhya Pradesh.

This criticism, however, must be qualified by understanding that while hindsight makes it clear that the uncharted forests of the Dandakaranya region turned out to be inhospitable to the Bengali settlers, the prevailing perception was that seemingly lush forests could easily be transformed into productive farms. Even B. H. Farmer, the British authority on agricultural colonization throughout South and Southeast Asia, could criticize other notable experts (including P. T. Bauer and Kingsley Davis) for their overoptimism in projecting the potential of India's "cultural wastes," and yet marvel at the "readily cultivable land for the modern era of government-sponsored colonization" of the Dandakaranya plateaux (Farmer 1974, 31, 56).

Still, in retrospect it seems odd that the Indian government did not draw a more pessimistic conclusion from the fact that these areas had resisted cultivation for thousands of years, and had been capable of sustaining only very small populations of largely nomadic tribals. Rather than viewing the forest and the marginal lands remaining as the residue of thousands of years of efforts to extend agriculture, the premise of the Dandakaranya project was that these lands were a frontier for new settlers. Perhaps the previously low population density was seen as the result of the endemic malaria, and therefore the officials expected that the eradication of malaria would unleash the productive potential of the area. Perhaps the government officials attributed the tribals' failure to domesticate the forest to their backwardness, and presumed that the more dynamic Bengalis would behave more like the European settlers in North America. Or perhaps the presumption was that "modern government-sponsored colonization" is capable of combining the appropriate financial, technical, administrative, and social factors to make an area like Dandakaranya work.

In any event, although there is controversy over whether there were adequate soil surveys (see Gupta 1965 and Farmer 1974, 144), soil studies were not published, often did not reach the top policymakers, or were disregarded in the planning of the project. As early as 1962 agronomists were reporting on the very poor soil conditions of much of the Dandakaranya areas (Gupta 1965, 16). When reports of very low yields of paddy reached headquarters with the endorsement of the Authority's director of agriculture,

> [t]he Chief Administrator . . . would not believe it and held that the yield must be higher, and an obliging subordinate officer of the Agricultural Department dutifully gave him a note in support, but the Director of Agriculture stuck to his view. To the Chief Administrator's statement that at least 60 percent of the lands given to displaced persons must be yielding 10 mds of paddy per acre if not more he observed that "the lands would then be very good indeed and there would have been no scope for us to find hundreds of acres in this tract unutilised" (Gupta 1965, 17).

This sort of reaction may be the key to understanding why there is so little evidence of "adaptive management" to rectify the false steps in the Dandakaranya project. Overcoming the reluctance to adapt, with the obvious political cost of implying that previous procedures and policies necessitate change, requires credible information. The information coming from the field was not only sparse, it was also bound to be questioned in the highly politically charged atmosphere of a troubled project that had become a partisan political issue heatedly debated in Parliament. Was the director of agriculture reporting information in a neutral, technical fashion, or playing intra-agency politics? The level of politicization of attitudes toward the Dandakaranya project is reflected in an article in *Modern Review* in October 1967, which argues:

> In ancient times, people were sent to Dandakaranya for Vanabash, as a punishment or for penance. . . . [Today] the sinners do not go to Dandakaranya but they arrange to send the people they have sinned against to those dismal regions. First came the West Bengal refugees, who were driven out of their homes in East Bengal by the soldiers of the new State of Pakistan which was created by a joint agreement between the Indian National Congress, the Muslim League and the British Parliament. The people who performed this treacherous act of betrayal against millions of innocent persons in order to achieve their ambitions are still enjoying power and prosperity while the victims of their sinful scheming are trying to build their new homes in the dense jungles or arid plains of the most inhospitable parts of India. (*Modern Review* 1967, 242)

Whatever one thinks of the hyperbole of this interpretation, it does make it clear why any criticism of the Dandakaranya project, whether internal or external, would have been interpreted from a political perspective.

Indonesian Transmigration

In contrast with the Dandakaranya project, which was impelled by the single event of India's partition and the subsequent problem of Bengali refugees, Indonesia's resettlement scheme has been a long-standing response to the continual population growth and overcrowding of Indonesia's "Inner Islands" of Java, Bali, Madura, and Lombok. Resettlement to the "Outer Islands" of Sumatra, Kalimantan, and Sulawesi began as early as 1894 under Dutch rule. More than 200,000 people were resettled on these three islands between 1905 and 1940; however, they were primarily moved directly into employment on plantations (rubber, tea, tobacco, and spice) or in oil and mining operations (Donner 1987, 43). Given the small scale of resettlement relative to the population increase of the Inner Islands, and the focus on providing laborers for export-oriented operations, this early experience was quite different from the Dandakaranya-like post-World War II emphasis on providing homesteads for huge numbers of settlers in forested areas.

The Transmigration program (*transmigrasi*) under the independent Indonesian government was unveiled in 1947 with the wildly ambitious target of moving 31 million people within fifteen years. In 1951 the target was revised to 48 million people for the period 1953 to 1987, or 1.26 million annually. In reality, fewer than 500,000 people left the crowded Inner Islands between 1950 and 1969 under the official auspices of the government program, an average of 26,300 per year (Donner 1987, 45).

Since 1969, *transmigrasi* has been part of the five-year development plans called Repelita I, II, and III. In terms of meeting the numerical targets, the results have been impressive. Repelita I (1969–73) achieved 110.3 percent of its targeted 40,959 families; and although Repelita II (1974–79) only relocated 22.4 percent of its targeted 250,000 families (Van Der Wijst 1985, 9), Repelita III (1979–84) exceeded its target of 500,000 families by 5 percent (Donner 1987, 253). Yet the quality of life of the settlers, the environmental damage to the forest areas, and doubts about the settlements' long-term sustainability have aroused very strong criticism.

In the initiation of the *transmigrasi* after World War II, the goal of resettlement was clearly to relieve the population pressures by providing the poor of the Inner Islands with the opportunity to exploit the undeveloped Outer Islands. For President Sukarno, Indonesia's population was not too large (he stated that the country could accommodate 250 million people (Oberai 1983, 250)); it was poorly distributed. The Outer Islands were a presumably bountiful frontier; the objective was to "fill up the empty spaces of the Outer Islands" (Colchester 1986, 100).

For the Suharto administration, encasing *transmigrasi* in the comprehensive five-year plans has increased the objectives attributed to it: national unity, national security, equal distribution of population, national development, preservation of nature, assistance to the farming classes, and improvement in the welfare of local peoples (the equivalent of the "tribals" in the Dandakaranya region) (*The Ecologist* 1985, 300). Van Der Wijst (1985, 4) adds that by Repelita II the program was also defended on the grounds of its presumed contributions to more equitable distribution of welfare benefits and employment creation, as well as increases in agricultural production and regional development.

All of these objectives are laudable and ought to be kept in mind while formulating policy. Yet attributing them all to the *transmigrasi,* which seems to have been motivated overwhelmingly by the short-run target of moving as many families as quickly as possible, had the opposite effect of stifling the examination of *trade-offs* among the objectives outlined above. While some conversion of virgin forest into farmland may have been desirable, there was no publicized analysis of what the optimal amount of conversion would be. Even so, in 1982 the Indonesian government acknowledged, in a joint study with the International Institute for Environment and Development, that "[t]he program as it presumably is implemented does not support the sustainable development of Indonesia's forestlands, or, for that matter, the settlements themselves" (Secrett 1986, 85).

In conceiving the *transmigrasi* project, the Indonesian leaders did not expect that resettlement would be the panacea to overcrowding, nor that it should be the only policy instrument. Suharto has initiated government-sponsored birth control programs; despite the overoptimistic public pronouncements about the capacity of *transmigrasi* to relieve overcrowding, it is not the only response to this problem. On the other hand, the fact that resettlement only affects a fraction of the population added each year to the Inner Islands does not mean that *transmigrasi* is necessarily ineffective— the situation would be worse if that fraction had not been relocated. So the question is not so much "Should migration to the Outer Islands be *the* policy to alleviate population pressure on the Inner Islands?" but rather "How much migration—official or unofficial—ought to be tolerated or encouraged, and at what price, given that both the Inner Islands and the Outer Islands have problems with absorbing more population?"

Another objective of the *transmigrasi,* at least under Suharto, has been the cultural and socioeconomic unification of Indonesia, tinged with vague national security implications. The government's unabashedly integrationist attitude toward non-Muslim, economically backward forest dwellers has drawn much criticism as being culturally chauvinistic, patronizing, and insensitive to the rights of the indigenous populations. The "nation building/national unification" perspective is at odds with the demands made by outside critics to preserve indigenous cultures.

The substantive flaw in scope of the *transmigrasi* was in overestimating the carrying capacity of the Outer Islands. Official statistics estimate that six out of eighteen receiving regions of the Outer Islands are already overcrowded, with a net overpopulation of over 1.6 million people (Donner 1987, 250). The government estimated in 1987 that the Outer Islands still had room for 8.3 million more people, but this has been strongly disputed in light of the fragility of the forests, the damage already done through slash-and-burn cultivation, and the abandonment of many farm sites. The discrepancy between the microevaluations questioning the sustainability of existing settlements and the estimate of 8.3 million potential settlers indicates that the macroestimate was made without reference to the specific conditions of the settlement areas.

The most ominous development has been that after Suharto banned virgin forest clearing in 1979, and therefore cancelled some of the latest settlements of Repelita III, he apparently reversed this policy for the *transmigrasi* of Repelita IV (1984–89), for which 80 percent of the sites are to be situated in previously untouched forest. This represents the loss of some 3.3 million hectares of forest, for official migrants' first settlement plots alone (Secrett 1986, 80). The recognition of environmental risk is not simply the hobbyhorse of government critics; yet, despite the government's own worries, the pressure to move families from the Inner Islands has been allowed to jeopardize the ecological balance of the Outer Islands.

This pressure on the Outer Islands has been exacerbated by unofficial spontaneous migration. Ironically, the phenomenon of spontaneous migration was not only anticipated by the *transmigrasi* planners, it was made a virtue. The "growth pole" regional development theory prevalent since Repelita I has been based on the idea that the effectiveness of official resources devoted to Outer Island migration would be magnified by the self-financed migration of other settlers. The attractiveness of land acquisition in the Outer Islands was great enough to draw settlers even without the *transmigrasi,* which, if successful, would provide the infrastructure to make resettlement all the more attractive. A more skeptical view, however, would be that the pressure on natural resources was not only greater than that represented by the planned resettlement, but also far less predictable.

Yet the resettlement program per se was, in a sense, very thoroughly preplanned. The notion of regional development embraced by the *transmigrasi* planners was rooted in the idea of the self-sufficient village. Each resettlement village was to be provided with all the necessary occupations (for example, carpenters, blacksmiths, teachers, and doctors). This finely balanced self-sufficiency would distinguish the planned resettlement from the spontaneous resettlement. Of course, this resulted in a mentality of planning from the center to create essentially "turnkey" settlements. Little allowance was made for the possibility of unforeseen occurrences or idiosyncracies; there were no effective mechanisms for on-site adaptation to unforeseen or special circumstances. To be sure, administration in the settlements under the local transmigration officials is helped by extension workers to provide advice on animal husbandry, agriculture, and education. Local elites, selected and trained by *transmigrasi* officials, are also used in the village-level administration. And after five years, jurisdiction passes to the Ministry of Home Affairs and settlers are granted voting rights. Yet the basic decisions on who shall form a settlement, where the settlements are to be located, how much land should be allotted, and the regulation of settlers' behavior are made at the center.

The lack of sensitivity for specific conditions, and the apparent lack of awareness of how the program was working out "in the field," are consistent with the policymaking mode adopted by the *transmigrasi* planners. All program planning comes directly from the central government. Spontaneous migration aside, the formal program was originally conceived with hardly any input from the Indonesian public. In the Indonesian political context, the enthusiastic support of an initiative by the top governmental leadership virtually assures that other officials will support the program and be very reluctant to voice criticism. President Suharto "has long been known to have an obsessional interest in transmigration. His personal interest in the project for many years has been such that no official has dared to oppose it" (Budiardjo 1986, 114). Moreover, Suharto has involved Indonesia's powerful military in the program, giving them some of the site clearance responsibility (Jackson 1978, 12–13). The extension of official programs into the Outer Islands is seen by the Indonesian armed forces as an instrument of unification for national security (see below). In short, as long as the top officials and military express commitment, *transmigrasi* will proceed, and only the rationales will change periodically to suit the spirit of the times. The key question then becomes: what magnitude? The official planned targets do not seem to have been formulated systematically in terms of available resources, judging by the severe shortfall for Repelita II and the scaling back of the 1986–87 target from 100,000 families to only 36,000 in December of 1986 (Lachica 1986, 12E).

The real determination of the resources devoted to the *transmigrasi* seems to be a two-stage process: the government proposal of the foreign exchange requirements of the project to the various international donors and lenders, and the responses of these agencies to the government's request. Within the limitations of this resource ceiling, there may be an additional constraint imposed by any guidelines coming from the government or the international agencies that could lead to delays in implementation under prevailing conditions of bureaucratic capability or restrict where settlement can take place. In other words, both the top Indonesian leadership and the international agencies share in the setting of upper bounds on the level of migration, both by the level of funding that is requested and granted, and by imposing further restrictions on implementation.

In these circumstances, the Indonesian governmental agencies that might worry about the adverse effects on the environment and on indigenous populations are not in a position to oppose the overall thrust of policy or the operations of the Ministry of Transmigration, even though environmental, health, and resource concerns are obvious. The Ministry of Transmigration, formed in 1983 to overcome the poor coordination of its lower-level predecessor and other governmental agencies, has the formal authority to oversee the implementation of all resettlement operations. To be sure, many other agencies are involved in the operations. The Department of Public Works is involved (along with the military) in planning and building the infrastructure of roads and land clearing; the Ministry of Home Affairs assists with land searches; the Ministry of Agriculture is involved in land preparation and agricultural extension; the Ministry of Education provides school facilities and teachers; the Ministry of Health provides medical care and disease control; and the Ministry of the Environment consults on land selection and land-use regulation. Yet these agencies play relatively little role in shaping the broad outlines of the *transmigrasi* program. The agencies that are proficient and eager to expand their activities, such as the Department of Public Works, have a strong incentive to support the expansion of resettlement. Those with responsibilities that would lead to objections to the pace and nature of resettlement, such as the Ministry of the

Environment, are up against the "pet project" of the president. What little discretion these other agencies have lies primarily in selecting their personnel to be lent for transmigration operations. Lending their first-rate personnel would be a way of increasing their influence, but it would also take some of the best personnel away from agencies already concerned about the thinness of their qualified personnel.

The Ministry of Transmigration's dominance over the resettlement program has been enhanced by three additional factors. First, there are *transmigrasi* officials sprinkled throughout the other agencies and in local government at the resettlement sites. Second, the power of the Transmigration Ministry has been manifested in its tendency to operate with minimal consultation with other agencies, thus keeping them short of information that might strengthen their ability to assert themselves in the shaping of the resettlement policy. For example, for many years there was practically no contact between transmigration authorities and the Ministry of Health, despite the fact that migrants represented new disease vectors.

Third, *transmigrasi* has been heavily funded by outside donors, including international organizations such as the World Bank (the largest lender), the United Nations Development Programme, and the Food and Agriculture Organization; bilateral government sources such as the United States, France, and West Germany; and NGOs such as Catholic Relief Services (Colchester 1986, 67). The combination of the Transmigration Ministry and its prestigious international collaborators could not easily be challenged in terms of expertise, experience, and political clout. Although all outside assistance must be matched by a certain percentage of local currency outlays and personnel commitments, the project's capacity to "earn" foreign exchange makes it a formidable political force. A quite parallel situation arose in Sri Lanka with the Mahaweli project (see chapter 6), where the inflow of huge amounts of foreign currency made the project attractive even if its usefulness was highly questionable. Yet in the case of Mahaweli the worst scenario is basically that the dams remain inoperative and the cost would be the lost opportunity to use the resources more productively. The worst-case scenario for the Indonesian resettlement is far more ominous: irreversible damage to Indonesia's forests and the stranding of hundreds of thousands of people in inhospitable areas.

One might expect that reliance on foreign donors and lenders would make the *transmigrasi* more accountable to these institutions. Yet until very recently there has been little responsiveness of either the Indonesian government or the funding agencies to criticisms from environmentalists and human rights activists supporting the rights of the indigenous populations. This may be explained by the fact that these agencies had also developed a vested interest in the progress of the resettlement program. Insofar as an international financial institution like the World Bank has to fulfill its mandate to lend large volumes of money, the unimpeded progress of a mega-project like the Indonesian transmigration project—to which the World Bank committed $600 million by 1985[4]—becomes a high priority. Even if the criticism of the international agency's involvement with the project mounts within the agency (as was also the case with Brazil's Polonoroeste project examined next), the institution's top leadership and especially the personnel associated with the project cannot be expected to shift their position without the greatest reluctance. In the case of the Indonesian transmigration project, the World Bank finally changed its emphasis on rapid resettlement to a greater concern for finding better sites. It earmarked $120 million of its loans for better site selection, making it more difficult for *transmigrasi* officials to obtain enough land to meet the targets (Caufield 1984, 27). The government ended up in somewhat of a double bind: the more stringent site criteria made it more difficult to adhere to resettlement targets, and the scaling back of targets prompted the World Bank to cut back on funding.

Beyond the macro-policy issue of the optimal scope of the resettlement, the key challenge for the *transmigrasi* planners has been the selection of sites. As with the Dandakaranya region, the hilly, heavily wooded resettlement areas of the Outer Islands have great local variation, with many sites so borderline in terms of cultivable potential that detailed soil and rainfall analyses are essential (Hanson 1981, 220). An additional problem is that flora and fauna unique to very small ecosystems are also at risk, with the possibility of the loss of hundreds of species of plants and animals (Secrett 1986, 78).

Thus selecting sites that both provide viable production for the settlers and avoid destroying unique ecosystems is particularly difficult in Indonesia. It is also a highly "expert-intensive task." The Transmigration Ministry and the international lending agencies have had central government personnel to assist them, but the caliber of personnel freed up by ministries already too thinly staffed with technical experts has been problematic.

On paper the procedures for selecting settlement sites seem impeccable.

Each potential site undergoes a separate analysis of its suitability, involving aerial and ground surveys to judge land conditions and soil quality; topographical and border surveys; meteorological and hydrologic surveys; and sociodemographic and economic surveys of the preexisting populations (Comte 1978: 31). However, the importance to the *transmigrasi* planners of relocating people as rapidly as possible is borne out by the fact that for every thorough site survey there have been many incomplete surveys (Van der Wijst 1985: 12).

In light of the variability in site quality, the issue of plot size becomes crucial, even if hopelessly poor plots are eliminated. In contrast to Dandakaranya, where there was little variation in plot size despite wide variations in soil and hydrological conditions, the Indonesian approach has been more sophisticated and less rigid. Where land was known to be relatively poor in quality or inaccessible, the settlers were given larger plots, expanding the usual range of landholdings to between two and five hectares (*The Ecologist* 1985, 300).

Finally, the *transmigrasi* officials had to contend with the issue of whether and how to regulate the settlers' use of the forest. The key issues were the size of each settler's plot, the question of whether conditions could be imposed upon the use of all or part of that plot, and the advisability of establishing government reserves on the land not allocated to individual families. This was all in the context of heavy pressures from ''nonofficial'' migrants, who did not receive the direct benefits from the government but who did not fall under full governmental regulation either. The decision was to allocate relatively small quality-adjusted plots, without requiring that the settlers maintain any fraction of their land in forest. In light of the inequities of land allocation in Dandakaranya and elsewhere,[5] and the abuses encountered in the Brazilian case that follows, the Indonesian decision seems wise. Yet it did impose additional analytic and administrative burdens on the *transmigrasi* administration to distinguish land quality differences and to make the allocations accordingly.

The Centralization Bias of Transmigrasi Administration

The Transmigration Ministry oversees operations by ten ministries or departments and fifty-four directorates general (Van der Wijst 1985, 5). Local-level administration is staffed primarily by central government career personnel, including the project manager, village unit manager, and their staffs. Extension workers also receive their orders from Jakarta. Block leaders and others given authority at the next lower level are local people selected by the administrators on the basis of their education, and are trained by the extension workers to teach skills to the settlers. Most training centers are located on Java (Donner 1987, 158).

This structure adheres closely to the social structure of the Javanese village, with the village leader (*bapak*) serving as educator, protector, and opinion leader. Most villagers accept the domination of the *bapak* (Jackson 1978, 35); thus the reliance on local elites has eased the central government's efforts to gain acceptance of its decisions and to convey information down to the settlers. However, there is little feedback flowing up from the villagers as to their problems, and the local leaders typically acquiesce to government plans, even when unworkable, to avoid "being crude" to people of higher social station (Jackson 1978, 39). Moreover, it has been found that the rise of a small elite within the settlement leads to inequality in terms of access to benefits and credit, and often the poorer transmigrant families become bound to wealthier families in an unequal patronage relationship (Van der Wijst 1985, 16).

Evaluating the Transmigrasi *Program*

The success of the Indonesian transmigration program has to be gauged by several criteria. One is the degree to which the expenses of the program are justified by the benefits to the settlers and others. While the program has been promoted for its impact on reducing overcrowding of the Inner Islands, population growth there has left *transmigrasi* with rather little proportional impact—Transmigration Minister Martono has stated that twenty million people would have to be moved from Java to significantly improve living conditions there (Otten 1986, 71).

Yet a more reasonable question is whether *transmigrasi* has improved the lives of the migrants. Here the answer seems to be yes, *thus far*. The targets of Repelita I and III were exceeded, and, in comparative perspective, the number of returnees has been minimal. Of the 527,000 people resettled under Repelita III, only 2,000 returned home, mainly because they had received land unsuitable for cultivation (Donner 1987, 253). Overall, the rate of returnees has been between 2 and 5 percent (Comte 1978, 34). This is a very low rate compared to the one-quarter return rate of Dandakaranya, although one must take into account the financial difficulty of returning from the Outer Islands without governmental assistance. The low return rate and the willingness of yet more people to be resettled indicates that most settlers perceive themselves to be better off and may be communicating that back to their families and acquaintances on the Inner Islands.

However, this seems to be a benefit of migration per se, rather than government-directed migration, since several studies indicate that the unassisted settlers are as well off as the official *transmigrasi* settlers (Suratman and Guiness 1977, 99–100; Fachurrozie and MacAndrews 1978, 102). Since official settlers receive subsidized transportation, initial food supplies, equipment, and technical assistance,[6] one might expect the official settlers to do better. Yet there is some evidence that the official settlers are assigned inferior land to what the spontaneous settlers can secure for themselves (Van Der Wijst 1985, 12–14; Hanson 1981, 220–21), and the spontaneous settlers benefit indirectly from much of the infrastructure provided for the official *transmigrasi*. Thus the comparison between spontaneous and official migrants, even if the spontaneous migrants appear to be better off, does not signify a program failure, nor that the official migrants would have been better off remaining on the increasingly congested Inner Islands.

The justifiability of *transmigrasi* expenditures in terms of the benefit and cost comparison naturally depends on who pays. From a strictly Indonesian perspective, the subsidies to official and spontaneous settlers are worthwhile to the degree that the settlers are truly better off, expenses are borne by concessional international loans or foreign aid, *and* these funds would not have been rechanneled to other Indonesian projects if resettlement were discontinued.

The second criterion is the long-term sustainability of the settlements. Here is where the greatest concern must be raised—will the settlers remain truly better off than if they had stayed on the Inner Islands? The cutbacks in the current plan targets were apparently driven by the difficulty of finding suitable sites rather than by funding shortages. This difficulty reflects the growing awareness that the pool of potential sites of long-term viability is more limited than previously believed; that environmental problems are not just unfortunate side effects but are jeopardizing the survival of the settlements. In 1984 Transmigration Minister Martono admitted that many transmigration settlements needed reconstruction, and, eighteen months later, recommended closing 18 of the 667 sites (Budiardjo 1986, 116). Many sites have simply lost their fertility, especially when subjected to the wet rice cultivation methods developed in Java but inappropriate on fragile lands reclaimed from rain forest. Thus the total pressure on the land resource is magnified not only by the spontaneous migrants, but also by the shifting of *transmigrasi* settlers to new land. The amount of land that ultimately has to be devoted to each family thus exceeds the initial plot of two to five hectares.

The third criterion is environmental protection. In addition to the unknown degree of environmental degradation that bears directly on the viability of settlements, the environmental situation includes the equally elusive issue of the importance of losing species diversity. Even if the myriad species were all identified and classified, their ultimate value for human welfare is unknown. Obviously, the potential that each species may provide the basis for new medications or plant breeding stock is unknown. While critics attack the resettlement program for the destruction of species, there is no indication that this nonquantifiable cost is balanced against *transmigrasi* gains in the government's deliberations. Nor are the possibilities of climatic change taken into account. These are sobering examples of the adage that the unmeasurable is often ignored.

An additional complication in evaluating the environmental impact is the interaction between official and spontaneous settlement. It is more likely that the unofficial migrants, less directly under the "guidance" of the Transmigration Ministry, are more prone to exploit the forests for quick profit and to encroach on the relatively fertile land held by indigenous people who are supposed to be protected by the *transmigrasi* program. Thus, insofar as the program imposes greater environmental discipline upon official settlers who would have migrated spontaneously, it is a clear benefit. However, to the degree that the program encouraged official migration of families who otherwise would not have migrated, and greater spontaneous migration as well, its benefits in relieving Inner Island population pressure must be balanced by the environmental costs imposed by the increased numbers of spontaneous and official migrants.

Unfortunately, there has been inadequate monitoring and evaluation of the movement of *transmigrasi* settlers onto new lands, let alone reliable statistics on the spontaneous migrants. The projections that 3.3 million hectares of Indonesia's tropical forests will be cleared in the next five years for *transmigrasi* would seem modest (aside from species loss), since it constitutes only 2.4 percent of Indonesia's 140 million hectares of forest (Secrett 1986, 77). Yet total deforestation, adding in unplanned clearing beyond the first settlements for official migrants, the clearing by spontaneous migrants, and increasingly frequent forest fires, constitutes a much greater but unknown potential loss.

Finally, on the criterion of participation, the *transmigrasi* has been deficient in several respects. The treatment of indigenous peoples has ranged from patronizing to exploitative. The *transmigrasi* program's dealings with indigenous populations have been very troubled, as one might expect from the government's national unification perspective. The results have been many claims of human rights violations, attacks by indigenous people on resettlement villages, deaths of indigenous people at the hands of the army, and land appropriation without adequate compensation or viable plans for resettling the displaced inhabitants (Colchester 1986, 102–3).

The fact that migrants are first congregated in groups of fifty to one hundred in staging areas on their home islands, and then travel together (with a typical travel duration of one month) to the Outer Islands, presumably has some effect on creating a sense of bonding among the settlers that may provide a first step toward building communities capable of self-expression. Once they are in a new settlement area, however, they are subject to a five-year period of "guidance," during which the Transmigration Ministry still holds authority over key decisions. After that point, the village attains the status of other villages in Indonesia—with the typical opportunities and constraints on participation (e.g., the dominance of the *bapak*) of other villages. Yet on one key issue the decisionmaking remains highly centralized: the Transmigration Ministry and the planning bureau, *Bappenas,* decide on how many more migrants will come into each of the settlement areas. There is no vehicle for one resettlement community to register opposition to the establishment of nearby settlements that might compete for access to natural resources.

Taking one step back to assess the Indonesian transmigration program, we can ask whether the more intensive *planning* of the *transmigrasi* of later years, inasmuch as it has been implanted within the five-year Repelitas and subject to analysis by the government's planning apparatus, has improved its effectiveness. The first answer to this question is that the coordination of site preparation, road building, and movement of official *transmigrasi* populations seems to have improved, even according to rather critical observers (Van der Wijst 1985). One might say that this is simply a result of learning from the mistakes of the past—transmigration under Repelita I was almost ad hoc, with many ensuing complaints of very poor scheduling and inadequate site selection; under Repelita II the coordination and advanced planning of settlements was still rudimentary (Van der Wijst 1985, 8). By Repelita III, it had become clear that greater advance preparation, provision of infrastructure, and staff were necessary. In this regard, finding ways to do things right and improving on past experience with coordination is where learning and planning converge.

The second answer is that taking into account the increasing difficulty in finding suitable sites, the *effectiveness* of securing and preparing sites for settlers may have improved, but the budget expenditures per resettled family have increased tremendously. During Repelita I, the average cost per family was just above $200; for Repelita II, it was $818. By 1979–80, the first year of Repelita III, the cost per family almost doubled from the last year of Repelita II; by 1982–83 the cost per family was $4,260 (Van der Wijst 1985, 7). Of course, some of these expenses, whether devoted to general administration or specific site preparation, benefited some of the spontaneous migrants. And to be sure, inflation accounts for some of the increase. Even so, the costs in *constant* dollars per official resettled family rose by a factor of five from 1969–70 to 1980–81 (Van der Wijst 1985, 7). The Ministry of Transmigration has built up a rather large empire, with the number of civil servants exceeding 13,000 by 1983 (Van der Wijst 1985, 8). The idea that migrants would be involved in the preliminary construction of infrastructure and site preparation was abandoned, as it was in Dandakaranya, and mechanized land clearing was emphasized at least until it was criticized in the early 1980s. Thus the state had taken over more of the responsibilities of providing for each officially sponsored family.

The third answer turns around the definition of success. It is certainly true that under Repelita III, the Transmigration Ministry was able to increase the number of migrants dramatically, and that their immediate needs and proximate environment were provided more effectively. Yet concerns about the carrying capacity of the Outer Islands bring the wisdom of this increase into question. The mechanization needed to clear land rapidly enough reduces the agricultural potential of the soils (Van der Wijst 1985, 17). Both the numbers of settlers (official and spontaneous) and the placement of some of them on substandard sites give additional impetus to slash-and-burn encroachments into the forests. Thus, planning as the initial *analytic* determination of the optimal scope of the program seems to have been neglected. *Coordination* seems to have improved, but *analysis* of the nature and boundaries of the problems was suppressed, presumably because of the ''political reality'' of unwavering support from the top administration, as well as the bureaucratic interests of the Transmigration Ministry itself.

It is important to conclude this survey of the Indonesian transmigration experience by pointing out that *evaluation* of such an experience is always less than satisfactory. In accounts of the *transmigrasi*—or Dandakaranya or any other such program—one can always find references to problems: settlers arriving to find that their promised homes have not yet been constructed; soils that were not as good as they should have been; delays in implementation, and so on. Yet we know, of course, that some problem or another is inevitable; reporting these problems, culled from fragmentary assessments, can certainly give a strongly negative impression. In one sense, every preventable error is unacceptable, but finding such errors does not tell us whether the undertaking was worth doing, or whether the way the project was carried out—in terms of administrative structure, timing, etc.— was appropriate.

Moreover, even if we knew the overall balance of success and failure for each family, there is no straightforward means of concluding whether the result is acceptable or not. Assuming that the resettled net benefit to the population is positive, we still do not know whether the combination of spending *and* the depletion of the natural resource endowment has been best used in light of alternative projects. Alternatively, we can take the resettle-ment scheme as a *fait accompli*, turn away from the question of whether it should have been undertaken (political commitment having made this a moot issue), and focus attention on how it can be best done.

Brazil's Polonoroeste Project

Our previous cases of resettlement range from the clear imperative seen by Indian officials to stimulate resettlement where little or none would have taken place without governmental impetus, to the Indonesian *transmigrasi,* where the government was strongly motivated to *augment* the spontaneous migration already directed to the Outer Islands. We turn now to the Brazilian Amazon, where a flood of migration had been occurring, partly as a result of governmental policy but not primarily under governmental direction. Land consolidation due to mechanization in Brazil's South, and high birthrates, especially in Brazil's impoverished Northeast, had resulted in millions of landless rural people. Many of the landless looked to the largely unoccupied Amazon region to obtain or regain some land. Govern-ment policy also enticed them by laws pertaining to public lands that in effect gave ownership to whoever cleared virgin land.

In the case of Brazil's Polonoroeste project, the government was more concerned with controlling rather than stimulating migration—though

Brazilian policymakers were well aware of both the population pressures in Brazil's South and Northeast and the fact that the Amazon region could absorb some of that population overflow. By 1980, the annual population growth rate in the Amazonian state of Rondônia reached 14.8 percent, and in Mato Grosso 8 percent. The questions were: how much migration, at what rate, and under what conditions, to allow for maximum sustainable development?

For decades, the migration of Brazilians into the Amazon region was not directly undertaken by government programs, although it certainly was stimulated by government projects. In the 1960s, Brazil developed and implemented the Plan for National Integration (PIN), the Trans-Amazonian Highway Project, and two Plans for Development of the Amazon (PDA I and PDA II). Therefore the primary objective of the Northwest Regional Development Plan (Polonoroeste) was not explicitly to promote migration—as was the goal for both the Dandakaranya and *transmigrasi* projects—but rather to improve migration patterns, and to promote productive, sustainable use of natural resources in Rondônia and Mato Grosso while accelerating the region's economic development (Fearnside 1986, 229). A World Bank specialist, José Botafogo, has described the primary objective of Polonoroeste as steering migration away from fragile areas and promoting sound agricultural practices (Botafogo 1985, 224).

A broad infrastructure for Amazonian development was in place, and significant patterns of decisionmaking and influence had been established.[7] Most decisions to implement Amazonian projects were made at the highest level of government, especially within the Ministry of Agriculture and the Ministry of Transport. These upper-level decisions generally have not been based on significant input from lower-level officials or specialists. Decisions on the Amazon region have been regarded as of the highest national security concern, a key element of Brazil's development path toward great nation status, and partly high politics. Whether the Amazon in fact presents issues of such importance is debatable, but the previous promotion of highly expensive Amazonian development initiatives certainly gave Amazonian development great importance in the eyes of many Brazilians. It is therefore understandable, if lamentable, that specialists on the scientific and environmental aspects of Amazonian development were relegated to "troubleshooting"; they were assigned basically to address the problems and reduce the damage caused by the projects, but were minimally involved in formulating the macrodesign (Fearnside 1986).

When the Cuiabá–Pôrto Velho Highway was opened in 1969, much of the pressure of population increases and increasing land concentration in Brazil's South and Northeast was directed into the fragile forest and swamp of the Amazon region. The migration by the 1970s was rapid and largely uncontrolled. Migrants came whenever the highway was passable, and settled on whatever land they found unoccupied. Violent conflicts arose between indigenous Indians and the settlers, as official and unofficial Indian reserves were invaded; violence also occurred when the migrants themselves disputed land. Slash-and-burn cultivation led to deforestation. Unlike long-standing communities of stable population that practice slash-and-burn rotation that permits previously cleared land to recuperate by the time it comes back into rotation, the flood of settlers pushed the clearing further and further into the forest, as settlers searched for soil more conducive to farming. By 1980, the situation in the Northwest territory (Rondônia and western Mato Grosso) was alarming and still deteriorating. Late in that year, the Brazilian government asked the World Bank to evaluate the situation.

World Bank specialists worked intensively with personnel of the Ministries of Transport and Agriculture. There were numerous complaints that the Ministry of Agriculture had been thoroughly penetrated by the special interest representatives of the Amazonian Association of Agriculture and Ranching Entrepreneurs, as well as individual landowners and extractive industry companies (Teece 1987). The Ministry of Transport was, of course, heavily involved because of the central role played by first the Trans-Amazonian Highway and then all the feeder roads designed to open up the region. Unlike both the Dandakaranya and *transmigrasi* projects there was no special government unit given overall control over resettlement, although the Ministry of Agriculture's National Institute for Colonization and Agrarian Reform (INCRA), established in 1970 to bring order to Amazonian colonization, was involved among other agencies.

The result of this collaboration was the Polonoroeste project: road construction, allocation of land to settlers in return for their commitment to manage it according to government guidelines, extension services and infrastructure development, and greater support for agencies in charge of environmental protection and Amerindian affairs. This combination gave the project a dual image. The kind interpretation was that the Brazilian government was addressing the fact of spontaneous migration by trying to channel it as constructively as possible. The skeptical interpretation was that the Brazilian government had packaged a continuation of the Amazonian road program in such a way as to make it more palatable to the World

Bank and other donors by adding some superficial conservationist trappings.

INCRA and the National Department of Roads and Highways (DNER) were allotted the greatest amount of money to carry out their parts of Polonoroeste, roughly 26 percent and 57 percent respectively. In the bureaucratic infighting, INCRA had several advantages. It was created by President Medici expressly to oversee Amazonian migration, and it has legal jurisdiction over federal lands. To a large degree it is self-financing (rather than being dependent on the federal budget) through its land sales to the private sector. Of course, this, too, gives rise to criticism over the influence of the private sector over Amazonian development. In any event, INCRA has been responsible for supervising land settlements. The government also established an "Institute for the Defense of the Forest" (IBDF), to serve as an institutionalized pressure group within the government. Whether the IBDF was allowed to be effective or was simply window dressing designed to deflect criticism has been a matter of controversy. Similar charges have been aimed at the National Indian Foundation (FUNAI), a governmental agency formed to protect the indigenous Amazonian population.

DNER receives such a large portion of total funding because of the emphasis on building, maintaining, and improving national roads and highways. DNER had the primary responsibility for the key Amazonian construction project, Highway BR-364, to which over half of the Polonoroeste budget was committed. DNER is required to work with INCRA, the state governments, and the military (which, like the Indonesian armed forces, gets involved in road construction). DNER maintains its preeminent position in highway management through the support of local and national private-sector interests, ranging from land developers and logging companies to highway construction contractors.

This was the policymaking terrain in place when the Polonoroeste project was launched. The objective of the project was to create regulated settlements for the 5,000 migrants arriving each month in the Northwest territory. The settlement sites would be selected and established by INCRA based on soil surveys conducted by the technical Agency for Research in Agriculture and Cattle Ranching (EMBRAPA). Further steps for establishing settlements would include: clarifying land tenure; providing credit, storage, transportation, and fertilizer; reinforcing extension and research; improving education; and improving health conditions through clinics, clean water, and anti-malaria programs (Goodland 1986, 18).

Individual families were given 100 hectares of land upon arrival, half of which was to remain forested (Fearnside 1985, 246). Compared to the Dandakaranya and *transmigrasi* projects, even the fifty hectares of legally exploitable land sounds extremely high. This original policy of allotting 100 hectares per family seems to have been a precedent from earlier Amazonian development policies—little research was done and the amount came under heavy criticism later on from a variety of critics. In light of the Dandakaranya and *transmigrasi* projects, the fact that the additional fifty hectares was given over to the settlers, rather than giving them just the fifty exploitable acres and leaving the rest under the direct control of the state or local government, also seems unusual.

EMBRAPA had an important role in the Polonoroeste project: to conduct two separate aerial land surveys of the region, the second at a higher level of detail. The survey maps were to be used by INCRA to classify the sites by soil quality.[8]

While INCRA has had the responsibility to select sites based on EMBRAPA information, the Institute for the Defense of the Forest (IBDF) has had the formal authority over all forest clearing and was charged with enforcing the regulation that no more than 50 percent of a given parcel could be cleared. Thus the IBDF has been responsible for demarcating forest reserve boundaries, maintaining a battalion of forest police, and monitoring deforestation in conjunction with the Space Research Institute via aerial and satellite information. IBDF is also responsible for encouraging sustained-yield forest management of the colonists' lands that are to remain forested. In practice, however, the IBDF has little influence over settlement sites and has been ineffective in policing forest use.

Similarly, the underfunded FUNAI was charged with the broad tasks of guaranteeing enforcement of the laws protecting the Indians and safeguarding their reserves (8,000 Indians on thirty-five separate officially designated areas were recognized in the project design). FUNAI has been responsible for notifying the Indians that settlers would be arriving, and then either trying to protect the reserve area or relocating the Indians elsewhere. FUNAI, with little money, no real enforcement power, and a politically powerless constituency, has had little success. It has been particularly weak in blocking road building into reserve areas, just as the IBDF has been ineffective in blocking incursions into forest reserves. This is hardly surprising in light of the political support and huge budget of NDER, compared to the 3 percent share of the Polonoroeste budget allotted to the IBDF and FUNAI together.

The planned settlements to be established by INCRA in 1981 were to be based on an EMBRAPA land survey completed before the settlements were to begin. However, understaffing at EMBRAPA caused a one-year delay in producing even the first set of maps. INCRA proceeded with establishing settlements on lands with almost no research, and apparently even the preliminary EMBRAPA research was ignored (Fearnside 1986, 229). By the time the EMBRAPA soil and land survey was completed in 1982, roads and settlement infrastructure had already been built on very poor agricultural land. The soil surveys showed that only 15 percent of the area under active settlement had soils requiring low or medium fertilizer and lime inputs; the rest would require applications of costly complex fertilizers for sustainable use. This compared with a total of 42 percent of viable soils encountered in earlier projects (Fearnside 1986, 233–34). As in the Indonesian Outer Islands, the soil surveys showed that the land remaining for additional resettlement was increasingly marginal.

INCRA was successful in demarcating landholdings and providing clear titles for some 12,000 families a year. Of course, in many other countries the problem of obtaining clear title to land has been a serious obstacle to agricultural productivity. But the rush to provide relatively large parcels of substandard land did not contribute to higher productivity.

The government's largesse in endowing each settler family with 100 hectares of land had a surprising consequence. The fifty hectares legally available for cultivation required too much labor and capital for full exploitation, whereas the option of felling as many trees as possible, without additional inputs, and then selling the land to speculators or ranchers, provided many settlers with an irresistible windfall. Thus, in addition to those settlers who simply managed their 100 hectares poorly, there were many who essentially transferred their land to the larger landholders, transforming the program into a short-lived subsidy for the settlers as well as furthering deforestation.

Aside from the policy of trying to reserve half of each 100-hectare holding for forest, the Polonoroeste plan maintained (but did not expand) designated forest reserve areas off-limits to development. One rationale for not expanding the reserve area, which covered only 1.8 percent of Amazonia, was the inability of the IBDF to monitor a larger area. In light of the initial plan's stated objective to steer migration away from ecologically sensitive areas, the absence of forest reserve expansion drew heavy criticism.

It appears that INCRA tried to respond to the economic failures of its previous settlement attempts by putting more emphasis on agricultural development, even at the expense of equity considerations. Kendall (1984, 226) quotes Ernani Continho Filho, INCRA director in Rondônia, as observing in 1982 that "of course, the prerequisite is still farmers who hold no land. But we have a selection process for farmers these days. We tend to favor people with experience in managing their own farms, people with some education and a stable family life. Those are the people who tend to succeed on the frontier." He continued, however, "That's the theory, anyway. In practice, the majority of pioneers who come to Rondônia are still totally unprepared people, poor and illiterate."

In late 1984 the mid-term assessment of Polonoroeste revealed that road construction and other physical infrastructure developments were ahead of schedule, but Indian protection, environmental protection, health services, and agricultural extension were very poor (Goodland 1986, 24). The negative reaction of the World Bank prompted the Brazilian government to hold back its application for disbursement of the World Bank loan, effectively suspending the project. But in the summer of 1985, President José Sarney called for adding two million hectares to the Amazon's protected reserves, removing illegal squatters, and improving the institutional structure of environmental protection. In August the disbursements were resumed.

It may be argued that the Polonoroeste project made some settlers better off through their subsidies, and perhaps some settlers were steered away from particularly fragile areas. Yet the project undoubtedly had some effect on enhancing rather than dampening the Amazon's image as a government-sponsored magnet for development and settlement. The inflow of people and the sale or abandonment of depleted land have resulted in significant unemployment within the region. As was the case in both Dandakaranya and the Indonesian Outer Islands, the infrastructure of extension agents and experienced on-site bureaucrats, though widely recognized as essential, was very deficient.

Thus the irony is that the Polonoroeste project, designed (at least according to the least cynical interpretation) to regulate migration, has exacerbated some of its problems. Now, perhaps one could say that the Polonoroeste project was not the cause of the "spontaneous" migration into the Amazon even after the decent agricultural land had been claimed. Yet the project has contributed to the abuse of the forest in several ways. First, it has encouraged settlers to try to exploit marginal land that they may have been bypassed were it not for the fact that they were given clear title to it. Second, whatever credibility the Polonoroeste project gave to the image of rational Amazonian development probably legitimated the efforts to open up the Amazon. For example, the Inter-American Development Bank's financing of the Pôrto Velho–Rio Branco Highway and the World Bank's general funding would have been far less likely without an apparent effort to provide regulation. Third, the provision of roads and public services subsidized spontaneous migrants as well as planned migration.

The World Bank and other funders have had growing reservations about the entire Amazonian development approach. The World Bank, in particular, had been under increasing pressure by environmentalists who blamed the Bank for continuing to support Amazonian development with inadequate provision for environmental and Indian protection. To be sure, many of these critics believe that there is no way to develop the Amazon without unacceptable damage to both. The World Bank, for its part, was caught in the same dilemma as the Brazilian government: a project designed (at least in part) to steer migration away from its most destructive manifestations still encourages further migration and abuse. In 1987 a large part of World Bank funding for Amazonian road construction was suspended on the grounds that the projects did not meet environmental standards. Further Trans-Amazonian Highway construction apparently has been stopped. The Polonoroeste project, at least under that designation, has been abandoned.

However, even as the Brazilian government was protesting the World Bank's decision and complaining that Brazil's national sovereignty had been violated by the interference in domestic policy, it was proposing that the World Bank provide a $100 million credit for an environmental protection plan (de Onis 1987). Whether this signals a new approach to balancing migration with environmental protection remains to be seen.

General Lessons from Resettlement Experiences

Whether resettlement programs are motivated out of concerns for equity, growth, or reducing environmental abuse, they are clearly among the most complex challenges a government can undertake. The relocation of hundreds of thousands of people to a totally new environment engages both the complexity of sheer size and the complexity of having to reshape entire communities. In all three cases—Dandakaranya, *transmigrasi,* and Polonoroeste—resettlement in forests has meant that the projects had to cope with uncertainty and wide diversity in soil conditions; they had to make do with the poor state of knowledge about the carrying capacity of rain forest. The preservation of biodiversity in varying ecosystems is a problem in all three cases; varying rainfall is a problem at least for the Dandakaranya and *transmigrasi* cases. For the Indonesian and Brazilian resettlement programs, spontaneous migration added immensely to the uncertainty of impacts.

Another aspect of the complexity of resettlement programs is the multiplicity of agencies that reasonably could be expected to be involved. Since all of these programs had multiple goals, the mandates of many government units were engaged: transport, public works, agriculture, health, community development, environment, education, welfare of indigenous populations, and so on.

An additional level of complexity comes from the diversity of interests that come to be focused on the resettlement area. Indigenous groups, official settlers, spontaneous settlers, and land speculators complicate the picture. Finally, the challenge of managing resettlement programs is heightened by the fact that once land is assigned, the vested interests of those who have received the benefit make it difficult to change course in order to correct mistakes.

There are several natural impulses to coping with complexity. Some of these can be seen in the three resettlement projects reviewed above. One impulse is to simplify by centralizing. For both Dandakaranya and the Indonesian transmigration program, a separate authority was given primacy; in Brazil the authority was, in practice, much more dispersed. The case of Dandakaranya clearly shows that while putting virtually all decisionmaking power in the hands of a single "authority" may reduce bureaucratic infighting and poor coordination, it also runs the risk of creating a "state within the state" that molds the initiative to serve its own purposes, with little accountability to higher or parallel authorities.

Another impulse in the face of daunting complexity is simply to disregard certain aspects of complexity, especially uncertainty, by presuming that adaptations to unforeseen conditions will be successful. All of the resettlement examples reveal a Pollyanna attitude toward the productivity and durability of forestlands. Even when soil survey procedures are built into the project, as in the case of Dandakaranya, the tedious process of conducting the surveys typically delays the dissemination of the results past the point in time when the project could be significantly restructured or cancelled without tremendous political costs to its sponsors.

All of the resettlement examples also show overoptimism about the capacity to move people into an unfamiliar ecosystem and get them to work productively within a short period. Particularly in the cases where spontaneous migration is also occurring, a resettlement planner may argue that any systematic structuring of the migration patterns is superior to the patterns that will otherwise prevail. Nevertheless, an overoptimistic official resettlement program will encourage settlers who otherwise would not have migrated, thus adding pressure to environmental and social systems that suffer from the strain.

5

Grandiose Designs:

The Construction of Large Dams

Large dams play three major roles in the macro-management of natural resources: providing power, irrigation, and flood control. Irrigation, discussed in depth in the following chapter, has been *the* major water issue in the Third World. Hydropower plays a crucial role in economic development; successful hydroelectric projects have contributed substantially to the economic well-being of many developing nations. Dams have the potential to control flooding, although some critics claim that dams can actually magnify floodwater damage (Goldsmith & Hildyard 1984, ch. 10). There are possible additional benefits of improved navigation, recreation and fishing. Given these multiple benefits, it is clear why large dams have been so extraordinarily alluring.

Yet large dams raise so many problems that a large body of opinion rejects the entire enterprise of large dam building. Brent Blackwelder, of the Environmental Policy Institute, argues that "the case against irreversible manipulation of river systems on a global scale is so overwhelming that we proceed with funding of these superdams at our own peril" (Goldsmith and Hildyard 1984, xxii). Reservoirs associated with large dams often submerge vast tracts of farming and forest lands, displacing longtime residents and wildlife. Upstream soil erosion often causes major dams to silt prematurely, reducing their effective lives and thus their economic returns, and keeping the silt from flowing beyond the dam may deny soil nutrients to downstream locations. In some instances, changes in water flow increase

Case materials for this chapter were initially prepared by Moira Quinlan and Alangudy Srinivasan.

the incidence of parasitic disease. Even under the best circumstances, dam construction ties up huge amounts of investment capital that could be devoted to other development projects; even if the funding comes from external donors, a large portion of that funding is typically diverted from other purposes.

Major development strategy decisions hinge on whether this drastic critique is justified, or whether the problems can be addressed by reforming the policymaking processes of designing and implementing large dam projects. There has recently been much soul searching, even among river-valley development specialists, as to whether any large dams can be cost effective, even in a country like India with glaring shortages of energy and water; given the *possibility* that large dams could be instrumental in lifting poor countries out of poverty, the reality is that they will be launched. The challenge for planners and policymakers is to ensure that social, environmental, and participation issues are adequately considered.

In this chapter we examine the planning, implementation, and assessment of dam-building projects in the neighboring countries of Sri Lanka and India. Sri Lanka's Accelerated Mahaweli Development Program, touted for both its irrigation and hydroelectric potential, has become the archetypical "boondoggle" project. Its sheer magnitude and financial resource requirements led to the domination of foreign aid considerations over those of rational resource use, environment, and even sound engineering. The result was a structurally flawed, hugely wasteful project. Major river valley developments in India began with the vaunted Damodar Valley Corporation, which foundered on interstate rivalry and lack of adequate coordination. The current agonies of the Narmada Valley's development—a long-delayed effort beset with bitter controversy and apparent official neglect of environmental and distributional problems—illustrates that the legacy of earlier setbacks may result in a stalemate of mutual suspicion rather than positive learning. Finally, we examine the Bodhghat (or Indira Reservoir) project, a medium-sized dam proposed in Madhya Pradesh—precisely where the ill-fated Dandakaranya resettlement scheme and the pine forest project discussed in chapter 3 failed miserably. While less majestic and certainly less significant for India than the mammoth dam projects already mentioned, the Indira Reservoir has gone through more thoughtful and better balanced consideration, although the whole gamut of environmental and distributional risks confronts this project as well.

The striking lesson to policymakers is the importance of addressing flaws in political and social organization. Certainly there is much technical analysis to be done in order for huge, complex ventures like multipurpose dams to be well designed and implemented. Yet in these cases the problem is not so much that the technical burdens are overwhelming, but rather that restrictive policymaking routines, lack of participation, and premature closure of problem definitions render good technical analysis either impossible or irrelevant. The obstacles amounting to the "implementation gap" mentioned in chapter 1—regional rivalries, political maneuvering, and bureaucratic inefficiency—are clearly operative in these cases.

The Accelerated Mahaweli Development Program

The Mahaweli Ganga is Sri Lanka's most important river, draining an area of approximately 4,000 square miles. Originating in the mountainous south-central part of the island, it flows for 200 miles into the dry zone before discharging into the Bay of Bengal. The river is the principal source of water for irrigating the dry zone. The Mahaweli Development Program, a monumental irrigation and hydropower project, was conceived to use this river not only within its natural basin, but also to divert the Mahaweli Ganga to seven rivers in the dry zone. The "scheme" involves huge dams, a barrage across the Mahaweli, an intricate canal system, and long tunnels.

Such a project is also a resettlement program for those displaced by the creation of reservoirs. Others are likely to move spontaneously, or to be moved by government programs, to take advantage of newly cultivable land. The objective was to shift population into the newly productive drylands area, away from the population concentrations in the areas of greater rainfall. Huge dam projects like the Mahaweli scheme thus add the socio-geographical complexities of resettlement to the major engineering challenges connected with building the dams and related structures.

Background of the Accelerated Mahaweli Program

Water engineering was certainly not new to Sri Lanka. In the sixth century A.D. and again in the twelfth century, stable and centralized Sri Lankan kingdoms constructed elaborate systems of canals, reservoirs, and tanks distributed widely over the dry zone (de Silva 1987, 47–49). In the following centuries of political disintegration these systems deteriorated, leading to the depopulation of the dry zone, yet the irrigation systems did indicate the capability of traditional irrigation to offset the climatic imbalances of nature. The ancient Sri Lankan population, however, was much smaller than it is today; Sri Lanka's current population is six times larger than the population of just one hundred years ago.

The original Mahaweli Development Plan of the 1960s proposed to irrigate 900,000 acres of land through projects scheduled from 1970 to the year 2000. Of this, 654,000 acres were undeveloped, while 246,000 acres were already under cultivation, 90 percent in paddy. The project was to cover a gross area of over 9,000 square miles—40 percent of Sri Lanka's land area. The original plan envisioned fifteen new reservoirs and eleven power stations, allowing double-cropping on extensive dry zone areas and a doubling in hydropower by the addition of 540 megawatts. According to plan estimates, over one million people were to have found jobs in agriculture, agrobased industries and ancillary services. The estimated cost of the project was Rs. 6 billion (roughly one billion 1970 U.S. dollars) over thirty years.

Obviously, a plan of this magnitude and complexity requires detailed feasibility studies and engineering plans. The government's initiation of such studies came in 1963 as a request to the Food and Agricultural Organization (FAO) and the United Nations Development Programme (UNDP) to examine the irrigation and power potential of the Mahaweli system. The study was undertaken, largely with FAO and local Sri Lankan personnel, from 1965 to 1968 (Iriyagolle 1978, 2–3). Despite this apparently long interval, the UNDP/FAO study did little beyond examining the feasibility of the first phase projects, and yet it gave estimates of what subsequent phases might yield in terms of water, irrigated acreage, and hydroelectric potential. All of this was accompanied by formulae and specific figures, but the UNDP/FAO mission was quite explicit about the superficiality of its analysis of phases II and III, calling it a "preliminary study" of a "reconnaissance nature" (Iriyagolle 1987, 2). Even the accompanying maps varied as to the affected areas.

According to Gamini Iriyagolle, a disillusioned Sri Lankan development official who published an exposé of the project in 1978, the World Bank found even the Phase I analysis so rudimentary that in 1969 it refused to fund this phase. This was a serious political cost for the United National Party (UNP) government, which had already announced that the project had been funded. After further negotiations, the World Bank relented and agreed to fund Phase I in three stages, but only if each stage were accompanied by further feasibility studies by foreign consultants acceptable to the World Bank (Iriyagolle 1978, 2–3). The World Bank provided roughly half the funding for the Phase I project. However, although this funding was almost lost because of dissatisfaction with the UNDP/FAO study and the lack of more definite feasibility studies, the Sri Lankan government later labeled the UNDP/FAO study the "Master Plan" for all of the Mahaweli Development Program. Neither the Sri Lankan government nor the World Bank produced a new "master plan" to replace the UNDP/FAO study.

Work on the first stage of the plan—the construction of two dams and power houses at Polgolla and Bowatenna—was started in March of 1970. Two years later, the UNP government was defeated by the Sri Lankan Freedom Party (SLFP), which criticized the "harsh terms" that the World Bank had imposed on Sri Lanka with the UNP's consent (Navaratne 1981, 6). As a result of the SLFP's poor relations with the World Bank and the impasse on lending terms, the project was delayed for two years.

Nevertheless, the government resumed work on the first stage of the Mahaweli program in 1972. This segment was almost completed when the UNP government returned to power in 1977. Soon after his election, Prime Minister J. R. Jayawardene presided over the opening up of 130,000 acres of newly irrigated land, with the accompanying resettlement and growth in agricultural production of this first-phase area.

The Initiation of the Accelerated Mahaweli Program

After consulting with the World Bank and several foreign governments, the Jayawardene government unveiled the "Accelerated Mahaweli Scheme." A new Ministry of Mahaweli Development was established to signal its importance. In the initial announcement, this program was presented as a telescoping of the remainder of the entire thirty-year program into five years:

> It has now been decided by the Sri Lanka Government to accelerate the pace of development with a view to complete all works envisaged in the Master Plan in five years. For this purpose, all works (other than the Project which is nearing completion) are grouped as 12 projects as indicated below which can be studied and executed as such (Mahaweli Development Board 1977).

The quote not only presents the acceleration of very complex construction as an exciting advantage, it also presents the decision as a *fait accompli.* Yet Jayawardene had been elected only in late June of the same year; obviously there had been no time for detailed feasibility studies.

Despite minor changes in the program's scope over the course of the following months,[1] the Accelerated Mahaweli Scheme remained extremely ambitious. While only two major dams to irrigate 130,000 acres had been constructed in the seven years of the original Mahaweli project, the Accelerated Scheme scheduled five dams to provide for 350,000 acres over five years. The ambitiousness was also evident in the project's share of the government's capital expenditure—on average, 30 percent of public sector investment, with the figure going above 40 percent in some years (Sri Lanka, Ministry of Finance and Planning 1985, 161–62). No one complained that the Accelerated Scheme was too slow, but many worried that the pace would outstrip Sri Lanka's capabilities. The World Bank's reaction was quite skeptical; ultimately the Bank funded only a relatively small part of the Accelerated Project.

Yet this ambition was a promotional and political virtue. The Accelerated Mahaweli Scheme was presented as the lead project of an integrated program designed to catapult Sri Lanka into the 21st century, a virtual panacea to Sri Lanka's problems. Gamini Dissanayake, the Minister of Mahaweli Development, stated in 1981 that the program's success held "the solution to all the major problems confronting the country, *viz.* self-sufficiency in food, full employment and energy to move the wheels of industry" (Sri Lanka, Ministry of Mahaweli Development 1982, i).

The Mahaweli Development Program was cast as the single most important key to the unemployment problem, the centerpiece of a revolutionary departure from the previous administration's "make-work" social welfarism. The Mahaweli Scheme was also presented as the remedy to Sri Lanka's heavy dependence on imports of food and other agricultural products. Since World War II rice production, the foundation of the rural economy, had failed to keep up with population. The Green Revolution had virtually bypassed Sri Lanka. The Mahaweli Scheme sought to liberate farmers from subsistence agriculture and to promote food self-sufficiency.[2] Greater paddy production was proposed as even having the potential to achieve an exportable surplus to decrease the trade deficit.

Increased irrigation capacity was seen to be the answer to the agricultural production problem. Approximately two-thirds of the resources allocated to agriculture in central government investment programs were earmarked for irrigation.

Finally, the Mahaweli Scheme proposed to solve the energy shortage that blocked Sri Lanka's industrialization. Lacking coal, petroleum, or natural gas, Sri Lanka was importing roughly three-fourths of its commercial primary energy, yet by 1978–80 energy consumption was growing at a rate of 12 percent, spurred on by improved living standards and rural electrification. In 1977 Sri Lanka was just entering a period of severe energy shortages that was to last at least through 1981, just when industry was surging. The desperation to build dams is thus understandable, since hydroelectric power is virtually the only source of domestic primary energy in Sri Lanka. The total hydro-capacity of Mahaweli was projected to reach 940 Mw, so that the total energy supply would be sufficient to meet demand up to 1990 (UNIDO 1986, 72).

With such challenging objectives, why was the project telescoped so drastically? The costs should have been obvious; the engineering, social, and infrastructural planning was hurried and proved to be terribly deficient. However, the government argued that if the project had been phased over thirty years as originally planned, there would be no "significant impact" on Sri Lanka's problems (Sri Lanka, Ministry of Mahaweli Development 1982, 72). The effects of development, it was argued, would be diluted. There was even a rather lame attempt to justify the accelerated schedule on the grounds that the longer period of the original project would increase the project costs through inflation—a specious argument given the importance of *real* as opposed to *nominal* costs, and the fact that public works wages would increase disposable income without immediate consumable output, thus contributing to inflation rather than reducing it. Indeed, the Accelerated Scheme was probably a major factor in the inflation that ensued in the late 1970s and early 1980s.

Yet the boldness of the Accelerated Scheme paid off politically; Sri Lankan historian C. R. de Silva (1987, 273) concludes that even by 1987 "it is as yet too early to make an assessment of the economic returns from the scheme but it is clear that it has caught the popular imagination and has been a factor that contributed to the electoral victories of the UNP after 1977."

In addition, the Accelerated Mahaweli Scheme still seemed to be a source of employment, as long as comparisons to the longer-term employment gains of a more drawn-out, labor-intensive schedule were not made. Yet more careful analysis would have revealed that the employment gains were illusory. The accelerated construction schedule dictated that heavy construction equipment—which had to be imported—would replace much of the labor-intensive construction of the earlier Mahaweli components.

The Accelerated Mahaweli Scheme was also to be Sri Lanka's greatest source of foreign exchange. Given the willingness of several bilateral lenders to subsidize the project, this was very attractive to a foreign-exchange-hungry government. Yet these two appeals resulted in a painful trade-off. To cash in on the maximum aid flows, the Accelerated Scheme required the most rapid construction methods, thus reducing the employment absorption of the project.

There may be little that is unusual about the case of the government of a country with a thin cadre of technical expertise overspending on a politically popular, grandiose development project. What makes the Accelerated Mahaweli Scheme particularly interesting as an example of Pollyanna optimism is the fact that the Accelerated Mahaweli Scheme involved the World Bank and several bilateral lending agencies of presumably impressive technical competence. This would seem to be the perfect opportunity for these agencies to play the technical watchdog role.

As mentioned above, the World Bank's doubts about the viability of several of the Accelerated Mahaweli Scheme's components put the Bank in the position of refusing to finance, or even to endorse, major pieces of the program. The World Bank did finance small pieces of the Accelerated Mahaweli Scheme, partly to preserve its access. Yet the Sri Lankan government soon discovered that although the World Bank urged scaling down the project, bilateral lending agencies were quite disposed to fill the breach. Sri Lanka has some geopolitical significance, serving as an excellent refueling point for tankers and military vessels. And many industrial countries had important but ailing industries producing the machinery needed for major hydroelectric and irrigation projects. Through "tied aid" (requiring Sri Lanka to purchase the earth movers, steel, turbines, and so forth from the donor country), the bilateral lending agencies could subsidize their national industries (and maintain domestic employment in those industries) while providing what must have been assumed to be a magnanimous gift to Sri Lanka. These arrangements resulted in financing from the United Kingdom, Canada, Sweden, West Germany, Japan, Kuwait, and the European Community.[3] The aid package amounted to 7,600 million 1982 rupees (approximately $365 million) by way of grants and import support on which *no* repayment was due. Sri Lanka had no incentive to be efficient in regard to time or money. It is no surprise that cost minimization and cost recovery seemed almost irrelevant.

Problems of Implementation

The Accelerated Scheme fell prey to the common paradox that haste causes delay. While inflation per se has little economic bearing on real project costs as long as relative prices remain more or less the same, the budgetary consequences of inflation, linked with rising real expenditures, plagued the scheduling of the program. Project costs, reflecting unforeseen expenses as much as inflation, could not be met by budgeted funds. Without reserve funds sufficient to cope with the overruns, project implementation was often delayed until further allocations were made, especially during the period of severe inflation between 1979 and 1983. In 1977 the total cost of the Accelerated Scheme was estimated at Rs. 8 billion. Due to cost overruns, inflation, and devaluation, the cost estimate at the end of 1980 was Rs. 31 billion.[4]

Though the greater portion of the capital was from foreign donors, Sri Lanka's own contribution of over 30 percent of public-sector investment meant that the Mahaweli's cost was viewed as restricting growth in other areas of the Sri Lankan economy and hence was fair game for cutbacks. The Ministry of Finance and Planning never settled on a clear plan for the pace of Mahaweli development under circumstances of fiscal stress, making delays commonplace and further planning virtually impossible for the Ministry of Mahaweli Development. In the first draft estimates for 1981, for example, the Ministry of Mahaweli Development received the biggest single amount of the budget—Rs. 4035 million—but by the end of 1981, the Ministry of Finance and Planning had cut the Mahaweli Development Scheme by 25 percent. It is not surprising, therefore, that the Minister of Finance and Planning, Ronnie de Mel, confessed in 1981 that "the government had reached the stage where it could no longer plan with certitude—*even for a year*" (Wijesinghe 1981, 40). This made it impossible to adhere to specified construction schedules.

The implementation of the Accelerated Scheme was constantly hampered by inadequate feasibility studies and shoddy technical projections. The lack of adequate studies on cropping patterns, farm productivity, water needs, farm size, and so on, left no basis for determining which components were cost-effective, for locating access roads or bridges, or for planning later stages. Iriyagolle reports that as late as 1977 the so-called "Master Plan" of the UNDP/FAO study was still the guiding document, despite the fact that it lacked specific engineering feasibility studies, cost-benefit studies, or even precise locations for canals and other essential works. In order to submit more credible proposals to the World Bank and to bilateral lenders, a Dutch consulting firm, NEDECO, was brought in—at the expense of the Netherlands government—to do feasibility studies for the "Implementation Strategy" of the Accelerated Scheme. The consultants, by their own admission, had woefully little time to carry out their work, and in any event the Prime Minister had made it clear that the Accelerated Scheme and its "Master Plan" had already been "decided" (Iriyagolle 1978, 4). NEDECO found many deficiencies in the UNDP/FAO study, declared that much information necessary to evaluate the project was lacking, and questioned Sri Lanka's administrative capability to handle a project of this magnitude. They warned that "if such an undertaking is not properly planned in all its details on the basis of lessons learned from past mistakes, a disastrous situation may develop" (Iriyagolle 1978, 5). Nonetheless, through a very optimistic interpretation of NEDECO's contradictory statement that their study confirmed the *outline* of the UNDP/FAO Master Plan, but that "firm conclusions therefore cannot be drawn as yet," the Jayawardene government launched the Accelerated Scheme.

Beyond the lack of feasibility studies and detailed plans, the crush of work required by telescoping the Mahaweli program led to the same kinds of inefficiency of haste that were encountered in the Dandakaranya, *transmigrasi,* and Polonoroeste projects. Surveyors who normally executed limited perimeter surveys for private clients were commissioned to survey up to 5,000 acres without survey department controls. Even when engineering surveys were carried out under supervision, channels were constructed that ran below the land to be irrigated. The dams themselves all suffered from major structural flaws.

The greatest technical omission of the Mahaweli Scheme, however, was in underestimating the amount of water necessary to irrigate the acreage of agricultural land proposed in the Master Plan. Assumptions in the UNDP/FAO study of the irrigation requirements of various crops were absurdly low, and the command area in all cases was stretched out excessively. The Ministry of Mahaweli Development greatly overestimated the annual water issue at 5,956,000 acre feet. Even so, 7,797,670 acre feet would be needed to irrigate the 900,000 acres proposed in the Master Plan. With the actual amount of water available, only 354,000 acres could have been irrigated (Iriyagolle 1978, 34–44). The plan also did not allow for water-use increases due to the influx of population into the settlement areas, or for increased industrial use. There was just not enough water to go around.[5] To compound the problem, shoddy construction due to the accelerated time schedule led to seepage losses of between 40 and 50 percent of all water issues at diversion points.

The above miscalculations and faulty technical estimates, aggravated by budgetary vacillations and uncertainties fed by inflation, led to revision upon revision and skyrocketing costs. At the commencement of the Accelerated Scheme in November-December 1977, the declared decision of the government was to complete the *entire* Master Plan (900,000 acres) in five years. Within a year, the time frame was extended—and obscured—by defining the remaining time frame as "five to six years." By mid-1978 the government decided to irrigate only 340,000 acres in five to six years. In early 1979 the command area was scaled down to 320,000 acres of new land under five new reservoirs plus an unspecified balance of other projects in five to six years. In 1980 the government accepted the main NEDECO recommendations and confined Phase I of the project to the Kotmale, Victoria, and Maduru Oya projects together with downstream works, but a *further* scaling down of the whole project became necessary at the end of 1980. The height of the Kotmale Dam had to be reduced in mid-project to reduce construction costs and allow for the decrease in water levels from the original estimate. The Randenigala project, begun in 1980, had to be put off for one year and then again in 1981.

One might be tempted to look upon these delays and deletions as a politically clever and technically reasonable way of bringing the project to a more feasible scope. Yet the delays increased construction costs by over 50 percent in *real* terms. The breakneck start-up pace resulted in poor articulation of related construction components that remained even after the schedule had been changed, and the commitment to the use of heavy equipment was irreversible, even though construction could have been labor intensive if a slower schedule had been followed from the beginning.

Of course, this description of the constant revisions plaguing the Mahaweli project is not to imply that all changes implemented in midstream are detrimental; obviously, it is better to remedy project deficiencies during construction than to cover up mistakes in order to maintain political credibility or favor. The criticism is that such costly revisions could have been avoided through intelligent prior planning. NEDECO had warned the Sri Lankan government in September 1979 that the scheme was "unrealistically ambitious":

> Developing and settling 120,000 hectares in 5 or 6 years implies an annual implementation speed of more than 20,000 hectares and the settlement of 140,000 persons per year. This is a *very high rate* and it is impossible to find examples from other countries of the world where such rates of land development and settlement have been achieved over sustained periods (cited in Wijesinghe 1981, 53).

NEDECO went on to express doubts about Sri Lanka's ability to provide the manpower and materials necessary for such "an undertaking of unprecedented scale complicated to a degree that would test the organizational skills of *any* country (cited in Wijesinghe 1981, 53).

The failure to come up with realistic preliminary cost estimates led to unjustifiable spending per beneficiary. Assuming the costs of irrigation, agriculture, and settlement infrastructure at Rs. 30,000 million, the overall capital investment per family receiving two and a half acres of irrigable land would have been Rs. 75,000—over $4,800 in 1978 U.S. dollars—in a country with a per capita income of roughly $250. According to Iriyagolle (1978, 46), the farmers would have to be the "best in the world" to give the country the minimum essential return for the "world's most expensive irrigation project to date."

The presentation of the Accelerated Mahaweli Scheme as a panacea also led to the neglect of many smaller cost-effective projects. There were approximately 10,000 small tanks that only needed minor reconstruction or renovation to be functional. It is estimated that 251,000 acres of land could have been made productive if 7,406 tanks were repaired and maintained. These smaller tank projects would have had much lower unit costs (Rs. 7,000 to Rs. 10,000 per acre) than those of the Mahaweli (Rs. 25,000 to Rs. 30,000 per acre), a much lower import content (15 percent) than that of the Mahaweli (40 percent), and much greater labor intensity. Yet, the government did not focus on these projects because they were not as glamorous or politically advantageous. Moreover, these minor tank projects, if they had been taken up full-swing, would have undermined Sri Lanka's claim for getting on the lending agenda of the bilateral lending countries. The emphasis of the government has therefore been on the size and number of projects, not on cost-efficiency and sustainability. As stated in *Public Investment 1985–89:*

> The emphasis in the past has been on the expansion of irrigated agriculture through large-scale projects. The neglect of operation and maintenance activities at the expense of new projects has resulted in the progressive deterioration of existing irrigation facilities and the wasteful use of water. The cost of providing additional irrigated acreage is thus becoming prohibitively high (Ministry of Finance and Planning 1985, 56).

It was only in 1982 that the Minor Tanks Rehabilitation Program was initiated, repairing approximately 200 village tanks at a cost of Rs. 670

million in order to bring improved irrigation to approximately 15,000 acres. While this program constituted a step in the right direction, it was practically negligible compared to the time, energy, and funds reserved for the grandiose Mahaweli Scheme.

Equity and Participation in the Mahaweli Resettlement Process

Significant population resettlement was an integral part of the original Mahaweli Accelerated Scheme. The colonization scheme had proposed to settle 1.5 million people. From 1975 to 1985, just over 47,000 families had been resettled (Central Bank of Sri Lanka 1985, 104). Even at six settlers per family, this was only a fraction of the targeted number. Iriyagolle (1978, 40) estimates more reasonably that roughly 140,000 families could have been allotted their 2.5-acre homesteads on the actual irrigable area. Even by this standard, the Mahaweli program, like the other officially sponsored resettlement programs we have examined, was seriously behind schedule—or permanently short of meeting the resettlement target.

Even the critics of the Accelerated Scheme acknowledge that some effort went into trying to learn from the country's earlier colonization schemes (Siriwardhana 1981). Nonetheless, the resettlement program is a glaring example of inequity in the allocation of resources and the absence of channels for grassroots participation. Both impeded the sustainability of settlement for many families.

The problem began even in the process of selecting colonists. The selection was to be based on the efficiency of farmers, yet in some cases this was impossible because land had been given as compensation to displaced individuals. Many solitary, old, unproductive farmers were given full-size allotments while many full families capable of efficient cultivation with their own manpower were turned away.

The greatest examples of inequity of distribution are to be found within the settlement areas themselves, following the distribution of allotments. From the start, too much emphasis was placed on construction and physical infrastructure, while the settlers were virtually ignored. An evaluation study by the research department of the People's Bank noted: "There was far more attention paid to land development, construction and capital investment rather than the socioeconomic requirements of the settlers as human investment" (Siriwardhana 1981, 46). The result was that quantitative considerations prevailed over qualitative ones regarding distribution within the settlements. In the eyes of the government, as long as each settler was given a plot of land, the distribution was an equitable one. The government overlooked the wide variations in the quality of the land parcels. Moreover, the government reduced the size of the allotment to 2.5 acres to allow a greater number of farmers to participate, leaving those allotted marginal land even less chance to farm successfully. In some areas, colonists sunk into abject conditions.[6]

The government also reduced the size of the settlement hamlets in order to foster ''greater social cohesion'' among the settlers. Yet the government ignored the potential for conflict arising from the fact that some settlers received plots of very poor soil far from the headworks, while others enjoyed highly productive plots with more than adequate water supply. This disregard for the equality of opportunity led to distrust within the colonies instead of community spirit.

The major factor behind the poor conditions of many colonists was the proliferation of forms of hidden tenancy and control over production and land, fueled by variations in the quality of land allotments. Many settlers simply never had the chance to make a living on their own allotment. It turned out that 55 percent of the sample area of Midellawa was not suitable for paddy cultivation (Siriwardhana 1981, 14). Poor land coupled with bad weather conditions caused many settlers to lose their investment capacity in the first season through crop failures. Without the initial capital to work their own land, their only alternative was to lease their allotments to individuals outside of the settlement areas or to settlers with better land and water resources. Many farmers were forced to lease their land simply because they did not have sufficient water resources to cultivate it. This problem was due to lack of both technical and social planning on the part of the government. Some farmers were placed at turnouts (water-issue points) that received more than ample amounts of water, while some were located at points receiving little or no water. From the social planning perspective, the size of turnout groups was virtually overlooked. Some turnouts supplied water to eight settlers while others of equal size were situated to supply water to sixteen settlers. Sample village studies show some extreme cases of land leasing.[7] Of course, not every village is necessarily reflected by the sample, so we do not know how widespread this pattern has been. As with the *transmigrasi* resettlement program in Indonesia, the post hoc evaluation is clearly incomplete. Yet the same lack of provision for careful soil analysis, equitable water access, sufficient land and inputs, and a credit safety net held for other resettlement areas within Sri Lanka.

The existing management and planning structures could not remedy these problems. These deficiencies originated in lack of communication and in the absence of grassroots participation.

The public had no role in assessing the advisability of the project or in evaluating its progress. According to Iriyagolle (1978, 48), "no correct account of the Mahaweli Project had as yet been available to the public or even some of the official agencies concerned . . . nobody, unless he has actually worked on the project has a chance of knowing what the project is, far from getting the advantage of a meaningful analysis. . . . The policy of those concerned officially with the project is to treat reports and other information as if they were for their private information only."

Similarly, communication among the government agencies overseeing the project was severely restricted. While the Mahaweli Development Board is required by law to present an annual performance report to the Minister of Mahaweli Development, by 1978 only *one* summary statement (in 1975) had been presented.

On the village level, an overly complex structure impeded communication among units charged with integrated development. In each village the management structure consisted of five separate units for water management, community development, agricultural extension, land settlement, and marketing. Rather than coordinating the functions necessary for integrated development, this structure was characterized by rivalry among the officials of each unit. To a greater degree than in the *transmigrasi* and Dandakaranya cases, these units reported to different ministries, blamed one another for failures, and operated without consultation.

The gravest communication failure was between field officials and farmers; it was exacerbated by inconsistency between what the government told the farmers to expect from the field officials and what field officials had the training and capability to do. Originally, farmers were told that extension officers would communicate their grievances to their superiors and that these grievances would be resolved. However, due to the lack of training and poor interunit communication, farmers' grievances were largely ignored and deficiencies of project implementation were not addressed. The regulation two-week visit of an extension officer called for only one day of discussion with the farmers; the rest of the time was to be spent in doing paperwork (Siriwardhana 1981, 65).

The lack of officials' responsiveness was also based on a perverse incentive system that seemed to base promotion on relations with the

Colombo officialdom alone. Inadequate supervision and evaluation techniques of settlement officials worsened the problem. The evaluation of the Midellawa settlement states:

> An assessment of the ability and efficiency of the field workers was not being carried out. Even the corrupt and inefficient field officials received the same treatment as the better officers and they were given good reports, promotions, etc. due to lack of proper evaluation and supervision. On the other hand, the promotions and good recommendations of field officers was dependent on the superior's judgment which may be based on their personal relationship. Therefore, in view of those factors, field officials were compelled to please their superiors and not the farmers (Siriwardhana 1981, 67).

Farmers' feelings of powerlessness and futility were heightened by lack of grassroots level organization and participation in project implementation. Farmers in the villages lacked capital, credit institutions, training, access to modern technology, and organized marketing facilities. Even the so-called "cooperatives" of the area were officially controlled institutions where farmers had little or no control. This was both politically exclusionary and perverse in terms of production. Sri Lankan farmers had practiced a form of well-coordinated, efficient tank irrigation for centuries, as compared to the government officials' limited knowledge of water development projects. While tank irrigation agriculture had taken place on a much smaller scale, the farmers' knowledge could still have been better used to achieve more cost-effective and time-efficient project implementation, better government-farmer relations, and increased responsibility and interest of the farmer in the sustainability and maintenance of the project.

The absence of grassroots participation reduced the cohesion of the villages and the incentives for socially responsible behavior. Not only did many settlers react negatively to the government officials (and ignored official advice on fertilizer use and the importance of transferring paddy), they often used wasteful amounts of water to kill weeds in preparation for paddy cultivation, defied official planting schedules, and obtained more water for household use than was permitted.

It is difficult to assess how widespread the mutual distrust and isolation among settlers has been throughout the resettlement area. Yet the problem was at least serious enough for the government to recognize it. In 1979 the Mahaweli Development Board established a system of turnout groups to remedy the lack of coordination, planning, and morale. The turnout group was to be used as the main channel for agricultural extension, community development, input deliveries, and government services. Yet this plan also failed due to the government's ignorance of one essential link for its success—a responsive organizational structure. For example, 48.7 percent of the farmers in turnout groups in Midellawa reported that the turnout leader, a settlement farmer selected and trained by the government for this position, "did not help them" (Siriwardhana 1981, 71). Most of the settlers with such negative opinions believed that the turnout leaders were taking advantage of their position for their own benefit. The turnout group thus simply became a management instrument of the officials and a source of power for the designated leader—not an independent grassroots organization.

In analyzing the deficiencies of the settlement scheme it is easy to cast the government as the villain. Yet the government did not intentionally ignore settlers' problems and let project shortcomings accumulate. It seems, rather, that the government instituted a village-level management system that could not offset the understandable tendency of officials to respond to their superiors rather than the farmers, and that the problem mushroomed from there. In the distribution of land allotments, there is no evidence that the government intentionally wished to promote income and resource inequities. Instead, it was easier and more convenient for the government to think in terms of quantity rather than quality—to redistribute standard-size parcels of land rather than to take discrepancies of land parcel quality into account and compensate for them.

Environmental Considerations

The Mahaweli Scheme largely ignored the environment. A deforestation problem predated the Mahaweli Scheme. Between 1956 and 1980 forested land dropped from 7.2 million acres to 4.1 million acres. This reduced the forest cover from 44 percent of land area to 25 percent, considered the minimum necessary to maintain soil fertility and conserve water (Wijesinghe 1981, 166). It is estimated that only 9 percent of the total land area of the wet zone, the catchment area of the major rivers of Sri Lanka, consists of forest cover. Yet the Mahaweli Scheme will reduce the net forested area by approximately a quarter of a million acres.

The government seems to have pursued a self-defeating conservation strategy. Under the Mahaweli Scheme, 700,000 acres of forest were to be converted to irrigated agriculture; to offset this, the government launched the Master Plan for Forestry Development to "ensure and develop forest resources" (Wijesinghe 1981, 166). Community forests were to be set up in the Mahaweli development areas and the settlers were to be provided with seedlings and technical advice in order to encourage preservation.

This plan, which has suffered from the weaknesses of extension and farming-practice regulations mentioned above, seems to be viewed by the Sri Lankan government as a sufficient response to environmental problems, in a sense legitimizing the rapid expansion of settlement areas. According to Goldsmith and Hildyard (1985, 52), "officials are totally ignoring the intangible ecological value of such benefits as soil preservation, water replenishment, climatic stabilization, air purification or wildlife shelter." There is a significant threat to biodiversity; eight species of fish, four species of amphibians, nineteen species of reptiles, eight species of birds, three species of mammals, and fifty-three species of plants—all native to Sri Lanka—are threatened with extinction (Goldsmith and Hildyard 1985, 57). Perhaps the most egregious lapse of environmental consideration has been the deforestation of wildlife sanctuaries. The program encompasses parts of the Pollunnaruwa, Serawila, and Allai Wildlife Sanctuaries; already, project implementation led to the logging of the Somawathie Wildlife Sanctuary (227, 275 ha.) by the State Timber Corporation. The scheme will also seriously disturb valuable wetland habitats along the banks of the Mahaweli, with the flooding of more than fifty biologically productive marsh areas (*villus*).

Beyond the environmental degradation brought about by deforestation are the ravages to the natural resource base due to organizational deficiencies or lack of supervision in the settlement areas. Settlers have taken environmental management (or mismanagement) into their own hands. Land and water management are neither integrated nor compatible with the needs of the village as a whole—the classic scenario of the tragedy of the commons. Villagers are motivated to the maximum exploitation of available resources, without consideration of the costs and benefits of this use to the community as a whole. Water wastage and overuse have been extreme. According to the Ministry of Finance and Planning (1983), "actual water utilization rates were and remain about twice their recommended rates." Water mismanagement in turn leads to salinization and erosion of the soil—undermining the entire agricultural base of the Mahaweli Scheme.

Conclusions

The most distinctive features of the Accelerated Mahaweli Development Program have been its magnitude and pace relative to the size of the Sri Lankan economy and the apparent importance of "ulterior" motives of employment and foreign aid generation. Sri Lankan irrigation had over a millennium of history of "small is beautiful," abandoned to take advantage of the opportunity for massive foreign aid and to provide public-works employment.

The government boasted of successful employment results. It reported that the Mahaweli program provided employment in opening up new areas in the Kalawewa region to about 50,000 people in agriculture and support services. The headworks at Victoria, Kotmale, and Maduru Oya employed approximately 8,000 persons. And, of course, successful farm families would be employed on their own land along with those employed in support services (Sri Lanka, Ministry of Mahaweli Development 1982, 1). Yet the public documents are strangely silent about the direct public-works employment on the construction of the Mahaweli dams, canals, and so on. Moreover, the truly relevant comparative question—how much employment would have been created by alternative uses of the capital—is understandably neglected in official Sri Lankan documents.

As mentioned previously, the reliance on heavy equipment rather than labor as well as the need to devote so much of the government's capital budget to Mahaweli, seemed justified by the volumes of foreign aid available for a breakneck program. Yet the opportunity costs of foregoing more efficient investments cannot be ignored and, unlike the Indonesian Transmigration Program, there was a high likelihood that bilateral aid would have been forthcoming for many types of projects.

Narmada Valley Development

The vicious circle that links objective conditions of inequality, environmental degradation, exclusion, and economic stagnation has a counterpart in the vicious circle of mistrust, biased analysis, and confrontation. This *political* vicious circle is fueled by suspicion and confrontation over how distributional, environmental, and participation issues will be resolved. It can either block natural resource exploitation or lead to counterproductive exploitation. Whereas the Mahaweli scheme is a prime example of inadequate planning that failed to address the physical complexities of planning and implementing large dams, the Narmada Valley development initiative is the epitome of political impasse. It represents the extreme outcome of natural resource projects left paralyzed, squandering both sunk resources and the opportunities for using the natural resource base constructively.

The political vicious circle is essentially the result of a perverse sort of learning. Bitterness and hostility remain when previous natural resource exploitation produced environmental deterioration, displacement, or impoverishment, or when relevant groups had been excluded. This atmosphere often untracks worthwhile projects or subjects them to very costly delays. To be sure, unwise projects may also be blocked, but the biggest loss is the reduced capacity to transform harmful projects into good ones and to accommodate the legitimate needs of otherwise excluded groups and objectives. This capacity is eroded whenever:

(a) nongovernmental groups are moved to exaggerate or otherwise misrepresent their circumstances and demands, out of disrespect or distrust of the government's willingness to use accurate information fairly
(b) the government loses the ability to distinguish between well-grounded criticism of its initiatives and criticism motivated out of partisan political objectives
(c) polarization prevents the government and its opponents from reaching reasonable accommodations for balancing growth, distribution, participation, and environmental conservation

This fate of the Narmada Valley development scheme in West India is particularly tragic because the valley's promise had been so apparent and the opportunity for constructive learning so great. Because of long delays in initiating action in the Narmada Valley, its exploitation could have benefited from the technical and procedural knowledge gained from decades of river valley development planning all over India. Yet instead of surmounting earlier ignorance or cultivating more advanced sensibilities toward environment and participation, the actors in the Narmada Valley drama were weighted down by accumulated mistrust.

The Narmada Valley is unique because its development was delayed in spite of its tremendous scope and potential. In its most ambitious version, the Narmada Project would be a system of 30 major dams, 135 medium irrigation schemes, and perhaps 1,000 minor irrigation projects, affecting 11.5 million people and costing 90 billion rupees—the equivalent of 11 billion U.S. dollars in 1983–84* (Kothari and Bhartari 1984, 908). The Narmada Valley could have been India's largest single-valley development project. Its projected five million hectares of irrigated area would give it more than twice the area of the most ambitious version of Sri Lanka's Mahaweli Scheme.

Normally, one would expect that the obvious large-scale irrigation and hydroelectric possibilities would have either been undertaken already or rejected as infeasible. But the Narmada Valley remained undeveloped because of the water disputes among the four states of the river basin, Madhya Pradesh, Gujarat, Maharashtra, and Rajasthan. The Narmada Valley Tribunal was formed in 1969, but only in 1979 did its report and the agreements among the states clear the official obstacles to development.

As of 1979, then, the conditions might have been thought to be ideal. There were few sunk costs to justify, few missteps to correct, and no feeling that the environment had already been despoiled to the point that little was left to preserve. With the exception of the Tawa Dam and a few other projects in this vast valley (the Narmada is India's largest westward-flowing river), the slate was rather clean. Moreover, since interest in developing the Narmada Valley's water resources dated back to Indian independence, some technical studies had already been done on the hydrology, topography, and soils of the region. Finally, in contrast to earlier times, the go-ahead for planning the project came at a time when environmental consciousness and awareness of the issues of participation and equity were already widespread.

The Ghosts of Past Failures

In another respect, however, the Narmada Project carried much of the baggage of previous experiences with huge valley-wide, interstate development projects. Most notably, the experience of Nehru's showcase project, the Damodar Valley Corporation, had soured many Indian planners on the feasibility of interstate cooperation. Billed as "Asia's TVA," the Damodar Valley's four huge flood-control, hydroelectric and irrigation dams, with additional thermal generation plants and a navigation canal, were to be constructed and operated by an autonomous public-sector entity shared by the states of West Bengal and Bihar and the central government. The modeling of the Damodar Valley Corporation on the Tennessee Valley Authority in the Southeast United States was quite explicit, both in the

*Chavan (1983, 20) estimates the Madhya Pradesh components at 3 billion rupees.

effort to structure the DVC so as to transcend state authority and in the engineering of the projects (a TVA engineer, Mr. Voorduin, designed the Damodar system) (Sinha 1977, 116).

Established with much fanfare in 1948, the DVC was the epitome of Jawaharlal Nehru's penchant for "thinking big"; it was also a development of considerable urgency, because of the flooding of the Damodar, which had been so severe that the river had taken on the name "River of Sorrow." Therefore the timeliness of planning, construction, and operation was not only a matter of securing the highest rates of return on investment (those calculated from the time that the investments are made), but also of averting the loss of life and property regardless of when the investments were made.

It was the inability to proceed with implementing the Damodar projects that discredited the approach of establishing a single interstate authority. The pressing need for flood control was frustrated by delays in resettlement that denied the flood-control engineers the storage space in two reservoirs; some flooding occurred in 1959 and 1963. The irrigation system had reached only 70 percent of its planned coverage by 1968 (Sinha 1977, 98). The navigation canal, scheduled for operation in 1958, was tested only in 1965 and remained unused for more than a decade after its scheduled opening because of jurisdictional disputes. Rapid silting of several of the Damodar dams resulted from the failure of the states to impose adequate soil conservation measures (Sinha 1977, 116).

In theory, the DVC should have been able to cut through the usual ministerial wrangling to bring these project components quickly to fruition. Instead, the DVC was frequently unable to proceed because one or more of the three governmental units refused to grant the necessary approval. On several occasions the West Bengali government incited local communities to resist authorized DVC actions.

Why did West Bengal, and, to a lesser extent, the other governments, turn on their own child? The fact that the West Bengal state government was Communist certainly was a major factor, but the lack of autonomy of the DVC was also a serious drawback. After the euphoria of the founding period, the Indian central government cut back on the real autonomy of the government member (and chairman) of the DVC board. Board membership in general became a part-time position of civil servants reporting (and owing their loyalties) to their three governments. Despite the formal equality of the governments of West Bengal and Bihar with the government of India in controlling the DVC, the state governments viewed the Corporation as another power struggle against the central government. DVC projects

in West Bengal and Bihar came to be seen as threats to the state governments, even though the financial resources would have to be secured
through the central government in any event. Thus, instead of enjoying a
measure of autonomy and reporting its decisions and progress to a board
kept at arm's length, the DVC became a highly constrained servant of three
feuding, veto-wielding masters. After prolonged and bitter controversy, the
DVC lost its control over Bengali irrigation to the West Bengali government,
and the Tenughat Dam was constructed on the Damodar River by the Bihari
government in spite of the idle but highly qualified DVC engineering staff.

There was no counterbalance to these reductions in DVC authority. Sinha
(1977, 112) points out that the DVC lacked the willingness, or perhaps
the political sophistication, to mobilize its local clientele to balance off the
pressures of the central and state governments. Selznick (1949) traces the
Tennessee Valley Authority's ability to fend off the incursions of seven
state governments to its success in establishing highly active grassroots
organizations, especially cooperatives. But the Damodar drama was restricted largely to the governments and to the people mobilized *against* the
DVC by the West Bengali government.

The Damodar disappointment in East India affected the later consideration of the Narmada Valley development through the reluctance of the
government of India to create an authority parallel to the DVC. Left to their
own devices, the four states were prone to view the valley development
issue as a purely conflictual matter of how to distribute a fixed volume of
water. Without a regional authority, polarization and stalemate over the
Narmada dispute could not be resolved.

Narmada's More Proximate Context

Thus the prospect of pulling together the government of India and the state
governments of Madhya Pradesh, Gujarat, Maharashtra, and Rajasthan on
Narmada development seemed extremely daunting. The states were encouraged in the 1950s and early 1960s to come to their own accommodation. This led to interminable negotiations without the forcing hand of the
central government. Finally, when in 1963 the states of Madhya Pradesh
and Gujarat reached an open impasse over the water allocation plan, the
government of India appointed an expert committee (the Khosla Committee) to see whether the discovery of a technical optimum could override the
politics of distribution. Not surprisingly, the report of that committee
simply led to more disputation, until the central government finally estab-

lished the three-man Narmada Water Disputes Tribunal in 1969, under authority of the 1956 Inter-State Water Disputes Act (Sinha 1977, 146).

It took the Narmada Water Disputes Tribunal a full decade to reach a judgment. The political difficulties were reflected by the fact that, even though it was fully involved in the Tribunal's deliberations, the Madhya Pradesh state government challenged the Tribunal's rulings. Only in August 1981 did a memorandum of understanding between the governments of Madhya Pradesh and Gujarat allow the major projects, most notably the Sardar and Narmada reservoirs, to proceed.

The legacy of Damodar was reflected in the lack of effort to set up a powerful project authority. The government of India represents the nation in dealing with external funders such as the World Bank, but the lion's share of project control is held by the state governments. The Narmada Control Authority in New Delhi is a modest liaison office (Kothari & Bhartari 1984, 909); Gujarat has the Narmada Planning Group and Madhya Pradesh has the full-fledged Narmada Project Ministry. There has been considerable friction between the Narmada planners of the two states, reflecting the long conflict preceding the initiation of the projects. Project implementation has been handled by a host of agencies working largely in isolation from one another.

The cost-benefit analyses of these projects were undertaken in a surprisingly limited way. For example, the Narmada Sagar Project Report explicitly admits that it did not assess the loss of wildlife or other ecological effects of submergence (Kothari & Bhartari 1984, 908). The Sardar Reservoir (''Sardar Sarovar'') Project got underway before the project plan received its environmental clearance from the government of India (Thakurta 1989, 90). No geological studies of possible earthquakes were done, despite the fact that the Narmada Valley lies within a seismic zone (Kothari & Bhartari 1984, 908). While as many as one million people may be displaced by the entire project, no comprehensive studies of the implications of such displacements have been undertaken.

The omission of these considerations from the ''cost'' side of the ledger was compounded by blatant underestimates of construction costs. Cost estimate increases from 23 billion to 40 billion rupees (approximately $2.2 billion to $3.8 billion) after the first year of construction in 1981 (Punalekar 1984, 353) cannot be attributed to inflation, but rather should be put down to an unwillingness to face up to the mammoth costs of such large-scale construction.

On the benefits side, the scope and pace of establishing the irrigation system were projected in very optimistic terms, in light of previous experience. The ambitious estimates of grain production from the Narmada Sagar project have been subject to widespread skepticism, and the future crops are valued without reference to price effects (Kothari & Bhartari 1984, 916).

This sort of Pollyanna appraisal should not come as a surprise—the Indian Planning Commission requires benefit-cost ratios of better than 1.5, and project planners are intent upon surmounting that hurdle. Yet, when impartial expert analysis is replaced by *partisan analysis* dedicated to open advocacy for particular projects, the planners not only arouse opposition, but also reduce their own credibility.

Most tellingly, the dam appraisals have been conducted separately, rather than within a valley-wide "systems analysis" framework as promised by the authorities. The "Master Plan" is a list of projects and specifications (not unlike the Mahaweli scheme's master plan), but without integrated analysis of impacts on production, overall water balances, forestation, or environmental consequences. The Narmada project has had the same kind of "unfixed" nature as the Mahaweli scheme in Sri Lanka. The specifics of a given component in such a large and interconnected cluster of projects remain uncertain because of the vagueness or changeability of other components. The timing of specific components is highly unpredictable, given both the sensitivity of each to delays in the others, and the importance of a few discrete, rather unpredictable funding decisions. Without a central project authority and a commitment of sufficient financial resources to complete any given set of components, even the definition of what would constitute a system analysis of the valley's development remains unfixed.

As the first steps were taken to get construction on the dams underway in the early 1980s, nongovernmental organizations emerged to defend environmental concerns and the populations targeted for displacement. No single project authority was in a position to negotiate or even to formulate a coherent response. Rightly or wrongly, these groups have consistently assumed the worst of the governments' intentions and competence. They have mobilized communities, particularly among the tribals, to demonstrate against the construction projects, thus contributing to the delay of the Sardar Reservoir construction and threatening the World Bank's crucial financial support of the project (Thakurta 1989, 90–91). The project planners cannot resort to the defense that the opposition consists of agitators maligning a well-studied project. The governments can hardly dismiss these groups as cranks when in 1984 the former Madhya Pradesh irrigation minister, Ramchandra Singhdeo, called for a review of the Narmada Reservoir plan on the grounds that the submergence could have disastrous economic and environmental consequences (Kothari & Bhartari 1984, 914).

In 1985 the World Bank had approved a $500 million loan, largely through its soft-loan IDA facility, for the Sardar Reservoir and associated projects. Earlier the World Bank had declared the Sardar Reservoir project a "model of irrigation planning," yet throughout 1986 and into 1987, the World Bank was still pressuring the Indian government to grant environmental clearance for the project; this only came in 1987 (Thakurta 1989, 91). The clearance seems to have come more from concern over losing World Bank funding than from definitive studies or changes in project design that would have reassured the government that the project's environmental consequences had been adequately addressed. Now, confronted with highly visible agitation over the displacement issue and continuing criticism from environmentalists, the World Bank may be reconsidering its commitment (Thakurta 1989, 90–91). By mid-1989, the World Bank had disbursed roughly $63 million for the dam, and the Indian government over $400 million (Thakurta 1989, 90). The rate of return on the project diminishes each year that passes from the time of their expenditure to the time the project starts to generate production benefits, and may virtually vanish if the project is never completed.

One of the key stumbling blocks in the implementation of the Sardar Reservoir has been the dispute between Madhya Pradesh and Gujarat over the disposition of some 70,000 of the villagers, mostly "tribals," of the submergence area. An agreement had been reached to give land in Gujarat to a large number of Madhya Pradesh inhabitants. While the Gujarati government was making provisions for this resettlement, opposition grew among Gujarati villagers who were to be displaced by the Sardar Reservoir. They claimed that the Gujarati state government, though bound by the high-level commitment to provide adequate resources for the Madhya Pradesh migrants, was shirking its obligation to Gujaratis.

The immediate provocation that ignited much of the opposition by nongovernmental organizations was the lack of provision for employment guarantees for the landless inhabitants who were to be displaced. Within the rather legalistic compensation approach of the tribunal and the state governments, loss of private property is considered grounds for compensation, but loss of access to common property is not. The landless people who derived their livelihoods from gathering firewood and other products from the forest were not even formally considered as oustees by the Sardar Reservoir planners (Kothari & Bhartari 1984, 915).

The governments clearly have been unsuccessful in mobilizing support for the projects. There was no central project authority with the incentive to generate grassroots support. The concepts of participation and grassroots involvement are at best only partially incorporated into the thinking and procedures of the planners. Consider the commitment made by Madhya Pradesh official S. B. Chavan: "The farmers have to be involved right from the beginning in planning, implementing and evaluating the success of the canal systems. The best results from the canal systems can be achieved only with the involvement of the farmers in the management and operation of the canal systems" (Chavan 1983, 20).

Contrast this statement with the conclusion of a study team that covered the length and breadth of the Narmada Valley in mid-1983:

> Nowhere during the planning have local people been involved. When asked about this, some of the officials we met seemed amused—their unstated attitude was obviously one of scorn for the abilities of the villagers; involving them in planning seemed quite absurd. Other officials admitted, however, that this was a serious fault in planning, and that this "we-know-best-for-them" attitudes in the past had resulted in the failure of several projects. A case in point is the Tawa Project in Hoshangabad district (MP), where some planners who were quite unaware of the ground conditions decided to introduce canal irrigation into the area. If they had only asked the farmers, they would have told them that many of the black cotton soil areas do not need irrigation since this soil has considerable water retention capacity. But irrigation was brought in, and serious waterlogging resulted in some areas (Kothari and Bhartari 1984, 909).

To be sure, this assessment was made by a group that has looked upon the Narmada Valley development with much skepticism—Kothari is currently a spokesman of the environmental group *Kalpavriksh* (Thakurta 1989, 91). Nonetheless, the point is that the government's efforts at encouraging and incorporating participation fell far short of what it would have taken to establish an atmosphere of trust between the government and other relevant actors. Nor did the governments apply even a modicum of political sensitivity in initiating the preconstruction phase of the project. One of the most provocative features of the Sardar Reservoir construction plan was that relatively lavish staff facilities were built just when villagers facing displacement were being offered what many considered to be meager compensation.

Conclusions

The Narmada Project vividly and tragically reflects the political vicious circle triggered by the polarization between the planners and an opposition driven to cynicism. Of course, from the perspective of those who categorically reject the feasibility of sustainable large-scale river development projects, stalemate means that bad projects have been blocked. The problems with this assessment are that resources are squandered even if projects are not completed; the opportunities for alternative accommodations are often lost in the polarized confrontation; and, finally, stalemate is sometimes overcome by governments by suppressing environmental, participatory, and equity issues—as was basically the case with the Mahaweli scheme in Sri Lanka.

The Indira Reservoir (Bodhghat)

The Indira Reservoir ("Indira Sarovar") project would be interesting in its own right, but it is particularly poignant inasmuch as it is situated in the Bastar district where Dandakaranya and plantation forestry both failed. A harsh reading of the Indira Reservoir case would cast it as the latest folly in an area where natural resource exploitation has been consistently "unnatural"—where the virtues of the virgin forest have been forsaken for ventures that impose settlers, plantations, or dams where they cannot be sustained. A kinder reading would bring out how social and environmental issues can be given consideration without the degree of polarization that marks the Narmada Valley development. To a certain degree, the experts involved in the Indira Reservoir planning have discharged their responsibilities to provide sophisticated interpretations of both benefits and costs of the project, including consideration of social and environmental issues. Whether they have done so adequately is at the heart of the debate. Public opinion has played a more positive role as well.

Background of the Indira Reservoir

The exploitation and development of very rich natural resources of the Bastar region of Madhya Pradesh has long been hampered by shortages of electric power. The railways and the National Mineral Corporation are the only two major consumers at present; power is being supplied to these industries from a thermal power plant which is more than 500 kilometers away, involving heavy transmission losses and therefore very high costs. A dependable and cheap source of power from within the region would take care of the full needs of the Bastar region and contribute to its all-around prosperity.

In the early 1960s studies were begun on the hydroelectric potential of the Indravati River. The project that took shape from these studies was regarded by many as having the potential to generate power at an extremely low cost, involve the smallest area of deforestation as compared to any other project of equivalent capacity, and displace a very small number of persons. Its supporters argue that the project poses the least problem of resettlement, has the shortest commissioning period, and will best contribute to the economy of the Bastar region on a sustainable basis. Therefore they pose it as the best alternative in Madhya Pradesh to achieve the energy objectives. There had been no opposition or agitation against the project until the early 1980s, and even now there is the suspicion that opposition to the project is politically motivated and based on distorted facts and interpretations.

The Indira Reservoir (formerly known as Bodhghat) was approved by the planning commission of the government of India in early 1979. The Indira Reservoir project, with an installed power capacity of 500 megawatts, was deemed as fitting very well into the predominantly thermal power system of Madhya Pradesh, since this system had an urgent need for peaking power.[8] The project had been examined by the Central Electricity Authority for its technical, hydrological, and economical viability. In accordance with governmental procedures, clearance was also obtained from agencies overseeing the environmental and wildlife-preservation aspects.

Policy Considerations

Because the hydroelectric capacity in the state is insignificant, the Madhya Pradesh power system suffers badly in its capacity to meet peak loads. Industries must run their own captive diesel generators to meet the power demand during peak periods. These are expensive to operate, and the larger generators must be imported. This drain on foreign exchange is compounded by the huge amounts of imported oil they consume.

According to projections of demand, there will be a sizable power shortage in Madhya Pradesh if the Indira Reservoir is not commissioned by

1990 or 1991. The capacity of the Madhya Pradesh power system to meet peak requirements is expected to worsen without new hydroelectric stations. The Indira Reservoir is one of the lowest-cost solutions of generating electricity.[9] With the project, thermal plants in the state could operate at a plant load factor of about 56 percent; without it, the state would have to add thermal capacity, which would substantially increase power costs by bringing down the plant load factor to 50 percent. Madhya Pradesh could not take advantage of gas turbines, which are very expensive to install and operate, require foreign exchange, and would not be approved by the central government for states with sufficient hydroelectric potential. The central government has also laid down the broad policy of achieving a thermal-hydroelectric power mix of 60:40 for the optimum operation of the power system as a whole. The short period to complete the project is an additional attraction, in light of the imminent capacity shortfall. Thus the Indira Reservoir project has been very popular—from an energy planning point of view.

World Bank Participation. Although the Planning Commission had directed the completion of the project within a period of five to six years, no progress was made due to lack of funds. The central government therefore decided in 1980 to seek World Bank financing. To meet the World Bank requirements and guidelines, the Madhya Pradesh Electricity Board carried out detailed investigations for the dam, the water conductor system, the submergence area, and the geology of the head race tunnel. The team updated the hydrological studies, taking into consideration the apportionment of water of the Indravati between Orissa and Madhya Pradesh states on the basis of the Godavari Tribunal Award. A comprehensive project report was submitted to the World Bank in April 1983.

The World Bank sent preparatory missions to India in June and October 1983. The Bank appeared to be satisfied with all aspects of the project, negotiated the terms of the loan, and approved a loan of $300 million in April 1984 to meet part of the estimated $700 million total. The loan agreement became effective in March 1985.

Project Implementation

After completion of designs by the Central Water Commission and the Central Electricity Authority of the central government, project authorities prequalified international contracting companies for participation in the project and invited international tenders for the major civil works. Tenders for the hydroturbines and generators have also been invited on a global basis—in sharp contrast with Mahaweli's tied-aid provisions.

In the meantime, the project authorities have undertaken the preliminary infrastructural works, such as accommodations for the project staff and roads and bridges for communication as well as basic civil works for the power house and tunnels. At the time of writing, an expenditure of over $25 million has already been incurred and the government of India has started drawing disbursements from the World Bank.

Environmental Aspects and the Virtues of High-Level Meetings

In contrast to thermal power plants that burn fossil fuels, hydroelectric projects provide renewable energy. But by the late 1970s, Indians were becoming increasingly aware that dams hold their own environmental risks. The Indira Reservoir project entails the submergence of land, including forest, and the displacement of the residents from the submergence area.

In 1980 the Indian Parliament enacted the Forest Conservation Act. As the physical transfer of the forest land for the Indira Reservoir project had not yet taken place, the Department of Forests of the Government of India decided to have a fresh look into the environmental and ecological aspects of the project. Although clearance had been obtained from the Department of Environment of the government of India and the Wildlife Department of the state government in 1979, and the same clearances were revalidated in 1983, the Department of Forests convened a working group consisting of representatives from the Departments of Power, Finance, and Forests.

The project authorities were naturally alarmed about these unexpected developments and were particularly concerned about project delays. Yet they seem to have been assured by the government of India that final clearance would be forthcoming if they prepared a comprehensive report for compensatory afforestation and resettlement, provided specific details of the nonforest lands identified for forest plantation as close as possible to the existing forests, and developed a resettlement plan specifying year-by-year requirements for implementation and funding.

A detailed project report was submitted to the central government in December 1985. The issues were aired in a high-level meeting attended by officials of the central government's Finance Ministry, Department of Forests, and Department of Power. The Madhya Pradesh government and the Madhya Pradesh Electricity Board were also represented. The Forest

Department expressed its concerns about the ecological effects of deforestation for the project. Forestry officials claimed that compensatory afforestation plans were inadequate, because the targeted land parcels were too small and scattered to be developed as a forest system. They argued that the loss of *sal* trees, an important native species, would be irreplaceable as there was no known method of managing that species in plantations. Finally, they questioned whether the power production was large enough to justify deforestation of 5,700 hectares of prime forest containing rare native species.

In light of these qualms, the Finance Ministry expressed concerns about devoting further foreign currency expenditures and expertise to the project. The Finance Ministry apparently went as far as advising the central government to withdraw the project from the World Bank if the Forest Department continued to have apprehensions about the environmental aspects. Although no final decision was taken, the project authorities were asked to review all implications of dropping the project and also to suggest alternatives, if any, for consideration by the cabinet and the prime minister.

Grassroots Movements

When it became known that even the central government was having second thoughts about proceeding with the project, various grassroots advocacy groups claiming to represent the oustees as well as the environment started to voice their protests in much stronger terms. In addition to raising environmental concerns,[10] they argued that the project would disrupt the lives and culture of the Bastar district tribals, who would be vulnerable to exploitative forestry, police, and revenue officials. Advocacy groups argued that development programs had brought little tangible benefits to a majority of tribals, while those more favored with economic strength and education would receive most of the gains of development. S. C. Dube (1987, 7), a well-known anthropologist of the region, argued:

> the tribals need the forest more than the power, even if it is given free of charge to them. Their habitat can never be replaced, for it has some special features. They build sprawling dwellings with many fruit-bearing trees in the vicinity. The government cannot give them comparable agricultural land or dwellings. Besides, the tribals have cultural links with the forest. Their earth god and ancestor spirits reside in it. It is pointless to ask who these gods are and what their worth is,

for they are a matter of deep-seated faith to the tribal people. A ham-handed approach is likely to be counter productive.

Of course, some past experiences justified the fear that future programs might be designed to refashion tribal ways of life rather than respond to the needs felt by the tribals themselves. Large-scale programs like the Bailadila iron-ore project and the Dandakaranya Railway project failed to provide stable economic opportunities to the tribals. Tribal advocacy groups accused these programs of marginalizing and subordinating the tribals.

Beyond the particular problems faced by tribal populations, the resettlement of residents in general raised questions about the adequacy of the government machinery for relocating and finding employment for the dislocated. The governments' inept handling of West Bengali refugees (for example, the Dandakaranya Project reviewed in chapter 4) is still remembered by a large segment of the local population. The advocacy groups accused bureaucrats of defining rehabilitation in the narrow terms of providing land, housing, and money rather than developing adequate social and community infrastructures.

Review by Madhya Pradesh Electricity Board Officials

Faced by mounting criticism from the public and from within government ranks, the Madhya Pradesh Electricity Board officials recognized the seriousness of the challenge to their initiative and took concerted action to assemble voluminous data in defense of the project. The Electricity Board is a close-knit and highly professionalized organization, but the board members and staff were unaccustomed to independent review of their proposals or public discussions of their activities. Their staffing structure and their charter did not equip them to handle problems involving multiobjective planning, environmental considerations, and interdisciplinary cooperation. The Indira Reservoir project, however, was a matter of great prestige for them and they felt that the criticism was based on a lack of full appreciation of the facts by the public and the bureaucrats in Delhi.

The arguments advanced by the Electricity Board in defense of the project began with an attempt to put the deforestation issue in a different perspective. The danger to the *sal* tree was, according to the Electricity Board, exaggerated in light of the abundance of *sal* that can be seen in vast tracts of Madhya Pradesh forests. The total forest area in Madhya Pradesh is about 16 million hectares, of which Bastar district alone constitutes 2 million hectares. Thus the small figure of 5,500 hectares of forest land requiring deforestation is less than 0.25 percent of the total. Sample enumeration surveys done within the submergence area showed that the percentage of sound *sal* trees was less than 3 percent of the forest growth, the rest being largely "fuel" varieties. *Sal* is more abundant in other areas of Bastar forests and at higher elevations. *Sal* is of economic value, but does not fall within the categories of rare or endangered species, and thus would be exploited in any event. Moreover, the collection of *sal* seeds by the tribals is a seasonal activity that has largely benefited the urban end-users rather than the tribals. Finally, while conceding that current knowledge for planting and growing of *sal* is inadequate, the Electricity Board argued that the success of *sal* reforestation can be achieved by continued research and improved techniques. For the Electricity Board, the furor over the *sal* trees was a distraction from other, more legitimate environmental concerns.

The Electricity Board responded to criticism of the compensatory afforestation program by countering that the program would be handled by expert foresters of the state Forest Department. The types and species of trees to be planted would be selected to serve the remaining tribals and to preserve the ecosystem, fully in accordance with the requirements of the central government Forest Department. One full-fledged forest division has been established exclusively for the plantation work. A single large chunk of 1,300 hectares of government-owned revenue land contiguous to the existing forests has been taken over and preparation has already started to raise nurseries for the first year's program.

The Board's study of the reservoir plan reveals that the *current* forest land of 5,700 hectares in the submergence area is made up of 25 to 30 different patches, with discontinuous tree growth even within each patch. Except in upper regions of hill slopes, the tree growth is very scattered in the plains and foothills.[11] The new forests will eventually get integrated with the old forests to preserve the "composite" nature. A commitment to take up an additional 5,700 hectares of forest plantation was made as well.

As for the financial aspects of deforestation, project officials admit it is difficult to work out the cost in monetary terms of the renewable forest wealth that is loss. However, the addition of new forests under the plantation scheme will gradually redress the losses. The monetary loss arising on account of land submergence, estimated at 5 to 6 million rupees (approximately $240,000 to $280,000) annually, is small compared to the net revenue earnings from the generation and sale of electricity. The

Electricity Board documents that the technical aspects of the project have been fully investigated over the years by the Central Electricity Authority and the Central Water Commission, covering the key issues of water availability, silt load factor, tightness of the reservoir, provision of dead storage for a 100-year life of the dam, power generation, and all other technoeconomic factors. The project's "stand alone" viability has been fully justified. Without the dam, the direct electricity-sales revenue loss would be combined with a huge loss of foregone benefits in agriculture and industry. In contrast with so many earlier off-the-cuff appraisals, the project costs do include figures for environmental losses from soil erosion effects on hydrological cycles, ecological aspects, microclimate, and so forth, as well as social costs of rehabilitation.

Project authorities have asserted that the rehabilitation of the tribals has the highest priority. They have argued that resettling 1,200 families is not so major as to pose any serious logistical problems; the resettlement areas are not far from their present habitat and very much within the tribal tract, far from other groups. Even so, a separate division is to be established to aid the tribals, with adequate autonomy, funds, and expertise. The resettlement of tribals will ensure that the same ethnic groups are resettled together. The oustees would be consulted at all stages of rehabilitation and the scheme would be implemented with their full consent and acceptance of the selected areas, habitats, and dwellings.

Along with these commitments *cum* clarifications, the project authorities offered their own interpretation of the origins of opposition to the project, arguing that land speculators and agitators are encouraging the tribals to cut the forests. Local administrators of Bastar maintain that unless tribals are given regular employment to improve their standard of living, agitators will lure them into antigovernment activities. The project authorities have promised that in addition to the free five-acre developed agricultural plots for each oustee family, one member of each family will be trained in the industrial training institute for employment in the project.

This combination of public pressure, skepticism within the government, and the Electricity Board's motivation to defend its own initiative culminated in a clearer, better-balanced action plan and more explicit commitments, than had been available a few years earlier. True, the Electricity Board seemed to deny the allegations of its critics, but each denial carried with it a more tangible commitment to address the potential problems. One might still argue that the promises are just words. Nevertheless, the explicit commitment of the project authorities to do more than they would have done otherwise puts significantly greater pressure on them to undertake these activities.

At this stage, the project authorities have carried out the first phases of these commitments. Senior local revenue officials have certified the availability and quick transfer of the areas selected for resettlement and re-forestation, and some areas have already been transferred to the project. The identification of lands is made by joint teams representing revenue, forest, and project officials. The lands exclude forest land, and as such are outside the purview of Forest Conservation Act.

The project officials are also focusing on the growing demand for extending electrification—today considered as basic a need as food, shelter, and clothing—to all tribal villages and promoting rural industries to provide stable livelihoods for the tribals. The Madhya Pradesh Electricity Board has already provided 17,000 single-point light connections to the tribals in Bastar district at very nominal costs to the tribals. It is also proposed to take up an accelerated electrification of villages. The project has faced no problems in its attempts to resettle tribals thus far. Lands belonging to seven villages have already been acquired with full compensation. The oustees from these villages have been moved to alternative dwellings with facilities to maintain their traditional ways of life.

Conclusions

The dispute over the Indira Reservoir project, if one is to believe the rather demanding project appraisals, may seem like political bombast, with the experts right in the first place but vindicated only after considerable delay. This conclusion, however, ignores the role of criticism as a prod to discipline. The project has emerged as a more fully analyzed undertaking because of the confrontation, and with more specific assurances to the potentially adversely affected parties. Whether one dismisses the critics as cranks or agitators, or accepts their critique, the fact remains that the Department of the Environment and the Wildlife Department both cleared the project *twice* from ecological, environmental, and wildlife angles, in an atmosphere of tolerance for skeptical opinion. The Madhya Pradesh government is under pressure to make good on its promise to provide especially favorable treatment to the displaced tribals.

It is, of course, significant that the Indira Reservoir project was amenable to reasonably comprehensive and rigorous analysis. Unlike the grandiose

Mahaweli and Narmada projects, the Indira Reservoir's unpretentiousness allowed for such analysis. In the Indira Reservoir case, the government did not produce perfect project appraisals the first time around, but adapted to criticism and maintained a modicum of credibility.

One might dismiss these comparisons on the grounds that the scale is so different. But that is in itself a central point. The Indira Reservoir project could be evaluated with a reasonable degree of rigor. But the vastness of the Mahaweli and Narmada schemes, combined with existing political, bureaucratic, and technical constraints, led to both inadequate planning and a political predicament that made it difficult to go back to the drawing boards. The burdens of planning a large integrated system are greater. To use the vastness of an integrated project as an excuse for not undertaking system-wide analysis is particularly perverse.

The Indira Reservoir and the Narmada cases demonstrate that although environmental awareness and concern for displaced populations can be important in the policymaking process, we cannot expect governments to "learn" this all by themselves. Governments cannot overcome all the pressures that limit their capacity to define natural resource policy with sufficient comprehensiveness or to give sufficient due to local knowledge and initiatives. Governments will remain vulnerable to demands for premature action, agency power plays, and simplistic problem definitions. These make it highly unlikely that the awareness of problems of equity, environment, and participation will consistently lead government agencies to do the right thing without continual vigilance and pressure from actors outside of government. The constant input by critics is part of the policymaking *process*—extending beyond governmental learning—that reflects "system learning" on how to cope with the natural resource endowment.

Nongovernmental voluntary groups can play a key role in maintaining social and environmental consciousness. It is revealing that the Gujarati oustees were more effectively mobilized than the Madhya Pradesh oustees (Kothari & Bhartari 1984, 915) because the nongovernmental organizations were stronger in the Gujarati districts.

Yet this social and environmental consciousness, in the general population and especially among university-educated activists, can lead to paralysis. In the Narmada case, the capacity to protest and to block action has been achieved through the mobilization of previously weak groups, but the capacity of the *system* to come to some accommodation has not been achieved.

How can the government proceed in such situations? Partisan analysis is not the answer; it undermines the credibility of accommodations to placate opposition or to gain the support of other parties. Even if opposition critiques are unfair, and some groups might oppose even the soundest planning, partisan analysis increases polarization and distrust. The only answer is honest government analysis combined with efforts to put the conflict on a footing of reasoned debate and mutual respect. The difficulty of achieving this state does not diminish the importance of pursuing it.

The design of irrigation systems offers the clearest window on the trade-offs of centralized knowledge and control versus localized knowledge and participation. It is also a window on the complexity of equity issues in natural resource policymaking. These trade-offs are part of the background to the dilemmas of promoting major or minor irrigation initiatives. This chapter examines some general characteristics of irrigation in India and two Indian case studies, in order to understand the issues of equity and participation in irrigation.

India has the world's second largest irrigation system after China, with roughly 40 million irrigated hectares (compared to China's 45 million), covering over 24 percent of India's cropland. A greater portion of India's land area is irrigated than China's (13 percent versus 5 percent) although 45 percent of China's cropland is more intensively irrigated than India's.[1] The vastness of India's system makes it particularly illuminating because of the great variations in climate, topography, and irrigation approaches taken by the various states.

The Indian case is also compelling because of the great gap between the governing center and the rural community in education, technical expertise, and differential familiarity with micro-conditions. Centralized knowledge proves to be remarkably fragile in Indian policymaking on irrigation. Therefore the lack of participation, rather than simply undermining equity as it does in so many other instances, can often paralyze irrigation altogether

Case materials for this chapter were initially developed by Arunoday Bhattacharjya and Merrill Buice.

or at least seriously impede irrigation operations. Another lesson concerns the importance of control and "political credit" issues in establishing whether irrigation will be undertaken through large-scale dam/canal structures, with their attendant environmental risks, or through minor tank or well programs.

On the issue of equity, the Indian case provides a rather surprising insight: equity has not been ignored, but it has been too narrowly understood in ways that probably have underestimated the contributions of irrigation to poverty alleviation.

Minor versus Major Irrigation

Given the high rate of population growth in countries like India and the close connection between the availability of water and food production, it has been generally conceded since the 1950s that the expansion of irrigation is essential. The real questions concern the forms of irrigation and how it should be administered.

The first quandary on the *form* of irrigation is the choice between *major* irrigation of dams and canals and *minor* irrigation of tanks (ranging from farm ponds to above-ground structures) and wells.[2] The distinction is not simply one of scale. Major irrigation is often of larger scale than minor irrigation, and certainly the component parts of minor irrigation are smaller than dams and canals. But there is no straightforward equivalence of major irrigation with large-scale irrigation and minor irrigation with small-scale irrigation, because dams can be rather small, and some *systems* of tanks and wells can be quite extensive.

One of the great puzzles of Indian irrigation is the persistence of the widespread bias in favor of the major irrigation projects of dams and canals. This bias is well-documented and widely recognized. Roy's (1979, 305) assessment of Green Revolution progress in northern India points to minor irrigation as the key to the most impressive productivity increases. Whereas studies in the state of Orissa indicate that minor irrigation has a greater potential than either major or medium-scale irrigation, nonetheless the bulk of the investment has been put into larger-scale ventures (Satpathy 1984, 67). Former government secretary B. B. Vohra led off a major 1982 Ford Foundation–funded conference on "Productivity and Equity in Irrigation Systems" by strongly criticizing the neglect of groundwater development in favor of major irrigation schemes (Pant 1984, xiv). This is not to say that minor irrigation is superior to major irrigation as a general principle.

Indeed, Dhawan (1985, 11–13) points out that minor irrigation has its own environmental problems in semiarid areas and where groundwater quality is poor, and that the groundwater potential is simply smaller than the potential for surface water irrigation. So the puzzle is not why minor irrigation fails to dominate, but rather why it has been underutilized relative to its potential.

This bias is puzzling at least insofar as there are several reasons to expect a bias *against* major irrigation. First, the environmental drawbacks of a general policy of major irrigation have long been visible. Contrary to the impression that environmental knowledge is an invention of the last few decades, the tendencies of dams to silt up, ancient canal systems to decay, and waterlogging and salinization to reduce soil fertility have been recognized for quite some time. Second, major irrigation puts the burden of finance on the always-strapped central or state government authorities. Whereas minor irrigation programs could unleash the initiative of the farmer, major irrigation ultimately may require the acquiescence and cooperation of the farmer but typically requires the government to bear the cost. Third, the coordination problems of major irrigation are, almost by definition, much more formidable than the coordination problems of minor irrigation. As Kamble et al. (1979) point out, the market aspects of land productivity and the costs of well-digging and maintenance establish a more or less automatic balancing of the number of minor irrigation units. There is even an equilibrium reached by the water table (inasmuch as water drawn by wells affects the water table), in that wells deep enough to reach a lower water table are more expensive to drill.

In searching for explanations of the bias in favor of major irrigation, *political* and *institutional* factors dominate over technical reasons. In some Indian states, at least, the evidence is clear that minor irrigation is underutilized relative to its intrinsic potential (Satpathy 1984, ch. 4). In this sense, then, the political and procedural constraints hamper India's agricultural progress.

Major Irrigation as a Gift. Ironically, the failure in irrigation systems to exact full water charges is a basis for the popularity of major irrigation over minor irrigation. If the farmers within the potential command area expect that an irrigation system will not require full cost recovery, then the decision to undertake the irrigation project is seen as providing them with a large component of "rent" (in the economist's sense of returns above the level that the risk-adjusted investment of available land, labor, and capital would have provided). In contrast, even when subsidized credit is available for village tank construction or repair, or for the drilling and construction of efficient wells, the village or the individual farmer still bears a substantial burden of cost and risk. In short, major irrigation tends to be seen as a gift, whereas minor irrigation tends to be seen as a risky (even if sometimes subsidized) venture.

The Political Attractiveness of Big Promises

There is a tendency, in India at least, to define larger-than-optimum command areas for major irrigation (Pant 1984, xvii); presumably, part of the motivation is to increase the support for any particular project by increasing the scope of beneficiaries. A similar political logic would favor any major over minor irrigation. Even if subsidies for minor irrigation development were extended to many *potential* beneficiaries, specifically who would receive them and what their gains in productivity would be (given the costs and risks mentioned in the point above) remains in doubt. The announcement of the boundaries of a command area for dams and canals is a more politically potent event than the announcement of a credit or grant program to facilitate the expansion of tank or well irrigation to the benefit of as-yet unspecified farmers.

Jurisdictions and power. In allocating resources for irrigation, the central or state governments find that major irrigation systems, by their very nature, are ventures *of* the central or state governments, whereas the contributions of these authorities to minor irrigation (basically loans and grants) are of necessity more distanced. Therefore, to the degree that the impulse to control holds sway, the major irrigation project will be preferred by the central authorities because it virtually guarantees their continued control, whereas the minor systems put control in the hands of local farmers and villages. This does not, of course, mean that the central authorities are simply motivated by power and self-aggrandizement. They may operate on the basis of the conscious or unconscious assumption that their expertise justifies their control. Or, especially in the Indian climate of hypersensitivity to distributional issues, the central authorities may believe that minor irrigation would strengthen local notables but centrally controlled irrigation could be designed to redress inequality. Whatever the motive, the result is a central authority bias in favor of major irrigation that reinforces the control by these authorities.

Exaggerated optimism. Major projects are simply more prone to the "Pollyanna optimism" discussed elsewhere in this volume. Assessing the benefits and potential problems of a new village tank or a stone-reinforced circular well is rather straightforward. But, as we see with major dam schemes, it is easy to wax enthusiastic about the potentials of large projects, dismiss each of the possible pitfalls as only modestly probable (without adding up the probabilities that *something* serious could go wrong), and conclude that the big projects have attractive rates of return. A general conclusion regarding major irrigation in India is that the *ex ante* cost-benefit analyses have a strong tendency to exaggerate the benefits because of unrealistic assumptions (Pant 1984, xvii). This is also a very common problem in the United States (Goldsmith and Hildyard 1985, 271–72), and in developing countries in general. Yudelman's (1989) assessment of $3 billion worth of irrigation projects funded by the World Bank indicates that while medium-term *ex post* evaluations show that three-fourths of the projects had return rates above the 10 percent hurdle rate, virtually all *ex ante* return rate calculations were greater than the actual benefits from these projects.[3] In other words, the Pollyanna optimism made these projects seem much more attractive in relation to other investments than they deserved.

Absence of recognition of coordination difficulties. A more specific reason for the Pollyanna effect is that potential coordination problems typically go unrecognized in project appraisals. To be sure, in some contexts a whole class of projects may become discredited because of previous instances of severe coordination difficulties. This has occurred with integrated rural development projects sponsored by the World Bank. But if a class of project is regarded as acceptable, the technical appraisal generally has no place for the notion that the returns may be lower because some participants involved, whether government agencies or local residents, will be at loggerheads. In the Jamuna irrigation project described below the possibility that the local residents would be unable to come to enough agreement even to initiate the use of the water, let alone utilize it effectively, was simply not anticipated. Why this happens is hardly mysterious. Within a government bureaucracy it is usually considered bad form to be explicit about the potential difficulties of dealing with one's counterparts in other agencies, or about the potential clashes with the very people the bureaucracy proposes to help.

Equity

As an essential aspect of the Green Revolution in India, irrigation has been part of the technological transformation that has saved millions from starvation. Farmers with truly marginal dry-zone lands have been granted impressive gains in productivity through irrigation. Yet irrigation in India has been plagued by criticism directed against its supposed inequality. One of the most frequent critiques of irrigation projects and, for that matter, most infrastructure improvements, is that the benefits are not shared equitably. Indeed, irrigation has often been the whipping boy of leftist critiques of natural resource policy. How can we understand this paradox?

The debate over agricultural policy in India since the 1960s has tended to frame the equity issue in terms of trade-offs between equity and production. Naturally, it was legitimate to ask whether irrigation, in pursuing higher production, might have the unfortunate side effect of worsening income distribution. But in the highly ideological context of the Indian development controversy, as soon as the question was framed in terms of the potential production versus equity conflict, the debate proceeded as if this were an established problematique. The combination of irrigation and the promotion of high-yield variety agriculture, with its relatively expensive inputs, was labeled the strategy of "betting on the strong."

As such the controversy focused on the two distributional issues that would inevitably seem to tarnish any irrigation initiative. The first was the disparity of benefits for farmers within the command area and those outside of it; the second was the distribution of water access for farmers within the command area. There is clearly no way to equalize the benefits to farmers within and without the command area. And it is virtually impossible to design an irrigation system that provides precisely the same amount of water to all farmers in the command area; some mechanisms can help to bring the distribution closer to equality, but some inequality will remain. Yet the distributive effects of irrigation go beyond these two.

Dimensions of Equity

The root of the paradox is that equity (or distributional justice) is not the straightforward concept it seems to be. Even aside from the different normative principles that can be asserted as to what the distribution of wealth or income ought to be, the very *basis* of defining equity is complicated. This is especially true for irrigation, because there are several distinct but important distributional effects that involve people within and outside the command area.

Effect 1. Irrigation typically brings greater agricultural production, which in turn often means more abundant, less expensive food. Some segments of the poor will be better off to the degree that they can afford more food—or other goods and services that can be purchased with disposable income left over after food purchases are made. The poor population consists not only of small farmers, but also of farm laborers and poor nonfarm workers. Workers in these last two categories, and even some small farmers, do not themselves meet their families' food requirements; they must purchase some or all of their food. Insofar as the poor devote a higher proportion of their income to food than do the rich ("Engel's law"), this has a progressive impact as long as a significant segment of the poor are net food consumers.

Effect 2. By the same token, irrigation brings production advantages to those who are within the command area.

Effect 3. Resources devoted to creating an irrigation system could have been used to benefit others. Therefore, the irrigation decision represents foregone opportunities for anyone who could have benefited more than the production or consumption effects of irrigation have brought.

Effect 4. The creation of the irrigation system may reduce the competitiveness of farmers left out of the system.

Effect 5. The definition and scope of the actual command area (where the water ends up, whether through design, seepage, or even illegal intake) establishes who will receive production benefits and who will not. Having irrigated land also gives the landowner an advantage in competing for other resources. For example, more valuable land serves as better collateral for more credit.

Effect 6. The promotion of water-intensive (for example, paddy) cropping or less water-intensive cropping determines how broadly or narrowly the production benefits will be spread, inasmuch as irrigation for water-intensive crops will restrict the scope of the command area. Cropping choices are not simply a matter for the farmer to decide, since they are heavily influenced by the design of the system as well as the agricultural policies applied to the command area.

Effect 7. The specific location of the canals and the headworks determines which farmers will be at the best locations for drawing water from the irrigation system.

Effect 8. The physical structure of the irrigation system (for example, lined versus unlined ditches) and the operating system of water sharing determines how much greater advantage can be enjoyed by farmers closer to the headworks of the irrigation system.

Thus a meaningfully comprehensive view of the relationship between production and equity must include the implications of the enhanced purchasing power of the poor in the context of increased production. Therefore the decision to promote irrigation will necessarily create some disparities among farmers, but this is a by-product of production opportunities to provide greater volumes of food and other agricultural outputs that benefit the poor. The key question is whether the poverty alleviation that results from more affordable food, as well as from increasing the incomes of the owners of otherwise marginal farms, is large in comparison with alternative uses of governmental resources and attention.

In the final analysis the production benefits of irrigation, evaluated in terms of the opportunity costs of foregoing other possible poverty alleviation uses of the same resources, may be as important or even more important than other factors in contributing to *overall* equity and poverty alleviation. The Green Revolution's greatest contribution was not higher incomes for the farmer—although this was certainly important and welcome—but rather averting mass starvation in both the cities and the countryside. It goes without saying that those at risk of starvation were the desperately poor.

Moreover, while one might presume that the political power of large farmers would result in a greater likelihood that they would benefit more from the spread of irrigation than would small farmers, this does not seem to be the case. Official statistics indicate that small farmers use scarce irrigation waters disproportionately to their share of land (Dhawan 1988, 215), and some careful empirical studies find that irrigation can bring greater income gains to small farmers than large farmers (Panda 1986, 530–31).

Equity and the Policy Process for Irrigation

While the above assessment denies the terms of the debate that pits productivity against equity, it does not deny that problems of equity do exist in irrigation, or that improvements in the equity of irrigation design are important and often feasible.

Equity and initiation. A number of distributional outcomes are largely fixed by the time the technical analysis of an irrigation project gets underway. First, as with other resource initiatives reviewed in this volume, irrigation may be defined solely in terms of productivity, thus leaving equity concerns out of the analysis (and provoking the critics to assert that productivity and equity are inevitably in conflict). Chambers (1984, 16) calls this "the trap of the single criterion," and cites examples of irrigation engineers defining their task strictly in terms of maximizing productivity or maximizing the efficiency of water supply. If the project is conceived as "major irrigation," then minor irrigation options may be ignored. If the broad parameters of the system's extension are taken as given, the intensity of irrigation may be seen as fixed rather than subject to analysis and possible revision. This premature closure in defining the irrigation project is particularly serious when irrigation is defined in terms of programs for the development of specific crops. M. V. Nadkarni (1979, 9) argues that "a shift to heavy consumers of water like paddy and sugarcane would restrict the extension of irrigated area and confine the benefits of irrigation to a relatively small part of land (and a small number of farmers), though at the micro-level the benefit appears to be conspicuous for the beneficiaries."

Indeed, Syed Hashim Ali argues that the single fundamental difference between the irrigation approaches of North and South India has been the Northern emphasis on "protective" projects that spread the command area relatively thinly in order to avert famine and the economic collapse of marginal farmers in times of drought. Ali notes: "The Canal design [in the North], therefore, was originally meant to distribute the available water over as large an area as possible to provide protective irrigation to rain-fed agriculture. It may, therefore, be said that these canal systems were designed for equity though this expression is not generally used in the Project Reports" (Ali 1984, 212).

In South India, the initial planning emphasis was based on identifying the highest-yielding cropping patterns, and then calibrating the scope of irrigation to accomplish this objective. This resulted in smaller, more intensely irrigated command areas. Ali cites an Andhra Pradesh irrigation official's blunt assessment: "[The irrigation projects] are planned for optimum yields of crops with supply of water as required for plant growth. There are no protective projects" (Ali 1984, 213).

Equity, analysis, and evaluation. When analysts do try to take distributional concerns into account in their thinking about irrigation, there is a striking discrepancy between the breadth of the equity dimensions they recognize as relevant *in principle* and the narrowness of the considerations they actually use in designing projects and evaluating their performance. A telling example can be found in an otherwise exemplary analysis by Robert Chambers (1984). Chambers, in specifying five "focal criteria" of irrigation performance, includes equity along with productivity, stability, carrying capacity and well-being. His model of criteria, objectives, and causal linkages includes the contribution of higher production to "cheaper food for the towns" (Chambers 1984, 18). But the only equity criterion that

Chambers deems worthy of defining operationally and monitoring is *equity in water distribution within the command area:*

> Equity in its broadest sense is a more difficult concept, implying equality, fairness and evenhanded dealing. It can be extended to include wide questions of who benefits from irrigation, including landless laborers, women, the public at large, officials, and others, and how they benefit—from employment, wages, cheaper food, health and so on. *Here equity is limited to the allocation and receipt of irrigation water* (Chambers 1984, 21–23; emphasis added).

When Chambers deals with the issue of the trade-offs between productivity and equity, which he regards as "obvious and important," he confines them to three: 1) wide distribution of water is more equitable but less productive because of transmission losses; 2) higher productivity in times of water scarcity would require concentrating the water in the areas where it would yield the greatest harvest; and 3) drawing down the groundwater table for increased productivity, even if replenished during years of heavy rainfall, would make it more difficult for smaller farmers to raise water, given their typically shallower wells (Chambers 1984, 35).

This is peculiar, because in recognizing the links among irrigation, higher production, and cheaper food, his framework allows for all of the eight effects outlined above, and yet the provision of more abundant and cheaper food—the accomplishment responsible for averting the starvation of millions of poor people—is ignored as an equity consideration.

Chambers offers no explicit explanation for this drastic limitation. Yet one might infer that the rationale for certain aspects of equity is the difficulty of conceptualizing and measuring them. The equity implications of changes in food production due to irrigation, balanced by the foregone opportunities to invest in other poverty-alleviating possibilities, are less demonstrable and more aggregate.

Another reason why the concept of equity may be so limited is that the focus on individual irrigation projects as the unit of analysis tends to obscure the "macro" effects on total food supply, food prices, wage rates, and so on. Dealing with each irrigation project individually, the overall supply and price impacts are typically so modest that they are ignored, and therefore the equity issue is defined simply in terms of the distribution of water to the farmers involved in the command area.

Finally, progressive distributional outcomes are typically difficult to grasp and measure because their distributional nature lies in the provision of benefits for the poor at the expense of foregone opportunities for others. The additional food that can be obtained by a poor laborer by virtue of governmental expenditures in irrigation comes at the expense of whoever would have benefited more had the resources gone to the next (marginal) project or program on the government's list, or to greater spending for one or more of the already-funded projects and programs.

If the evaluation of irrigation proceeds without explicit measurement of these more diffuse—but nonetheless terribly important—equity effects, then at least it should be recognized that these effects tend to offset the more easily measured "micro" effects that inevitably highlight the inequitable aspects of irrigation.

Equity and the project design process. The next question is how, for an irrigation system of given potential and command area, the allocation of water can be handled most equitably. For our purposes the most interesting insight is not that there are clever ways to increase equity, but rather that choosing the right mechanism and managing it effectively typically requires in-depth *local* knowledge and cooperation.

Indeed, Chambers (1984) summarizes dozens of very clever means of enhancing both the productivity and the equity entailed in irrigation, including sophisticated routines of water scheduling, staggered cultivation schedules, and crop choice. There are traditional systems, such as the fixed-proportion allocation *warabandi* system in place in Haryana for over a century, that perform quite well in their given social, political, and economic contexts (Malhotra, Raheja, and Seckler 1984). However, these options require expertise, coordination, and compliance. Therefore the unanswered questions regarding these technical possibilities are administrative and political: Can irrigation planning and management come close to determining the best options *and* enforcing them? The conclusion that emerges from the case studies that follow is that the equity aspect of water allocation (albeit not the only aspect of distribution involved in irrigation) has been best addressed through *locally specific* mechanisms that are very difficult to administer from afar.

When project design suffers from exaggerated optimism, there is an additional, perverse effect on the potential for equitable water distribution within the command area. In both North and South India, the overoptimistic early assumptions of minimal seepage and system losses and low water requirements for particular crops greatly reduced the pressure to establish control structures for fair distribution, since there seemed to be enough for all within the command area (Ali 1984, 213). Once it was realized that overuse at the head and system losses throughout did indeed create great inequities in the distribution of water from the head to the tail, the challenges of "retro-fitting" control structures such as the *warabandi* system in already-functioning systems have been difficult to meet. These structures are likely to be seen by the farmers near the headworks as provocative challenges to what has become, in their eyes, their entitlement of abundant water. To all concerned the imposition of the new control structure may seem both alien and a violation of the original understanding of how the system would operate. In other words, structures for fair water sharing, though they may be successful if they are compatible with the local culture and were designed into an irrigation system from the outset, cannot be easily grafted onto existing systems that lacked such structures before. Overoptimism makes it more likely that these structures will be grafted onto the irrigation project rather than included in the original design.

Equity and ex post appraisal. One final obstacle to the assessment of the equity effects of irrigation is worth noting, since it is closely linked with the capacity to learn from experience. The problem is the very considerable time lag between the initiation of an irrigation project and its ultimate operation. A typical irrigation system may take fifteen or even twenty years to reach this point, and then more time for the ultimate impacts on production and distribution to emerge. The obstacle to learning, then, is that analysts are not yet in a position to judge the empirical results of recent *planned* innovations in system design. Thus the debate as to whether new approaches will work remains a largely theoretical one since the empirical results pertain only to systems that were initiated in the 1970s at the latest.

Cooperation

The issue of cooperation is more central for water management than for most other aspects of natural resource exploitation. The so-called "hydraulic theory of civilization" goes so far as to credit the need for the co-ordination of irrigation and water management as the force behind the emergence of centralized authority in ancient Egypt, Mesopotamia, Peru, and other cultures. For many other natural resources, exploitation is in the hands of the state (for example, oil and mining) or is at least policed by the state (for example, forestry). But for irrigation, and in particular for major irrigation, the relationship between social arrangements and cooperation is essential. The social—and therefore political—issues concern water sharing and the upkeep of irrigation facilities. The archetypical issues of irrigation are the direct and indirect conflicts of distribution and the dilemmas of a public good that requires sacrifice for its maintenance but offers strong temptations to abuse it. Major irrigation requires water to flow from one farmer's property to another, and requires joint efforts at maintenance. Agreement on who should get what is crucial and the compliance of the farmer at the onset is a key to both efficiency and equity.

Coordination is so important, indeed, that its collapse can mean not only a decline in efficiency and equity, but the collapse of an entire irrigation initiative. As the following case study demonstrates, the calculations of production increases and distributional consequences are moot when irrigation initiatives are paralyzed by the lack of coordination.

The Jamuna Irrigation Project (Assam, India)

In the late 1960s a rather straightforward irrigation project was launched in Assam state in northeastern India. It did not have the engineering challenge or significant international implications (such as foreign assistance and foreign exchange) of the Mahaweli program in Sri Lanka. Whereas the Mahaweli was notable—or infamous—in its grandiose design and the intricacy of its resettlement requirements, Jamuna was an unprepossessing irrigation system. Engineering was not the most significant challenge; the fundamental challenge of effective irrigation turned out to be *social organization*.

The Jamuna irrigation project was an apparently sound component of the Third Five-Year Plan. Actual work on the project was started in January 1965 and was scheduled for completion by May 1969. However, while the main headworks, diversion works, and canal system were completed by the scheduled time, the planned irrigation could not be provided to most fields in the command area for a number of years beyond the time limit for the last phase planned for full utilization of the irrigation capacity, that is, 1973–74. It is this failure, more than any other, that has drawn the attention of planners, project formulators, and the Indian government in later years to try to identify the loopholes in design, preparation, implementation, or related policy decisions.

The most interesting aspects of the Jamuna irrigation project[4] revolve around the relationships between the project's implementors and the small farmer beneficiaries of the project, particularly in regard to the issue of popular participation in planning exercises. The project was not an unpopular venture imposed upon the local inhabitants by outsiders; indeed, it had strong popular support within the command area. Nonetheless, the problems encountered by the project reveal the relevance of popular participation in the policy choice process for natural resource projects having popularly demanded and supported policy objectives. The case demonstrates that when a central government launches or finances a major irrigation program, issues of *local* social organization often prove to be paramount. Because these issues are extremely difficult to master or monitor from far away, decisionmaking from the center is particularly problematic.

As in most developing areas, agriculture in the Jamuna region had been dependent on rain-fed agriculture, resulting in low productivity and uncertain harvest. Population increases and land tenure pressures, particularly in the postwar decades, made the investment of significant resources for irrigation increasingly compelling, in order to meet the seasonal needs of particular agricultural crops as well as for year-round cultivation. The Jamuna Irrigation Project was initiated in the late fifties to ensure a steady flow of water from the Jamuna River for agriculture in the command area, which had been subject to alternating floods and droughts.[5] The annual rainfall is again often concentrated to the rainy season of June through August. Moreover, because of heavy rains in the adjoining hills, Nagaon district, like other plains districts of Assam, was subject to heavy rainy-season flooding almost annually. The cropping season for paddy coincides with the flood season and therefore rain-fed paddy crop often suffered high losses. However, the areas of the district that were most vulnerable to high recurring floods were excluded from the irrigation command of the Jamuna project.

An adequate and timely supply of water had long been recognized by the people in the region as essential for high-yield agriculture. The project, therefore, was a popular one in terms of its objectives (although the case study shows the very limited participation of the beneficiaries in the command area).

Genesis of the Project

The project was designed to tap the Jamuna River near Bakuliaghat by constructing diversion works and by extending the canal system on its left bank. This would create a gross command area of 33,846 hectares, about 5 percent of the total geographical area of the district. The cultivable area was estimated to be 80 percent of the gross command area. Allowing for land that cannot be irrigated for one reason or other, the irrigable area was taken to be 95 percent of the cultivable area.

The Jamuna irrigation project was the first major venture in the state of Assam aimed at providing irrigation to cultivators, who were almost exclusively small and marginal farmers with land holdings varying from 0.5 to 10 hectares. Since agriculture was, if not their only, at least their primary source of livelihood, they were extremely vulnerable to vagaries of nature with their rain-fed cropping system. The demand for irrigation had been recognized for many years and gained momentum after Indian independence in 1947, when the five-year plans for economic development of India in the early 1950s designated irrigation as a governmental responsibility. In the Jamuna area, it was believed, irrigation would provide a clear improvement for the cultivation of paddy, which is the main staple food crop, but also for traditional cash crops like jute, sugarcane, oil seeds, and pulses.

Apparently, increased production of these crops was the only central concern of the project considered at the level of governmental planning. The sole explicitly stated purpose was to provide irrigation to reduce the risk of drought and to facilitate the change from traditional low-yield mono-cropping to high-yielding, short-duration, multiple cropping. There was no overt consideration of equity or of the environment. To be sure, the progressive reduction of inequality had been a central objective of planned economic development under the five-year plans. But, when this project was initiated during the Second Five-Year Plan in the latter half of the 1950s, the implicit belief or assumption involved in the policy choice seems to have been that the growth triggered by irrigation in the area would automatically contribute to poverty alleviation. The policy initiation exercise also did not recognize any ecological problem in tapping the water of the Jamuna River for irrigation; "environment" was simply not an explicit concern. In any case, the irrigation to be provided by the project was assumed, albeit tacitly, to help improve the ecology of the command area by countering the effect of drought. The initiative was thus the outcome of popular demand and the efforts of well-to-do influentials in the region. The influentials managed to bring in the technical experts of the governmental machinery to draw up an irrigation project. This was where the project's problems began.

Expert Analysis and Technical Consideration

At the request of the state government of Assam, the project report was initially prepared as a technical survey of the potential command area by the Central Water and Power Commission of the Indian government (CW&PC) in 1959–60. Besides the CW&PC, the Geological Survey of India undertook a geological study required for the river irrigation project. The soil exploration of the possible headwork sites was carried out by the Directorate of River Research Station and the Flood Control and Irrigation wing of the State Public Works Department (PWD). The model headworks designed by the CW&PC was further studied by the Pune station of the CW&PC. The final survey of the canal system and its design from the works engineering requirement was done by the Flood Control and Irrigation Wing engineers of the PWD.

The technical project proposal was a canal system comprising 261 kilometers spreading over the whole of the command area. Apart from the main canal, there were three principal distributaries and a host of minor and subminor canals for the irrigation network designed to feed the command area.[6] The total estimated cost of the project was 39.6 million rupees (then equivalent to approximately $5,000,000).

No comprehensive cost-benefit analysis was made in the project report. The cropping intensity was estimated to increase to 151 percent for conventional variety and to 153 percent when high-yielding short-duration varieties were introduced.[7] With the prevailing conventions of project evaluation, the exercise in project selection aimed at cost-effectiveness in achieving the purpose of the project. An *ex post* cost-benefit analysis of the project was, however, carried out at the evaluation stage (discussed below).

Formulation and Approval

The project, as formulated by the technical engineering experts, was analyzed and approved by the State Planning Department and the Planning Commission of the Indian government. All of the concerned administrative and technical departments of the government were involved in the prescribed ways. The project had general popular support and had been positively evaluated even on *ex post* equity and environmental dimensions.

And yet the decision to go ahead with the project did miss a central concern of popular participation in initiating and formulating how to implement the less technical but no less vital aspects of the provision of the detailed field-channel network for water flow within the command area. The experts who designed the project in terms of its technical capabilities and financial aspects did not comprehend the problem of the varied individual preferences of the potential beneficiaries. There was no recognition that problems would arise in designing the field channels to individual plots of various sizes and shapes and at different heights held by cultivator-owners or tenants of different economic means and political or social standing in the area. This was the problem that long delayed project benefits, even after the government-financed works were completed. The lack of participation of the intended beneficiaries in working out the details of the project, which had been entirely controlled by professional engineers, stopped the project dead in its tracks.

Implementation

The implementation of the project was entrusted to the engineers of the Flood Control and Irrigation wing of the Assam PWD. They completed the major civil works by the scheduled date of May 1969, although the field channels needed to bring the water to the agricultural plots remained to be commissioned. The cost of the works completed, however, amounted to 69.8 million rupees (approximately $8.8 million) as against the estimated total project cost of 39.6 million rupees. The field channels were to be built in a phase-by-phase sequence thereafter; the project report envisaged bringing 20 percent of the targeted area under irrigation every year after the 1969 completion of the construction works of the main water-head and canals. Thus by 1974 the irrigation capacity created through water-head and canal works of the project should have been fully utilized for irrigating the target land in the command area.

Yet by 1974 only 31 percent of the target area had been brought under irrigation. Apart from this dismal coverage, the failure to supply water in the dry winter season and to adopt the projected cropping pattern even in the irrigated portions of the command area created serious concern within the state government and volleys of public criticism. At this stage, the State Planning Board of Assam launched an *ex post* evaluation of the Jamuna irrigation project to identify the reasons for the poor performance and to formulate remedies. The facts brought out by this study[8] are summarized in the following evaluation.

The project's cost overruns, the failure to deliver the water to the bulk of the command area, and an unexpectedly high maintenance cost aroused strong criticism from the public and in government circles by 1974. Both the implementing and formulating authorities were blamed for the failure. Alternatives for getting the irrigation to the cultivable fields were developed, including pipes and lift irrigation pumps, but they were even more costly than the original scheme and neither the state exchequer nor the beneficiaries could afford them. The delay in implementation and the attempt to de-emphasize project components like the field channels damaged the morale and trust of implementors and recipients alike, further hampering utilization of the irrigation facilities. A perception spread that the project had been deliberately initiated to help a narrowly targeted group of cultivators. The rather minor component of the project, namely the provision of field channels, had become the Achilles heel for the implementors.

Ex Post Evaluation

The *ex post* evaluation study was conducted from 1973 to 1975 through field visits and a sample survey of 99 households in ten targeted villages in the command area, and 23 households selected from three control villages bordering the command area. Along with the failure to extend the irrigation system beyond 31 percent of the targeted coverage, the diversification of the cropping pattern, intensification of cropping, and adoption of high-yielding varieties of crops through a package of improved practices also did not materialize to the extent envisaged in the project report, even in the pockets where irrigation facilities were made available.

The evaluation team discovered that the root of the greatest setback to the project—namely its failure to provide field channels for 69 percent of the cultivable land—was the presumption of project authorities that the construction of the canal system would automatically stimulate the farmers to construct their own field channels to connect the canal to their fields. No obstacle was anticipated because it was also presumed that the cultivators would willingly devote their own labor, without any effort on the part of the project authorities. Yet these potential beneficiaries were not associated with the project at the stages of policy choice and project initiation.

This disastrous oversight was engendered by the project initiation approach of the experts and authorities concerned. The simple techniques of constructing field channels were either known to the cultivators or demonstrated to them. The farmers had the time and physical resources to construct the channels. Yet the channels were slow to come, particularly to the majority of fields that were not contiguous to a canal. The obvious reason for this, which the project authorities did not anticipate and failed to learn because the beneficiaries were not involved in project design and implementation at the initial stages, was that the farmer closer to the headwaters had no incentive to devote his own (or hired) labor to constructing channels that would conduct the water through his own field into another's. In some cases the farmer refused to allow down-channel potential recipients to construct the channels on his land. In short, no provisions were made by the project authorities to require the farmers closer to the canals to provide channels, to develop cooperative arrangements to induce these farmers to build the channels, or to take direct responsibility to construct the channels by government-hired and sanctioned labor. Since the project was a commonly desired one, the beneficiaries were likely to have agreed to provide the entire network of field channels voluntarily and in a cooperative manner if that had been a precondition for undertaking the project and its indispensability had been explained to the people. The behavioral aspects of the beneficiaries' incentives and the attitude of confrontation versus cooperation were ignored by the technical experts whose decisions shaped the project.

The evaluation study revealed other problems and shortcomings. Some of these problems were responsible for underutilization or inadequate access to water even where irrigation was available through field channels or outlets from the contiguous canals. These problems were:

(a) Absence of levelling of the fields to facilitate water flow through channels.
(b) Defective alignment of the canals making water flow to fields at higher levels, which were kept off the canal course, more difficult and often impossible without lifting arrangements.
(c) Lack of integration between the canal and channel networks to ensure equitable and adequate water flow to all fields.
(d) Inadequacy, faulty locations, and control of outlets from the canals, favoring certain fields and depriving others of water flow.
(e) Inappropriately designed tax measures, especially a betterment levy, which, because it was based on acreage rather than benefit, was virtually unenforceable.

These problems, or at least their crippling effect on the project, would have been minimized if the beneficiaries had been involved in the policy process and implementation exercises at least through consultation to ascertain their preferences and their knowledge of the local requirements and impediments relevant to the project. However, corrective steps were considered by the project authorities only after considerable time.

Reforming the Jamuna Approach

Based on these findings, the evaluation team made some suggestions for reform. This provided some indirect input from the potential beneficiaries. These suggestions were then examined further by the Irrigation Department of the state government. The Department offered its comments on these suggestions for final consideration of the issues raised by the State Evaluation Committee headed by the chief secretary of the state government.

The essential task of constructing the field channels was pursued by announcing that the government would, if necessary, resort to compulsory acquisition of the required tracts of land from some of the cultivators' fields for laying the channels by the project authorities themselves. At the same time, the Irrigation, Agriculture, and Revenue Departments and the local leadership of the *panchayats* (local self-government bodies at the village, development block, and subdivision/district levels) undertook concerted actions to mobilize activism on the issue through community awareness. The farmers who had quietly monopolized the benefits by neglecting to construct channels through their fields were confronted with greater community opprobrium. By 1976 these recalcitrant farmers acknowledged that such channels would have to be constructed. The resistance of the intervening field owners or cultivators ended once they were aware that the authorities would have no option but to intervene directly. At that point, cooperative participation and voluntary involvement seemed in the best interest of all the beneficiaries. It was then only a question of being compensated relative to the sacrifice of land use.

Pending the construction of the field channels, the most immediate action was the decision by the project authorities in consultation with the Agriculture Department *and* the local people to irrigate some of the previously excluded fields through flooding from the canals. Field management committees were constituted under the aegis of the Agriculture Department and with adequate representation of the beneficiaries in the command area for ensuring regular and timely supply of water to the fields from the canals. This proved a great success. By the end of 1977, more than 80 percent of the command area's cultivable fields were receiving irrigation for at least the principal paddy crop. In the meantime, construction of field channels was also taken up in a phased manner and the project was revitalized. However, the government's ability to collect water charges and the betterment levy, as called for by the project report, had to remain in abeyance. Without these mechanisms for making the project more self-financed and self-sustaining, the government had to provide funds for the construction cost of channels for feeding the high-elevation fields away from the canals.

Thus, ultimately the lack of rapport among project authorities and beneficiaries of divergent interests was rectified through governmental efforts and conscious public leadership. Once the situation had become critical, the power arrangements and the policy regime were able to be *reconstituted* in a more effective manner. And yet, the foregone opportunities of bringing the bulk of the irrigation system into use more than four years after its targeted date entailed a huge reduction in the rate of return of the project as a whole.[9]

The Jamuna case also highlights another aspect of the policymaking problem: even when some popular participation shapes natural resource policy choice, the nonpoor ''local notables'' often have a greater voice than the poor. In particular, the successful resistance to collecting water charges and the betterment levy precluded the government's ability to disengage from continued subsidization of the installed Jamuna system in order to initiate further irrigation or other poverty alleviation projects beyond this command area. Because the canal system and the water lead for the project continue to be maintained by the Irrigation Department of the Assam state government and the irrigation facility is provided free of cost to the individual beneficiaries, government resources are still tied up in what should be a self-sustaining program.

The Nalganga Irrigation Project (Maharashtra, India)

The Nalganga irrigation project, while similar to the Jamuna project in that it was the first major project in its district, differed in several important respects. There was a strong effort at pre-feasibility studies of soils, hydrology, geology, and agricultural potential. For example, the hydrologic studies established that dam and canal irrigation was necessary because of the greater salinity of well water than water directly from the Nalganga River. The agricultural studies dictated the planning of the crop mix to be promoted within the command area. There was a rather heavy emphasis on cash crops, in that just under half of the 21,000 acres of the command area was earmarked for cotton production, with the rest for food production. The decision to irrigate for cotton came largely from the local farmers' demands, reflecting their view that pre-monsoon sowing could increase the cotton yield by almost 100 percent. This region had already been one of India's major cotton-producing areas. Of the 52 percent of the acreage to be devoted to food production, a significant portion was planned for nonstaples such as bananas, chilies, and vegetables. The project seemed to have little objectionable distributive impact, since 62 percent of the cultivators had under two hectares of land, while only 2 percent had over five hectares. The incomes of farmers with less than four hectares were projected to increase by 200 percent once the irrigation system was completed, while the improvement for farmers with over four hectares was calculated at 176 percent. While these increases seem remarkably high, they would require loans for additional inputs of seed, implements, and fertilizer. The project planning documents specified the role of the Maharashtra Rural Development Department's responsibility for monitoring and facilitating these inputs through affordable loans.

In short, the Nalganga project, though only half the size of the Jamuna project in terms of command area and the length of the main canal, had more *ex ante* evaluation and feasibility studies than the Jamuna project. Indeed, crop performance was tested on a trial/demonstration farm with a staff of six established within the district. Even plans for food and cotton processing installations were part of the project's elaborate preparation. Finally, the six subareas of the command area were divided, with boundaries that seemed quite arbitrary, into six cultivation zones designated for particular crops. The planning documents do not specify whether these designations represent preferences expressed by the farmers, but judging by the uniformity of the zones and the regularity of their shapes it seems unlikely that the diversity of farmers' preferences was represented. The crop designations were to be enforced by the government through its water charges; for certain crops the government would delay or reduce water charges for farmers planting the "right" crops.

Despite these concerns with the appropriateness of the crop mix, the Nalganga planning, like that of Jamuna, did not explicitly consider environmental issues. Indeed, the whole series of late-1950s to 1960s irrigation projects undertaken by Madhya Pradesh and later (after reorganization) Maharashtra state government followed a boilerplate model of analyzing soil and topography, crop patterns and agricultural research, water rates, financial considerations, and infrastructure, without analyzing impacts on the water table, potential soil degradation, or other possible environmental consequences.

Construction on the 1 1/2-mile long earthen embankment dam began in 1958, employing over 2,000 laborers, followed by the construction of the 19-mile-long major canal. Thus by 1963–64 the headworks were sufficiently completed to allow for the irrigation of 4,000 hectares of land, *and yet less than one-tenth of that area received irrigation water*. In 1964–65, nearly 4,400 hectares could have been irrigated, but only 830 hectares actually were.

The problem, just as with Jamuna, was that the central planners had left the cutting of the field channels to the local authorities, who in turn apparently presumed that the channels would be constructed voluntarily by the farmers closer to the headworks. Many farmers either refused or were unable to construct their own channels. This occurred despite the fact that the pre-feasibility studies and the demonstration farm had alerted the community to the economic and employment potentials of the irrigation. In 1958 the government had already recognized the reluctance of farmers to build and maintain the channels to take the water into their fields. The response of the government was to lower the criteria for the field channels (and thus make their construction easier) and to issue a government circular fixing the responsibility for the field channels on *both* the government and the cultivators. By 1963, much reduced water charges were introduced as well as concerted efforts by the government to stimulate local actions through efforts at mobilization and threats. Thus legislation was pending "making it obligatory on the part of the beneficiaries to construct water courses and if they fail, empowering Government to construct them at their cost" (Maharashtra State 1970, 22).

In the evaluation of why the project had faltered, the very common discovery that the project cost had been underestimated was again made. Most importantly, the successful adaptation by the project authorities entailed lowering the criteria for individual channel construction and giving the local Rural Development officers the responsibility to complete the channels through governmental action and farmer cooperation. The resistance of farmers close to the headworks was overcome, as in Jamuna, through *force majeure*: legislation was enacted to require farmers to allow the channels to be cut to the next farmer's land. If neighboring farmers could not agree on the path of the channel, the local government was empowered to judge the shortest distance between the canal and the fields.

The block development officers and additional staff under each officer's supervision were deployed to ensure that the construction and agricultural extension were carried out.

Another change that helped overcome the project's paralysis in the early 1960s was the offer of very impressive subsidies for participating farmers through cheap loans and low prices for seeds, fertilizer, insecticides, and plows. Loans for the development of production bore no interest for five years, and a policy of loan recovery in kind was also instituted. With their risks much reduced, previously unenthusiastic or even resistant farmers were more eager to comply. Had these measures been part of the project from the start, and linked to the completion of the project, the farmers might have been willing to construct their channels initially. On the other hand, the notion of cost recovery had been almost entirely abandoned. And the farmers who had been benefited by receiving irrigation were further benefited through the subsidies in these other inputs.

The government also tried to create marketing cooperatives that would relieve the individual farmer's need to transport crops to market, but also avoid what were seen as exploitative merchant-class middlemen. These cooperatives failed, partly because the farmers chose not to wait for the cooperatives to collect and sell their produce, but rather to sell it themselves at the markets or to the private merchants. The government's reaction was to add additional "cooperative officers," thus increasing the bureaucracy but not appreciably increasing the attractiveness of the marketing coopera- tives, which still lacked the financial resources to pay farmers in advance.

In comparison with Jamuna and many other projects that hit major difficulties, the hallmark of the Nalganga project was the adaptability of its design and management. To be sure, the same oversights of presuming too much of the voluntarism of people largely left out of project approval, and disregarding the individualist incentives in designing cropping and market- ing strategies, were present. But the Nalganga authorities were quick to inquire, restructure, and make adjustments *in both objectives and pro- cedures*. Instead of trying to force the cropping pattern, the objective of achieving the government's conception of crop balance was postponed if not altogether abandoned.

The Nalganga project also shows that governmental penetration has been useful in overcoming the conflicts of interest within the local populations, but the imposition of preconceived patterns such as the cropping plan and the marketing cooperative initiative was much more problematic. And the impulse to resort to greater bureaucratic staffing—rather than providing the financial resources that would allow market forces to operate—was evident in the efforts to save the marketing cooperatives.

Finally, both the Jamuna and Nalganga experiences bring into question the information-monitoring capabilities of the Indian administrative structure. Clearly, the communities' willingness to contribute to the projects— not just to accept benefits—was the central issue, but the development officers apparently were not capable of discerning and transmitting a correct diagnosis of local conditions to the project designers. If one takes into account that the development officers were typically transferred over from the district revenue offices (Maheshwari 1985?), it seems likely that the *government-generated* linkages between localities and central authorities may not have been adequately trusted. The local *panchayats* did not do much better—but they were not given the opportunity to play a large role in the project planning until each project confronted serious problems.

Progress?

These rather "early" experiences with irrigation planning and administration—both the Jamuna and Nalganga projects were the first major irrigation initiatives in their respective areas—occurred well before the consciousness of environmental risk became a central topic, but also before the importance of social organization in irrigation management was given adequate recognition. Syed Hashim Ali (1984, 214–15) notes that it was not until 1974 that the Andhra Pradesh government established command area development authorities that were charged with the "multidisciplinary work . . . previously considered to be an automatic consequence of the completion of the engineering phase . . ." In Orissa, the command area development agency was established in 1975 to optimize the use of irrigation water (Panda 1986, 529).

Is environmental consciousness being translated into action? C. J. Joseph reported in 1986 that the major problem of silting and weed infestation of the canals in the state of Kerala—in contrast to the adequate maintenance of the barrage and field channels—was due to poor extension service (the water guards and farmers "were almost ignorant of the modern devices in desilting and weed elimination"), lack of funds and organization for maintenance, and unclear responsibility for maintaining the canal as the "commons" (Joseph 1986, 541–42). A. J. Pujari (1986) cites the recent approval in Maharashtra of the Ujjani Right Bank Canal's irrigation of the Mangalwedha area, despite the highly adverse soil conditions. Pujari accuses the government of approving the project before any adequate survey of the command area had been undertaken.

Without minimizing the seriousness of the environmental problems of salinity (or alkalinity) and waterlogging, it must be said that there is considerable irony in the fact that these result from water wastage by farmers near the headworks, and offer a unique opportunity for reconciling growth, equity, and environmental protection. First, waterlogging and salt deposits are truly the wages of selfishness and overindulgence on the part of the farmers near the headworks. Their practice of flooding their fields, and their resistance to putting labor and money into maintenance to prevent seepage, have resulted in productivity losses of more than 50 percent in many instances (Joshi 1987, 418–19).

The silver lining is that these environmental problems, with their all-too-apparent costs to productivity, are demonstrating the drawbacks of *too much* water use near the headworks. In order to preserve their own productivity, farmers near the headworks now have an incentive to support spending on lining the canals, providing better drainage, and general maintenance that can provide more water for the hitherto-denied tailenders. The positive signs are that most irrigation command authorities are now devoting more resources to subsurface drainage and greater efforts in canal lining have been undertaken (Joshi 1987, 421–22). Finally, the obvious tendency of well irrigation to lower the water table has led to greater efforts to combine canal and well irrigation so that the latter can offset the water table increases due to the former (Joshi 1987, 422).

Yet, except for these hopeful stirrings, the problems of inequitable distribution of water within the command areas have not been solved. Command area development agencies and authorities have not been very effective in reducing the overirrigation by the headwater farmers and the underirrigation left for the tailenders, as, for example, is reported by Panda (1986) in Orissa. In many areas the water rotation systems designed to ensure fairer distribution between farmers at the head and farmers at the tail have failed to be implemented. In Kerala, the state's proposal to establish water users associations was rejected by most farmers (Joseph 1986, 542); to many it seemed more like the penetration of the public sector than community participation. The *warabandi* system simply has not carried over to many of the locales where it had not been part of traditional practice. In Maharashtra (where the Nalganga project is located), Suryawanshi reported in 1986 that the "concept of outlet committee and [w]arabandi do not seem to have percolated at the grass-roots level. A better rapport between farmers and irrigation officials can help to address the problems of farmers and popularize the system. Very few farmers are aware of the problems of soil deterioration by the use of excess water" (Suryawanshi 1986, 541).

7

The Policy Process and Complexity

in Natural Resource Policymaking

It is obvious from the case studies that many policies impinging upon natural resource use have undesirable, unplanned, and often unanticipated impacts. These include ineffectiveness in raising incomes, inequalities in distribution, and negative—sometimes permanent—impacts on the environment. What goes wrong? Are there distinguishing patterns between successes and failures? Are there points in the policy process where failures occur frequently enough to warrant greater attention in the design of policymaking structures?

The key aspects of the policymaking process that deserve our attention can be identified by exploring where in the policy process the most obvious problems of balancing growth, equity, environmental protection, and participation have emerged. Our case studies have revealed many pitfalls, from the preliminary stages of defining policy problems to the later stages of implementing, ending, and evaluating specific policies and projects.

To a greater or lesser extent these pitfalls are distinctive to specific phases of the policy process. The theoretical perspective that motivates distinguishing different phases of the policy process rests on the recognition that there is no single policymaker who determines how resources are used, and no discrete "moment of decision." Our case studies amply demonstrate this point as well. Policymaking is a sequence of many actions by many actors, each with potentially different interests, information, roles, and perspectives (Lasswell 1971, ch. 2). No one can guarantee that policy will

The analysis in this chapter benefited greatly from comments and elaborations by Doreen Crompton.

"optimize for the system as a whole"—although there may be institutions (such as planning agencies) created to do so. Each of the phases of the policy process is populated by somewhat different official agencies and interest groups; each faces different analytic and political challenges (Brewer and deLeon 1983). Their efforts to coordinate or to contest with one another, and their limitations in grappling with the complexity of policy dilemmas, are typically left out of the texts on natural resource economics and management. Yet these interactions, what we call the "policy process," often spell the difference between success and failure in resource use.

Therefore a simple differentiation of the phases of the policy process can help to map out where natural resource policy can go wrong. Adopting the Brewer and deLeon terminology (1983, 20), we can divide the policy process into the following sequential stages:

(a) *initiation:* problem identification and agenda setting
(b) *estimation:* expert analysis and technical consideration
(c) *selection:* policy formulation, debate, and authorization
(d) *implementation:* greater specification and policy application
(e) *evaluation:* ex post appraisal
(f) *termination:* discontinuation or revision of policy.

The Policy Process and the Pitfalls in Natural Resource Policymaking

Problem Identification and Policy Initiation

The common failure to introduce all four of the objectives of growth, equity, environmental protection, and participation early enough in the policy deliberations can often be traced to the simple fact that the initial definition of the issue is cast in terms of one simple combination of diagnosis and solution. In the case of the Green Revolution, for example, the very broad issue of how to increase the Third World's food supply was quickly narrowed to the much more specific question of how to genetically improve basic grain crops so as to increase their yields. This made the problem easier to solve, but it also made it more likely that social and distributional problems outside of the scope of plant-breeding techniques would be ignored or neglected.

Such simplistic problem definitions often lead to the domination of policy by the single agency that has the relevant mandate or technical expertise.

Defining the food supply problem as a plant-breeding problem inevitably meant that plant geneticists rather than economists or land tenure specialists would be given most of the responsibility for dealing with it.

In irrigation projects, responsibility is invariably assigned to engineers—who presumably know how to deliver the water to where it is needed—to the exclusion of soil specialists or extensionists who are essential for planning the actual agricultural use of the water. Case after case of both irrigation planning and resettlement reveals the paucity of soil surveys, reflecting both the inability of the engineers to undertake the surveys and the lack of interest on the part of qualified agencies to help with projects from which they have been otherwise excluded.

The result of both single-problem definition and single-agency domination is that the concern that first puts the issue onto the policy agenda has a tendency to dominate—both conceptually and administratively—to the exclusion of other concerns that ought to share the focus of attention.

Obviously this result stems in part from the psychological tendency to frame a project or policy in terms of one dominant objective, to the exclusion of others. Yet this psychological tendency is often reinforced by a political consideration: those who wish to promote actions to address a particular concern, whether it be growth, poverty alleviation, or environmental protection, perceive a threat to the fullest achievement of that objective if other concerns are introduced. Development agencies are clearly concerned about the inhibiting effects of environmental considerations. For example, Brazil's National Department of Roads and Highways gave short shrift to environmental and indigenous cultural concerns in pushing the road system deep into the Amazon.

Moreover, when a project or policy is first identified, there is often an exaggerated optimism that good planning and design will mitigate problems with regard to other concerns. Secondary consequences, because they occur "unplanned" rather than being part of the initiative, are typically less well understood. Assertions that they will occur are not only arguable, they may also seem to be petty obstructionism. In many instances, the nay-sayer becomes tainted with the reputation for disloyalty, narrow-mindedness, and pessimism. This has frequently occurred with environmentalists who—despite their protestations that they are merely pointing out flaws in specific projects—have been seen as "anti-growth."

Another reason for the failure to pursue multiple objectives is the presumption common to conventional public administration and planning theory that objectives and goals ought to be clarified and *ranked* from the outset as an analytical (as well as political) exercise. The underlying premise of this advice is often that poor policies emerge from muddled, implicit goals; good policy requires an explicit hierarchy of goals. While it is certainly true that ambiguity makes policymaking more difficult, there is an equal danger in imposing priorities. Sometimes goals are in conflict with one another and must be addressed in light of these conflicts rather than by placing one goal over the others by fiat. Often the setting of priorities in the initiation stage of policymaking means that the center gets to decide on priorities, rather than allowing for other actors to express their preferences and to engage in the contentious but important *continuing* debate over priorities.

A common variant of this single-objective initiation is the simplistic focus on one factor—whether growth or redistribution—as the ultimate solution to achieving the other objectives. This can divert attention from the short- and medium-term problems with the other objectives, as when long-term aggregate growth is viewed as "ultimately" solving the distributional and environmental problems or, conversely, as growth is assumed to come eventually even if immediate redistribution does grave damage to short- and medium-term growth prospects.

Pollyanna optimality. A closely related bias in the initial consideration of a natural resource policy or project is the presumption that there need be no political clash because the initiative can benefit everyone. Because in theory any aggregate improvement can be distributed to benefit everyone, a vaguely defined proposal may be assumed to allow for the flow of benefits to all parties. We term this the assumption of "Pollyanna optimality"—the expectation that everyone will be made better off by the project. This leads to impossible expectations. For example, the discovery of vast oil reserves in Mexico in the late 1970s led to the expectation that oil could make all Mexicans better off. In fact, there were beneficiaries, but by no means did this group include all Mexicans. In making it possible for the government to postpone needed reforms, many individuals ended up worse off. The sharecropper who loses access to land when the Green Revolution makes large-scale mechanized production possible, or the farmer who is outside of the irrigation command area, will lose out despite the *theoretical* possibility of compensating all parties. If it is not clear that everyone will benefit immediately, then the argument of ultimate overall benefits may be invoked. Invoking aggregate improvements that contribute to the "general welfare" leaves little room for identifying specific groups, let alone individuals, who might lose out.

In the euphoria of "discovering" that a natural resource venture could hold the key to solving a serious problem of stagnation and poverty, long-term consequences are often given too little importance, even allowing for reasonable rates of discounting the future. Optimism about dealing with as-yet-poorly defined future problems is in keeping with the romance of grand schemes, political platforms, and asserting an agency's "can-do" mastery. The resettlement cases of Dandakaranya, Indonesia's *transmigrasi,* and Polonoroeste in Brazil are particularly graphic examples of downplaying the long-term consequences of tampering with fragile ecosystems.

The locus of initiation. When policy initiatives come from the center, they are often conceived as part of the expansion of responsibility of one or more central state entities, whether governmental agencies or semi-autonomous state enterprises. Indeed, since local initiatives often do not filter their way to high governmental circles, there is often an imbalance in problem identification in favor of the issues and ventures that are identified at the center—and, at least in part, serve the institutional interests of the agencies of the central government. Therefore there is a common tendency to take for granted that initiatives must come from the center and that the center must be in charge. In many cases, and particularly in major irrigation projects, the centralization of governmental financial resources precludes local or even state-level initiatives unless the central government is involved. Naturally, the central government's involvement, when it holds purse strings, frequently leads to central government dominance.

The first liability of central government dominance over the initiation of projects or policies lies in the distance between central planners and the multidimensional reality on the ground. It is in the "micro-environment" that the pursuit of a single, simple objective clashes with other objectives and values. For example, increasing the grain yield through Green Revolution technology seems straightforward and laudable in the abstract, but we have seen how the distributional issues arise on the micro-level of one farmer displacing another. It is in the forests of Indonesia and Brazil that rare species are disappearing, not in Jakarta or Brasília. It is in the fine-grained behavior of the farmer and the local irrigation manager that the allocation of water is determined, the problems of waterlogging arise, and the willingness to dig the necessary field channels is determined. In short, the highly aggregated analysis of the centralized planners often masks distributional issues; and remoteness makes it much more difficult to identify and appreciate unanticipated secondary consequences.

Indeed, conventional administrative theory finds no vice in having broad, simple policy established at the top, as long as the implementation of policy down the line can be adapted to the nuances of specific situations. The problem, however, is that simple, single-objective policy articulated by top leaders often stifles the introduction of other low-level considerations. Setting a single dominant objective puts the implementing authority in the hands of the agencies with this objective; the official evaluation of performance is likely to be dominated by this objective, while those who invoke other criteria can be dismissed as simply lacking commitment to the main goal.

The second liability of central initiation lies in the preoccupation of the central authorities with the high political payoffs of bold, exaggeratedly single-objective policies and projects. Local authorities are often aware that the pursuit of a single objective will create problems that they will have to confront, but central leaders may get large political rewards from the symbolism of simple initiatives with an impressive single performance measure—for example, number of settlers moved, total foreign grant money for huge dams, total irrigation expansion, and total grain yields. Moreover, when it comes to adapting projects and policies that begin to manifest other problems, the political symbolism of the big project often leaves little room for pulling back from the major objective; the bigger the venture, the more the central leaders' reputations are on the line.

However, allowing the initiation of policy to come from the local communities raises its own set of problems. Local initiation often allows the nonpoor local notables to have a greater voice than the poor. In plantation forestry projects, larger landowners are often able to get access to subsidized seedlings; the same is often true of subsidized fertilizer and pesticides in agricultural development projects. To the degree that irrigation projects can be skewed to favor the wealthier and more influential farmers, locally formulated proposals may reflect this bias. Again, because the weak information resources typical of developing countries make it difficult for the central government to know detailed conditions in local communities, the local notables—more articulate than their poorer neighbors and more likely to have contacts within the central government—can more easily define natural resource policy issues to reflect their own preoccupations.

The local initiation of policy concern is also a favored vehicle in many countries for local politicians to capture the attention of the central government. In political arenas where the capacity to mobilize populations is an entree to positions of greater authority, rousing a population to oppose a new project or to demand greater services is a common ploy whether or not the demands are reasonable in light of the nation's overall needs and resources.

However, this does not mean that local control necessarily dooms a program to domination by local elites; program design that gives an important role for the nonelites can increase their bargaining power over the distribution of the benefits. For example, if farmers must work together to maintain a small-scale irrigation system, the labor of the poor farmers may be as essential as the labor contributed by the rich farmer. If governmental agencies undertake the projects and money becomes the important resource in pursuing them, then the poor farmer is in a weaker power position in such a "monetized" context. In short, decentralization certainly has its pitfalls related to dominance by local elites, but the right combinations of local autonomy and project design can avoid these dangers.

Expert Analysis and Technical Consideration

The delay in expert assessment. The essential role of experts to design natural resource ventures and to assess their feasibility is often engaged too late to formulate a careful design, or to get a project or policy stopped if no design modification is possible. Typically, it is the bold scheme with fuzzy boundaries that captures the political imagination. The tendency to emphasize a single objective often leads to exaggerated initiatives that leave the realm of technical concerns for balance and efficiency and enter into the realm of political symbolism and romanticism. Many programs and projects designed to exploit the natural resource base are marked by breathtaking boldness—eleven huge dams to provide water to 40 percent of Sri Lanka's territory; the Aswan High Dam's mastery of the inconsistency of the Nile flood; the resettlement of hundreds of thousands of land-poor people in the forests of Brazil, India, and Indonesia. By the time technical considerations are permitted, it may be too late to reshape the project.

Sober technical analysis may be rejected outright. Boldness colors the initial stages of conceiving a natural resource undertaking. Bold initiatives are often undergirded by simple, defiant, heroic messages: the forest will yield; the river will be tamed; the land will be settled. Indeed, the political credit redounding to a government that tries to wrestle with socioeconomic problems by reshaping the environment can be greater simply by virtue of the fact that nature is defied.

It is difficult—though not impossible—to do the detailed engineering and economic assessments when the scope, location, and time frame of a policy or project remain poorly defined (sometimes deliberately so) or change with the political winds. Just as raising problems in the initiation phase is often taken as negativistic or obstructionist, the same thankless fate often awaits the technical specialist who raises objections early in the conceptual development of a project or policy. Yet once political support for a natural resource venture has been mobilized, experts work at a crippling disadvantage. Political leaders not infrequently stake their reputations on bold natural resource projects (for example, dams, resettlements, and oil policies), and can often bury the experts' objections or make sure that the analysis is not undertaken.

Pollyanna feasibility. Out of similar political pressures, the benefits of policies or projects are often exaggerated, and the costs understated, thereby reducing the legitimacy of arguments made against the initiative. Such distortions are possible because even "technical assessment," although the term connotes a cut-and-dried impartial evaluation, requires an enormous amount of judgment. Therefore when the technical problem is to explore the unplanned consequences of a planned venture, it is very easy to take the planned outcomes as given and to dismiss any possibly unintended liability as unlikely. Or, when unintended consequences are recognized, their seriousness is often underestimated. After all, uncertainty makes any given contingency uncertain, particularly if there is no policy intent to bring it about; the very fact that unintended consequences are unplanned thus makes any specific prediction of low likelihood. It is thus easy to be lulled into dismissing each danger one by one, without recognizing the likelihood that *something* is highly likely to go wrong in many natural resource ventures. In short, the intended consequences are typically perceived as likely because of the will to achieve them, but the unintended adverse consequences are given little credence because they cannot be well defined or accurately predicted.

We have seen this exaggerated optimism in virtually every large-scale project examined in the case studies. Resettlement programs have unanticipated costs of duplication and wastage resulting from poor interagency coordination; large dams regularly run into unforeseen geological problems that require more expensive approaches; the problems of salinity, water loss, and silting of irrigation projects occur chronically and yet are consistently underestimated. The prevalence of these problems is a good indication that there is a systemic tendency to underestimate costs and exaggerate benefits.

Biases in expertise. When experts do have a relevant role in natural resource policymaking, they sometimes operate without a comprehensive and systematic evaluation framework. Without an explicit way to balance growth, distribution, environment, and participation, analysis favoring any policy or project is vulnerable to the criticism that one or more of these objectives has been given inadequate weight. When the government is politically vulnerable, it may not be able to respond to such criticism by pointing to a balanced decision. Thus governments in this situation are prone to great volatility in the stance they take toward particular natural resource policy issues. A strong challenge may result in a total defensive denial of the critique, or in a complete policy reversal. Thus the very existence of the Narmada and Sardar reservoirs of the Narmada Valley in western India hangs in the balance; they may be pushed into construction over the objections of their critics within and outside of India, or they may be cancelled altogether. The Mahaweli scheme in Sri Lanka was telescoped from a thirty-year project to a seven-year project virtually overnight; but the number of reservoirs went from fifteen to seven. For want of a holistic way to assess the net benefits of the major resettlement schemes, huge undertakings such as Brazil's Polonoroeste and Indonesia's *transmigrasi* have been highly prone to abrupt changes in direction and funding levels.

Therefore it is understandable that analysts put forth ostensibly comprehensive cost-benefit frameworks that purport to provide the definitive answer to how costs and benefits across all relevant considerations add up. The analytic exercise of making the whole range of costs and benefits as explicit and comparable as possible is indeed essential. Yet ironically these techniques hold the potential pitfall of claiming comprehensiveness even when they do not give a fair weight to one or more relevant concerns. Typically, these methods implicitly weigh different concerns simply by including and excluding particular types of data, emphasizing the measurable (and particularly the quantifiable), considering only first-order consequences or consequences of well-understood relationships.

Whether or not formal or quantitative methods are used, the commitment to "rigor" on the part of many technical experts wishing to maintain their professional standards grants greater attention to those concerns that can be captured in specific information. Thus when information on one or more of the primary concerns is limited or poor, greater attention is paid to the other concerns. A parallel bias is introduced when the understanding of causes and effects associated with one or more of these concerns is so limited that greater attention is paid to the other concerns. In short, being rigorously scientific often boils down to focusing on the easily measured and the easily understood. Since distributional issues, participation, and long-term environmental effects are rarely as well understood as are short-term economic impacts, these concerns are often given inadequate attention by the most careful experts.

This problem is often exacerbated by the pecking order within the technical fields. The higher prestige and power of particular professions may impart inappropriate priorities in balancing the concerns of growth, equity, environmental protection, and participation. Typically, economists and engineers have more clout than the anthropologists or political scientists who track participation and distributional impacts of natural resource policy choices. As we have seen in the cases of agricultural modernization, resettlement schemes, and large dams, the training of anthropologists, sociologists, and political scientists inclines them to point out where governmental policy has gone wrong by disregarding the secondary consequences on life and culture, thus putting these social scientists into the position of seemingly querulous nay-saying. "Environmentalists" in many contexts still suffer from the stigma of their alleged lack of hardheaded rigor and their single-issue obsession.

No matter which technical experts do the analysis of project or policy feasibility, their decisions often dominate over the preferences of the citizens affected by natural resource policy choice, even when these citizens' knowledge of the micro-conditions of their particular contexts offers important guidance on how natural resources ought to be managed. The local population's choices of land use, the areas they avoid, their cropping patterns, and so on, often reveal aspects of local micro-conditions that escaped the notice of centralized planners and experts. This has been a recurrent theme in agricultural modernization, forestry, and irrigation. Consequently there has been much criticism of technocrats, and much polarization in the debate between local knowledge and scientific expertise. However, as the cases of the Narmada Valley and the Indira Reservoir demonstrate, the real challenge is to blend these different but *complementary* knowledge bases.

Policy Formulation and Selection

Poor coordination in governmental decisionmaking. Because well-balanced technical advice on natural resource policy choices suffers from the problems outlined above, and may be rejected in any event, balancing the inputs of governmental agencies mandated to uphold particular concerns becomes essential for good policy. Yet although diverse concerns are typically under the jurisdiction of different government agencies, poor coordination among agencies often prevents or delays appropriate actions. Bureaucracies are designed for vertical communication, yet the coordination of activities of several agencies obviously calls for horizontal communication.

At the other extreme, government agencies charged with pursuing a particular objective are often either excluded from policymaking over specific projects or policies or their influence is very limited, thereby diminishing the priority of the concerns they represent. The fact that horizontal communication is difficult—and that multiagency coordination often goes awry—can be used as a pretext to pursue bureaucratic and political motivations by excluding rival agencies.

This dilemma of whether to include or exclude bureaucratic units in formulating and implementing natural resources policies is based on the inevitable trade-offs between complicating the decision process and ensuring the representation of all relevant factors. Complicating the decision process has two obvious drawbacks. First, the more voices and bureaucratic procedures involved, the greater the likelihood of delay, confusion, and duplication. Second, the ultimate issues of progress and societal welfare can be obscured by the more immediate issues of intra-governmental rivalries over jurisdiction—the so-called "bureaucratic politics."

These "complications" may be necessary, however, to ensure that each of the considerations of growth, equity, environmental protection, and participation is adequately incorporated into decisionmaking. Whenever an environmental agency, health ministry, or other governmental unit is excluded or marginalized from policy deliberations on the grounds that the situation would have become too complicated, the factor represented by that unit may simply be overlooked. One might wonder whether political jockeying is obstructing the formulation and implementation of a sufficiently comprehensive policy.

The governmental agencies more likely to be excluded from natural resource policymaking are the weaker agencies with less capability to defend themselves in the bureaucratic political jostling. Just as there is a pecking order among experts of different disciplines, some governmental agencies have more power and prestige than others. Environmental agencies and agencies dedicated to aiding indigenous populations or the poor are frequently weaker than the major spending ministries or the large-scale state enterprises. Agencies for mobilizing popular participation sometimes capture impressive political power at propitious moments, but their ascendance is typically short-lived because of the threat that mass mobilization poses to governmental control. Initiatives often become the captive of one agency, typically one with great financial resources and a strong political constituency that has its own agenda. For example, the Polonoroeste Project in Brazil came to be dominated by the National Department of Roads and Highways, which controlled more than half of the total project expenditures.

The other dimension of possible poor coordination is the division among subnational jurisdictions. Rivalries among states or provinces often block the achievement of the optimal policy or project. This is particularly true when people or resources cross subnational borders: population resettlements, dams, industrial projects entailing downstream or downwind pollution, and so on. Since subnational governmental authorities are charged with pursuing the interests of their jurisdiction rather than the country as a whole, their reluctance to exchange the welfare of their own people even for the greater good of the nation as a whole is not only understandable, it may be a requirement of their formal responsibility. This problem plagued the Damodar Valley development at the beginning of the Indian independence period and the Narmada Valley efforts later on; learning how to overcome this problem is difficult indeed.

Both for agency competition and rivalries among subnational jurisdictions, the answers to poor coordination are not simple. The virtue of concentrating decisionmaking power into a single-program agency (or authority) is that such an authority must take the coordination of different facets of the program as its own administrative problem. One potential weakness of the single-authority strategy is that such an agency may become impervious to other voices. The Transmigration Ministry in Indonesia may very well be in this situation. Another potential weakness is that the single agency can develop its own internal coordination difficulties if it takes on too broad a mandate for its administrative capacity.

Overcontrol. There is widespread inclination to respond to threats to resources by imposing more formal control through the governmental apparatus. Often the presumption is that resources must be protected from those who are too preoccupied with survival to pay attention to the environment—the poor are often perceived as the problem rather than as the beneficiaries of the solutions. This reaction often leads to the conclusion that greater managerial control is necessary, and that such control requires greater formality in property ownership and use. Yet this shift from informal to formal exploitation of a natural resource removes opportunities for the poor to use those resources. This has been frequently observed in forest policy in India, where schemes to improve forest management through social forestry have eroded the traditional forest-use rights of tribal peoples.

Implementation

While the implementation of natural resource policy brings additional actors into play, the same problems that occur in the initiation and formulation of policy emerge. In theory, the implementation of policies by a nation's public administration does not make policy, it merely applies policy. In practice, though, the considerable discretion inevitably left in the hands of administrators requires that they shape outcomes through their decisions, thus creating policy in the most concrete sense.

Benefit "leakage." Because socioeconomic groups try to capture benefits and avoid costs, the targeting of natural resource policy benefits to the poor often fails. Ventures designed to help a narrowly targeted poor population tend to be extended to the point that they lead to wasteful resource use without even being progressive in terms of income distribution. This results not only from the typically superior organization of nonpoor groups as compared to the poor, but also to the political fact of life that if a benefit is popular, extending it more broadly will make it more popular, especially if the costs are disguised or postponed. Overexploitation of natural resources thus becomes a politically expedient—albeit shortsighted—policy choice.

Limitations of state enterprises as natural resource managers. When the state implements natural resource policies through its own enterprises, the idea of regulation of the natural selfishness of the private sector fades into the background. Yet, as a natural resource exploiter, the state often fails to meet its promises of targeting benefits to the poor, or protecting the environment, even though these are among the primary justifications offered for foregoing the presumed greater efficiency of the private sector.

Although state enterprises are typically created out of the belief that they are in a better position to address externalities of distribution, environment, and participation than are private-sector ventures, they often fail to meet this promise. State enterprises are often pushed by their own employees to channel the benefits of resource extraction to these employees themselves. They are sometimes required by the highest political leadership to make short-sighted payoffs to the politically powerful; the squandering of oil revenues in many countries is a flagrant case in point.

Ironically, state enterprises are often underregulated because the fact of ostensible public ownership, and consequent formal control by the government, alleviates these entities from the regulatory control assumed to be necessary to keep private-sector ventures under control.

Poor coordination of implementation. The same problems of bureaucratic confusion, rivalry, and sometimes exclusion pertain to the implementation phase as they do to the formulation and selection of policy. Indeed, since implementation typically involves larger numbers of personnel, the bureaucratic political stakes of who ends up implementing a program or project are often higher, with correspondingly greater infighting among the agencies involved. Delay or de-emphasis of project components may damage the morale and trust of implementors and recipients, thereby hampering successful implementation.

Ex Post Appraisal

The accurate assessment of policy success and project performance is essential for two reasons. First, short of market signals, ex post assessment or appraisal bears the burden of signalling when and where resources are misallocated. Second, appraisal, insofar as it serves as the basis for rewards (whether political popularity for leaders or promotions for officials), has a crucial impact on the incentive structure that shapes policy choice. However, the very fact that appraisal is so intimately connected with rewards and punishments frequently leads to distortions in the appraisal function.

Insensitivity to criticism. When critics of the balance among the objectives of growth, equity, environmental protection, and participation try to influence existing policy, they often find that natural resource policymakers are particularly impervious to criticism. It is a peculiarity of natural resource policy that many of the officials involved look upon themselves as crusaders, innovators, and defenders of the public good. They also often credit themselves with superior technical knowledge and hence are superior both to the other officials and to the public in decisionmaking. Therefore they are prone to stereotyping their own critics as the opponents of progress. In short, policymakers and administrators convinced that they are "doing good" are often less receptive to criticism and suggestions on how to balance the objectives better. For example, while the critics of large dams may view the planners as callous technocrats willing to gamble with the well-being of the population and the ecology, the planners typically view themselves as righteous crusaders for more accessible and productive water, electrification, and flood control. Since from their perspective they hold both the moral high road and technical superiority, the *warrant* for criticizing their decisions lacks legitimacy in their eyes.

Limited learning from experience. "Learning" from previous natural resource policy mistakes often seems minimal. There are many causes. First, the complexity of causes and effects of natural resource policy outcomes makes it difficult to pin down definitive lessons. Because many resource policies draw down natural capital stocks, the results are not seen as unprofitable projects but rather as income obtained from liquidating natural resource assets. Only sound projections of future income losses would show which of these seemingly profitable projects are indeed unsustainable.

Second, natural resource policies are typically complex and of long duration. By the time a clear lesson from a given project or policy can be discerned, the context has changed, and whether the putative lesson still holds remains an open question. We have seen in the case of large dams and resettlement schemes that when a thorough assessment of a completed project reveals weaknesses in that project's design, there is a strong tendency for current planners to dismiss the lesson on the grounds that "we don't do it that way any more." To be sure, designs are continually evolving, but we have seen only mixed evidence that the policymaking process and the substantive approaches to dams, irrigation, resettlement, or other natural resource initiatives have changed fundamentally from past patterns. Third, comprehensive follow-up efforts to determine long-term effects are often inadequate. This results from both technical and political factors. From a technical perspective, the critical problem is that the effects of a project or policy become increasingly diffuse as chains of cause and effect are triggered, making it increasingly difficult to trace these effects. Thus it is easy enough to assess the direct effects of the dam per se: Does it retain the anticipated volume of water? Does it leak? But the indirect consequences of lengthy causal chains (for example, increased downstream agricultural production reduces overall food prices, thus reducing the incomes of other farmers outside of the command area) affect more people and ever-widening geographical areas. The political factor is that governments responsible for resource projects that appear to be successful in terms of the most immediate criteria—such as solid dams and resettlement programs that actually move the projected number of people—have little incentive to devote the resources to comprehensive evaluations that may very well prove to be embarrassing.

Termination

The termination of natural resource policies or projects runs into the standard pitfalls of ending any public policy initiative. Once a natural resource policy choice has been seen as benefiting a particular group, any change or elimination of the policy risks being opposed by such a group. Such benefits come to be defended as entitlements, and the termination of benefits is typically seen as a punishment regardless of whether that group had been receiving more than others.

Furthermore, the termination of a program or project, even if the targeted policy had been appropriate and had simply outlived its usefulness, runs the risk of giving the appearance of policy failure. Political leaders are, of course, loathe to admit defeat, let alone allow themselves to appear as having failed just because the elimination of a policy or program gives that impression.

Finally, bureaucratic politics makes it difficult for an agency to acquiesce to the reduction of its jurisdiction by allowing its existing programs to be eliminated or scaled back. Even if other activities are possible, the conservative approach to defending the standing of the governmental unit is to defend existing activities to the hilt.

Understanding Why Natural Resource Policy Problems Occur

Aside from simply pointing out the problems listed above, the challenge for a constructive approach to improving natural resource policymaking is to understand why these particular problems arise so frequently. Explanations are given along with each pitfall mentioned above, but it is also useful to draw some general insights from the patterns we have identified. On the basis of these insights, recommendations for improved procedures can be derived. We begin with noting the peculiar *complexity* of natural resource issues as a class of policy problems.

Complexity

It is quite common for policymakers of all sorts to complain about the complexity of the issues they face. Yet natural resource policy is complex in rather distinctive ways, owing to the interconnectedness reviewed in chapter 2 and to the long time period involved. If one thinks of natural resource policy as the continual dilemma of whether, how, and when to convert resource endowments into capital and consumption—and for whose benefit—in the context of both positive and negative externalities, the complexity seems formidable indeed.

The case studies of natural resource policy choice and the pitfalls outlined above reveal the double-edged implication of the complexity of natural resource issues. The neglect of this complexity, for the multiple reasons outlined in this chapter, is responsible for many of the failures to uphold appropriate standards of growth, equity, environmental protection, or participation.

The opposite danger is that the recognition of complexity sometimes stimulates an overreaction that puts too much authority in the hands of technical experts mistakenly thought to be the masters of complexity. Since there are political and sociological dimensions to the complexity of natural resource policy choices, however, handling such issues as strictly technical matters is yet another pitfall of oversimplification.

Ignoring complexity. From a political perspective, both private and governmental actors are often motivated to deny the multiplicity of objectives that must be balanced in natural resource policymaking, so that the concerns they give the highest priority will dominate in the choice of policy. A particular private economic interest—for example, a lumber company—would rarely receive the greatest reward if all four objectives are pursued. In the case of a lumber company bidding for the right to harvest government timber, the concern for promoting GNP growth and export earnings would help its case. Environmental protection for long-term sustainable development may or may not be in the narrow interests of that company; but neither distributional equity concerns nor popular participation in resource management are likely to be of any benefit to that company.

This natural selfishness of private actors can be constructive or destructive, depending on how the state has structured the policy environment and the policymaking process itself. But the state, too, is vulnerable to ignoring the complexity of natural resource issues. Because agencies within the bureaucracy have specific responsibilities to address particular issues, each such agency also has an interest in denying complexity. As in the case of private actors, it is not necessarily a matter of evildoing that a bureaucratic unit would be bent on pursuing one object at the expense of the others. It would be surprising, and even troubling, if a government agency entrusted with export promotion failed to push ardently for this objective in the face of other concerns. The key, of course, is *balance*: How can governmental units, each pursuing a particular mandate, be organized so as to ensure that natural resource policy choices are based on an appropriate balance of concerns over growth, equity, environment, and participation?

Thus there is a parallel to the government's external role of balancing private-sector pressures; it must also balance public-sector interests derived from mandated responsibilities as well as bureaucratic politics. Just as the state has the potential to create an environment in which private interests can mesh constructively, the highest levels of government have the potential to mesh the agencies involved in making natural resource policy choices. This is particularly difficult when there are multiple levels of government managing a resource or where there are state enterprises with partial autonomy from governmental control. Yet because these state agencies have been given a degree of autonomy from the central government, the challenge to balance the four central concerns of natural resource policy is complicated by the partial independence enjoyed by state enterprises.

It cannot be said that centralization is a panacea or even necessarily desirable. There is considerable evidence that centralization can pose serious problems of poor information and clumsy control, as policymakers in the capital lose touch with the specifics "on the ground." The issues of centralization, decentralization, and devolution are complex indeed, as we see the obverse problems of control from too great a distance, and local control that runs the risk of playing into the selfishness of local elites.

Complexity also helps to explain why natural resource policymakers so frequently do not anticipate the problems that almost inevitably arise once policies are enacted. Throughout all the phases of policymaking, ignorance and uncertainty tilt in favor of the planned rather than the unplanned. By the same token, a given agency pursuing its own natural resource policy objectives is unlikely to have good information about low-priority concerns. While complexity implies the need for good information, the *uneven* quality of information influences the focus of attention.

The time dimension. Because resource use is an ongoing activity, with costs and benefits strung out over long time periods, resource policymakers face the dilemmas of weighing the present against the future. While rational men and women can certainly differ over how much the future ought to be discounted, our case studies provide ample evidence that policymaking often yields resource exploitation patterns that correspond to no one's time preferences. The problem here is not simply that the appropriate weights for present and future are always controversial, although that is true enough. The problem is that what little certainty we have about interactions between resource uses and relevant outcomes dwindles as we project out into the more distant future. This does not always mean that the future is slighted, as we have seen in the cases of current and short-term sacrifices made for some utopian vision of long-term benefits for all. But it does mean that careful consideration of sustainable development—if this is taken to mean the optimal provision of social welfare over time—is a very difficult technical challenge.

Politics In and Out of Government

The next key to understanding how policymakers and administrators deal with the complexity of natural resource policy is to recognize that their motivations are as complicated and "multiple" as are the objectives that must be served by such policies. The public choice theorists have contributed the insight that the interests of the "state" are important, but they often lost sight of the fact that these interests are varying and complex. In various combinations, their motivations are to:

(a) enhance the standing of the agencies in which they work
(b) promote their own careers within these agencies (or elsewhere)
(c) adhere to the highest professional standards, either for the sake of professionalism per se or to attain respect from professional peers
(d) pursue partisan political objectives
(e) pursue a particular *a priori* policy objective (such as environmental protection at any cost).

Thus, any official's reactions can be understood in the context of weighing these motivations. Although the observer might frown on these motivations as detracting from the simple pursuit of the public interest, in the eyes of the individual official these objectives may well be seen as compatible with placing him or her in the position of having the greatest scope to "do good." The career of Gifford Pinchot, the founder of the U.S. Forest Service, provides abundant examples of this type of behavior. The fact that policymakers and administrators can be motivated to enhance the standing of their agencies or their positions within them, and often do so proudly, explains much of the bureaucratic politics that marks policymaking in general.

The final key insight is obvious, although working out its implications is always complicated. Natural resource policies always imply benefits and costs for various socioeconomic groups (including state enterprise personnel and even government officials). Even though natural resource policy obviously addresses the question of how to pursue the "public good," the fact that particular policies will indulge or deprive specific groups tends to mobilize them to shape the policies in their interests. Even the ideally honest and impartial public servant will find that the definition of the public good is too vague to specify precisely what must be done, thus giving wide range to varying interpretations of how to proceed.

Convergence of Technical and Political Pitfalls

Although each phase of the policy process presents technical and political problems that can be separated *analytically*, in the real world they converge. Technical constraints often offer the opportunity for the pursuit of political agendas that depart from the public interest. This seemingly unfortunate circumstance is actually the key to offsetting the negative aspects of bureaucratic politics and narrow partisan politics, because it opens up the possibility of restructuring the technical structure of natural resource policymaking so as to avoid many of the political pitfalls. By the same token it also allows for political actions that can reduce some of the technical weaknesses in formulating and implementing resource policies and projects.

First, one of the most potent connections between the technical and political aspects of the policy process is the access to *information*. There has been a large volume of research confirming the importance of capturing and controlling information as a source of bureaucratic power (Cleaves 1974). The volume, availability, and precise forms of information shape many aspects of how resource issues are viewed and addressed: the focus of attention, the way problems come to be defined, and the ways that success or failure (that is, post-hoc evaluation) is attributed to a project or policy. For example, we have seen how different pieces of information on the performance of the Indonesian *transmigrasi* resettlement program (and different interpretations of that information) could lead to drastically different conclusions about its viability. It is, of course, much easier for a particular interest to use information to its political advantage if it holds a monopoly or predominance of control over information. With multiple sources of information on the same issue it is much more difficult for this sort of control to be manipulated. Thus much of the criticism of India's water and forest policies was possible only because of India's active and free press.

Thus one remedy to the monopolization of information is the establishment of alternative sources of information and the development of diverse measures. It makes sense to devote greater effort to reinforce the informational resources on facets that are typically undermeasured, such as distribution and environmental impact. The proliferation of "state of the environment reports" is a healthy step in this direction. There have been complaints that such measures are often misleading, and yet the same can be said about the conventional measures of aggregate growth. Any measure can be more or less useful depending on how much effort is devoted to interpreting its significance in specific contexts.

Second, to the degree that technical expertise is the admission ticket into the deliberations on resource policy, the possession of expertise is valuable in the same ways that information is valuable. In less developed countries, technical expertise is a relatively scarce commodity, often held predominantly within government. Particularly with respect to the issue of popular participation in natural resource policies, the lack of technical expertise among the local populations has severely reduced their credibility as participants in policy deliberations.

However, two very positive developments are evident with respect to the more equitable sharing of expertise. First, there has been growing awareness that the technical educations received in institutions of higher learning are not the only sources of expertise. Local lore about the land, the seasons, and the flora and fauna have proven time and again to be important. In a fascinating section of his critique of the Mahaweli Program, Gamini Iriyagolle (1978, 44) demonstrates that the "folk memory" of viable dry-season irrigation (as opposed to the project plan, which provided for irrigation only in the wet season) is retained in the Sinhalese word for "dry season," inasmuch as it corresponds to the term "agricultural season." Similarly, there are many instances of resettlement schemes that have failed in their attempts to cultivate land that local people had left alone despite the lack of "scientific" reasons for their neglect.

The other heartening development is that even conventional expertise is becoming more widely shared. In most countries, including very poor ones, well-educated people are devoting themselves to the service of the environment and the poor, ensuring that expertise is not monopolized by the beneficiaries of policies that might have unacceptably high costs to the environment, equity, or participation. There is increasing diffusion of expertise through local and international NGOS.

Third, the technical problem of lack of intra-governmental coordination provides the opportunity for each agency to pursue its own agenda, and especially for the more powerful agencies to minimize the influence of other agencies representing other concerns. Whereas in theory the allocation of various interests to different ministries and agencies provides support for each concern within the government, a disjointed decision process may permit one or more agencies to ignore the input of others. Our case studies show that a single authority in charge of a complex resource-related program can be effective as long as that authority is charged with the balanced pursuit of the four primary objectives. This requires careful choice of leadership and personnel within the authority, and clear political and technical arrangements to ensure that no interests are frozen out of the process.

Fourth, the many technical tendencies to simplify the complexity of natural resource issues by focusing on a single objective have been reinforced by the political appeal of particular single objectives. Thus the potent appeal of the Indonesian *transmigrasi*—to clear the marginals out of the overcrowded Inner Islands and provide them with a presumably better life on the Outer Islands—came at the expense of considerations of environmental protection and the sustainability of development. As long as these simplistic objectives retain their political potency, it is probably quixotic to expect that natural resource policymaking will typically be well-balanced. However, there is often a strong possibility of endowing *balanced development* with a strong political, ideological appeal in its own right. In several countries, from Mexico to India, the protection of the "national patrimony," and the role of government as the "steward of the nation's resource endowment" have had some potency in the policy debate over resource exploitation. As sustainable development gains currency as the central desideratum, it may become easier to reveal the limitations of quick-fix, single objectives.

8

Reforming

Natural Resource Policymaking

Few things are more difficult for policymakers to do than to pursue multiple objectives simultaneously. So many things seem to stand in their way—the pushing and tugging of interest groups, the self-interest of specialized government agencies, the complexity of the interactions within the system in which policy is to operate, and the possibility for unexpected, even perverse, side effects. These factors are compounded in Third World societies which often must contend with severe shortages of trained personnel, poor information, limited fiscal capacity, and fragile political relationships among groups and regions. In natural resource policymaking there is the additional problem that access to resources must be allocated not only among the multiplicity of current interests, but between the present generation and future generations. As we have seen in the previous chapters, the possibilities are almost endless for natural resource policies that are ineffective, inefficient, or inequitable.

We believe natural resource policymaking can be reformed. Rather than denying its complexity and the need to pursue multiple objectives, policymakers should work toward creating virtuous circles in which the pursuit of one objective reinforces another.

There are two main tasks in creating such circles. The first is to improve the transmission of information among the various parts of the policymaking system. This will lead to the early identification of sources of perceived inequity—and hence of potential resistance to the policy—as well as to the identification of unwanted environmental impacts. It also will give policymakers a better idea of when policies already in place should be modified or terminated.

The second task is to provide each of the parties affected by policy, whether they are private corporations, local governments, or individual farmers, with a clear incentive to cooperate actively in achieving the policy's goals. This can be done through regulation or other negative sanctions—for example, requiring that trees which are cut are replaced by new seedlings, with fines for noncompliance. Or it can be done through incentives—particularly the opportunity to provide inputs in designing projects and the establishment of property rights that give individuals a private reason for doing what government has determined is in the public interest.

Participation by those affected by policies is an important goal in its own right, but it is also—as our case studies have made clear—very important in accomplishing the tasks of providing information and creating incentives. As our examples from irrigation projects and from the Green Revolution indicate, technological innovations affect individuals quite differently depending on geographic location, access to land, capital markets, risk bearing ability, and education, among other factors. Lessons learned from implementation experience are valuable but often very costly in terms of failed and delayed projects and distribution of benefits in unintended ways. Early participation allows those who have potentially useful information to bring it to the attention of those responsible for the project or policy being considered. And it also enables those who would be hurt by the project or policy—or who simply would not benefit as much as would their neighbors—to express their concerns verbally rather than in later resistance to implementation. The essential difference between the Indira Reservoir project and the Narmada impasse lies in the constructive role of criticism in the former case.

Comprehensive Planning and Realistic Alternatives

Since the first serious attempts by governments to encourage economic development in the Third World immediately after World War II, there have been attempts to balance multiple policy objectives by comprehensive planning or (in the terminology of Lindblom 1976) "synoptic planning." This has been widely applied in economic planning (Mahalanobis 1965), in regional development planning (Friedmann 1964), in urban planning (Kent 1964), and in resource and environmental planning (Paley Commission

1952; McHarg 1969). Our cases demonstrate that comprehensive planning in its most ambitious form—the formulation of global, binding, long-term plans—is utopian, but the effort to strive to overcome the typical fragmentation of analysis and action is essential. The limits to comprehensive planning include the uncertainty that persists even when the best analysis is applied; the sheer complexity of efforts to transform the natural resource endowment; and the realities of institutional rivalries and bureaucratic politics. Thus if planning is to be a useful means for internalizing a long-term perspective within governmental policymaking and for committing resources to analysis, then it should be conceived as the coordination of long-range analysis across governmental and nongovernmental agencies. This conception also encompasses the synthesis of scientific knowledge from the center and the local knowledge of micro-conditions at the sites of resource use.

Planning is often regarded as synonymous with centralized, top-down analysis and decisionmaking generally monopolized by national government agencies. In two respects, however, planning does not have to proceed this way. Nongovernmental organizations have produced impressive environmental assessments and environmental plans in the guise of "state of the environment" reports and "national conservation strategies." Provincial and local plans, produced by decentralized units of government, have long been extremely important in most developed countries.

For planning to overcome fragmentation, there must be some point at which analysts examine whether the elements of the plan fit with one another. Yet this does not require that the elements be generated from an initial grand scheme originating from the center. Locally initiated proposals can be aggregated and shaped to ensure that they are compatible. The analytic questions are: "Given that there are projects that promise enough benefits to have been initiated by local authorities or communities, do they fit together as a whole? What adaptations have to be made for them to be compatible? Do they maintain their attractiveness if these adaptations are made?" Indeed, most "national plan" documents consist of lists of projects initiated from various sources, including diverse central government agencies and some subnational governments. The key step, all too often missing, is to undertake the thorough examination of compatibility.

For example, irrigation planning in India has focused increasingly on encouraging the creation of small- and medium-scale irrigation proposals spurred on by government offers of grants and credit. The set of projects that is ultimately deemed acceptable by the government will constitute a "comprehensive plan" insofar as the government planners and policy-makers examine the systemic effects of the whole set of projects (for example, impacts on the water table); reject or modify the projects that impact negatively on others or have insufficient returns in light of the other projects; and, if necessary, augment the system with the necessary infrastructure (for example, electrification to power motorized pumps).

The case of government-sponsored transmigration schemes provides a good example of a situation in which planning must be *holistic,* but need not be centralized. Transmigration has impacts both on the area from which the migrants come and the area to which they go. A number of agencies are necessarily involved—agriculture, transportation, education, and health. The need for holistic planning seems evident. Yet as our case studies have demonstrated, planning from above tends to ignore local conditions that might be readily apparent to planners operating in the localities affected. The transmission of information and the design of appropriate incentives could be greatly improved if a major part of the planning were done within the sending area and within the receiving area.

Planning must also be prepared to acknowledge partial ignorance in exploring how each given project would do in different contexts. Because planners can never expect to know with certainty how related projects will unfold—financing can be held up, designs can change, or implementation can be delayed—no single, definite context can be taken for granted. Therefore the planners must ask the following crucial question: "Is this a well-designed project in light of the *several* plausible scenarios regarding how related projects and trends might evolve?" A robust project design is one that makes sense across the whole range of contextual possibilities. In most circumstances, this would serve as an antidote to the overoptimism that so often plagues project designs. When planners are required to think through the consequences of several scenarios rather than the most sanguine projections, they cannot help but be sobered by having to think through the implications of less optimistic scenarios.

Thinking About the Issue of Size and Complexity

It would be foolish to conclude from the difficulties of huge projects that they ought to be rejected out of hand simply because of their size. This trap of incrementalist thinking has been thoroughly discredited for its inability to transcend low-level equilibria, to prepare for impending disasters, and to take advantage of the possibilities of drastically different policy regimes

(Dror 1968). Indeed, in many instances of natural resource exploitation, even relatively small projects must still be assessed in terms of their impact on the entire ecosystem; thus incrementalism of this sort does not avoid the burdens of undertaking comprehensive analysis, although the temptation to dispense with such analysis may be greater. The Narmada project, a massive river valley development scheme planned as a series of small projects, illustrates how problems of coordination cannot be avoided by simply ignoring their existence.

While "thinking big" may be appropriate, however, it must be understood that to undertake a significant change in the face of nature may well require a correspondingly significant change in how the state and the population are organized to deal with natural resources and the environment. Richard Norgaard (1981) has labeled this the "coevolution" of social and environmental systems. New systems of authority and control must be established as the standard arrangements of ministries and functionally specific agencies prove to be unequipped to handle the new challenges.

As argued above, massive projects require both contingency planning and greater coordination. The coordination issue often requires a parallel development of institutions to correspond to new activities and policies. The establishment of project authorities designed to oversee the coordination of complex projects is discussed below.

Multidisciplinary Involvement

Another way to improve planning is to broaden the range of disciplines represented among the people doing the planning. For better or worse, economists have traditionally dominated both planning and evaluation. Indeed, economists have many advantages in doing this type of work, among them a strong set of theoretical tools, quantitative skills, an orientation toward economic growth, a "systems orientation" via the understanding of how individual production and consumption decisions produce general equilibria, and a reputation for being objective and hardheaded in dealing with political constraints. In the Mahaweli project, for example, more explicit attention to the fundamental question of economists—what does it cost to obtain a given benefit?—would have revealed that the cost per beneficiary ($4,800 per family) was unacceptably high.

Economists, however, also tend to have characteristic blind spots. Among them are a tendency to brush aside distributional concerns, inattention to how policies might be resisted at the village level or by bureaucrats, and, until recently, a lack of comprehension of the extent and complexity of environmental side effects. In the case of the Green Revolution, for example, earlier involvement by economists might have identified the prospect that some regions and some landowning groups would disproportionately benefit. But it is unclear whether this would have led to recommendations for more equitable distribution or to even greater emphasis on "early adopters" and eventual "trickle-down" of benefits. Almost certainly, economists would have been unlikely, at least in the context of the 1950s and 1960s, to foresee the possibility of negative environmental impacts.

We believe that planning can also be improved by encouraging the participation of biological scientists and of a broader selection of social scientists, including political scientists and anthropologists. This does not have to be done in a formalistic manner, with each project and policy subjected to rigid analysis by a carefully balanced interdisciplinary team. Instead, analysts outside of economics should be encouraged to comment on groups of policies or projects. The work of the United Nations Research Institute for Social Development in analyzing the distributional impacts of the Green Revolution offers a good example of how new perspectives can be brought to bear on a complex problem. Another example is the World Bank's current system of dealing with environmental issues—rather than setting up a special "environmental sieve" for projects, the Bank concentrates on doing broader environmental research and disseminating the results widely among its project analysts.

Better Evaluation

Evaluation serves the dual purpose of providing specific feedback for deliberations over modifying or terminating existing projects and policies, and general learning to be applied to future initiatives. It also focuses attention on particular objectives and problems. Thus, one antidote to the usual problem of overly restricted problem definition is an evaluation mechanism that stresses the *breadth* of the criteria of evaluation.

This means, obviously, that good evaluation, like good planning, requires a multidisciplinary approach. It also means that evaluation must attend to both micro- and macro-effects. While a "systems approach" is important for gauging a project's overall impact—for example, the crucial issue of the impact of irrigation on the prices of staple grains or the overall demographic impacts of the resettlement schemes—is must also ask about the finer details of distribution and environmental impacts on site. The recent emphasis on assessing the environmental impacts of irrigation projects, dams, and resettlement schemes provides abundant opportunity for perfecting methodologies for such studies.

Evaluators must resist the temptation to try to reduce performance evaluation to a single quantified indicator, inasmuch as this tends to focus on aggregate growth, which is typically more easily quantified. But this is not a blanket condemnation of quantification. Indeed, quantification of the distributional and environmental impacts of policies can help to offset the usual preoccupation with economic growth over distribution and environmental protection.

Evaluation is intimately related to the rewards and punishments meted out to government officials involved in natural resource policymaking. The criteria for evaluation determine in large part the incentives for the behavior of these officials. Inasmuch as it is a political fact of life that governmental agencies are loathe to provide negative self-evaluations, some autonomy on the part of the evaluators is essential. Planning agencies often serve this function, but they are sometimes limited by the pressure to maintain the government's reputation for competence. In some countries, the institutions that were originally insulated from political pressures in order to monitor financial matters have extended their jurisdictions to appraise the effectiveness of programs and policies. Thus in the United States the General Accounting Office has taken on this function; in Chile the *Controlaria* has assumed the authority to evaluate programs.

In addition, the nongovernmental organizations that undertake "state of the environment" studies or evaluations of particular programs and policies often provide important feedback on the performance of natural resource policies, and frequently a counterweight when governmental evaluations are too rosy. The cases of Indian river valley developments, however, show that nongovernmental critiques, to be constructive, cannot afford to be so hypercritical of the government's every effort that the evaluation loses its capacity to discriminate good policies from bad and its credibility in the eyes of the government policymakers.

International organizations, with their technical expertise and usual detachment from the partisan politics of the countries with which they interact, can often play this constructive role of evaluation and critique. They—like the development agencies of donor governments—have the additional advantage that governments of the less developed countries generally have strong incentives to heed their advice. However, the evaluations of these organizations are useful only as long as they too do not fall prey to self-serving evaluations of projects involving their own participation.

Easier Termination

The results of project evaluations would be used more effectively if projects and policies were easier to modify or terminate. One help in doing so would be for agencies and politicians to make less sweeping claims when projects or new policies are initially announced. If Pollyanna optimality—helping everyone and injuring no one—cannot be achieved in practice, it is counterproductive to claim repeatedly that new policies will be uniformly beneficial. Admitting at the start that there will be mistakes and that there will be side effects would give agencies more space to modify their actions as experience accumulates.

Public choice theory (McLean 1988; Stroup and Baden 1983) has repeatedly demonstrated how agencies and individual bureaucrats acquire vested interests in the policies that they implement. Admission that a given policy is failing threatens the agency's budget, its personnel, its credibility, and perhaps above all, the political standing of its minister. Bureaucratic rewards and punishments should make more allowance for the fact that mid-course corrections and even the abandonment of some policies are normal parts of the policy process. A special problem here is that some policy changes remove a problem from the jurisdiction of one agency and give it to another.

Centralization and Decentralization

Centralization of authority has been used in virtually all societies as a way to improve both information flows and the ability to implement policies. Yet the major problems identified in our case studies are so consistently attributable to overcentralization that it seems indispensable to explore whether decentralization would be beneficial, either as an analytic strategy, an implementation strategy, or both.

Centralization has four distinct aspects. It can refer to the concentration of authority in the hands of:

(a) central (national) governments rather than states, provinces, or localities
(b) mainline (cabinet) ministries or departments rather than semi-autonomous authorities or corporations dedicated to specific development programs
(c) local authorities rather than local communities
(d) local community elites rather than the broad spectrum of community members.

One of the principal rationales for centralization is that technical expertise becomes increasingly scarce as one moves from the center to the periphery of a given society. This is thought to be particularly true in developing countries, where the total number of skilled people is often very small and where educated men and women tend to be concentrated in urban centers. We have learned from the case studies, however, that centralized expertise all too frequently fails to understand and respond to specific local conditions. Recall the finding of Kothari and Bhartari (see chapter 5) that if the Narmada project planners had only asked the local farmers, they would have learned that certain areas had no need of irrigation, and indeed were prone to waterlogging.

Time after time, the planners in New Delhi, Brasília, Jakarta and so on were limited in their knowledge of the local conditions of soil quality, weather variation, and other physical micro-conditions. Nor could the centralized experts plumb the minds of local inhabitants whose cooperation is often crucial for the success of projects.

Much of the essential information has to do with the willingness and motivations of the local communities to carry out their part of the activities necessary for project success. A classic and very widespread example is the unwillingness of recipients of irrigation water to cut field channels, despite the fact that they are the most direct beneficiaries of the projects. This was encountered in the Jamuna, Nalganga, and Damodar projects, as recounted in our case studies. Sinha (1977, 99) noted the same phenomenon in India's Nagarjunanagar, Chambal, Mahananda, and Rajasthan Canal projects, leading him to label it "the classical example of bad planning." The reluctance of communities to take advantage of what the planners consider to be attractive opportunities is also echoed in the unwillingness of Dandakaranya settlers to remain in their settlements, and the failure of many Polonoroeste settlers to continuously cultivate their land after the initial clearing. The penchant of planners to equate the attitudes of the presumed beneficiaries to the benefits calculated in their plans is a direct outgrowth of the incompleteness of the information obtainable at the center.

Another rationale for centralization is that it increases efficiency by allowing multiple local efforts to be coordinated. This is true in some ways. For example, it is easier to secure a single $500 million irrigation loan from an international agency than to finance a hundred $5 million projects. Centralization also makes it possible to do relevant research and to make sure that needed materials and personnel—agronomists and fertilizer, for example—are available when projects go into operation. The obverse of this advantage, however, is that projects are likely to be imposed on local people or local authorities who would much rather devote the same resources to other purposes. They may be willing to take the central government's money, but they frequently do so halfheartedly or even try to divert the resources to ends that are higher among their own priorities.

Yet another reason for centralization is the view that local elites will restrict the spread of benefits to deserving groups. To be sure, there is abundant evidence of social stratification in provincial and village societies, along with political favoritism and economic exploitation. Centralization, however, has at least three problems of its own. First, the least powerful members of rural society may be exploited by local elites but they are often literally invisible to centralized planners. In many cases, the intricate ties between local elites and underclasses provide at least some rationale for wide distribution of the benefits that flow to the area from the center. Second, national elites often find ways of dominating centralized policymaking. These are not exclusively the rich, but include unionized workers, bureaucrats, and, in some countries, favorably situated regional or tribal groups. Third, centralized agencies generally wind up dealing with the local notables in any case, partly because of political connections and partly because the local elite simply is more articulate than the mass of the population.

State Corporations and Regional Authorities

A common form of decentralization is to assign certain functions to state corporations (sometimes mixed state-private entities are used) or to multi-purpose regional authorities such as river basin commissions. Ironically, the concentration of power over a project in the hands of the staff of a decentralized agency is, in a sense, a type of centralization, insofar as functions diffused over several ministries or agencies are now combined within one.

The value of a single authority lies in its potential—not always realized—to:

(a) coordinate the various aspects of the project with greater efficiency and less interagency conflict than the mainline ministries would
(b) pursue a balanced set of objectives defined in terms of the overall success of the project rather than pursuing the typically narrower set of functions that characterize each mainline agency
(c) transcend the geographical boundary biases and disputes that arise when state, provincial, or local agencies make the definitive decisions on the parts of the project under their jurisdictions
(d) mobilize local participation in order to generate grass-roots project support.

Project authorities of this sort have proven to be effective when they are endowed with sufficient resources and are granted sufficient real discretion. Thus the classic model of the Tennessee Valley Authority in the United States surpassed the Damodar Valley Corporation in India in staffing, autonomy, and success. Without sufficient power, the Damodar Valley Corporation has not been able to rein in the competing state agencies over which it was intended to exercise jurisdiction. In Indonesia, the *transmigrasi* resettlement operation has maintained a reasonable level of coherence—which is not to say that the project is without problems—through the efforts of the *transmigrasi* authority; in contrast, the resettlements in the Brazilian Amazon have suffered from bureaucratic rivalries and the lack of coherent definitions of objectives and policies.

International organizations and governmental donor agencies can increase the level of discretion granted to a dedicated project or program authority by expressing a preference for interacting with such an authority in planning and implementing internationally funded projects.

Local Governments

Project planning and implementation in developing countries typically bypass local governments, which are assumed to have no skills and little ability to implement effectively. This becomes a self-fulfilling prophecy. Starved for resources and with no responsibility for the really important projects, local governments are unable to attract trained employees. With no experience in planning and managing projects, local governments are unable to generate ideas for new projects. They are widely regarded as possessing limited competence and creativity.

Yet it appears that local governments have distinct strengths that can be used to great advantage. For one thing, they are likely to be superior to centralized agencies in determining the mix of projects that local people really want. One village may be desperate for a new school or clinic, for example, while another might prefer a fuelwood project. Local governments and other village-level institutions are also likely to be more effective than centralized authorities in managing common property resources (Ostrom 1988). Ironically, attempts by national and state governments to "institute scientific management" of natural resources have often replaced effective local institutions with ineffective centralized ones. Bromley and Chapagain (1984) have shown how the extension of centralized governmental authority over common lands in Nepal destroyed long-standing local customary systems of managing them, which had been based on voluntary restraint among people organized in small communities. The ill-fated attempt by the Indian government to improve forest management by imposing massive tree plantations on tribal groups in the Bastar (described in chapter 3 above) is an excellent example of the price that project planners often pay when they ignore local peoples and their institutions.

Public Participation

One may distinguish between basic interest organizations—such as village cooperatives, labor unions, and peasant leagues—created to represent the direct interests of its members, and NGOs created to represent general public interest positions (for example, environmental groups) or the interests of other, usually disadvantaged populations (for example, organizations in India and Brazil devoted to defending the welfare of tribal peoples). Both types of organizations have important roles to play in the policymaking process. In developing countries, the NGO has become an increasingly important channel for the activism of university-educated people with expertise in the formal disciplines of economics, anthropology, ecology, and so on. Therefore, as explained above, they have the potential to provide a credible counterpoint to governmental evaluations when such evaluations lack objectivity and honesty. By the same token these activists may be motivated by ideological or partisan political objectives. While these objectives may be valid in their own right, they ought not be allowed to undermine governmental initiatives that are reasonably sound relative to other options.

The input of basic interest organizations or of individuals in the affected areas is not only the essence of participation—valuable in its own right—but also provides the local knowledge that so often fails to be incorporated by centralized planning. As shown so clearly in the irrigation cases, the voices of farmers could have relayed crucial information on objective conditions such as soil quality and on subjective matters such as whether the farmers themselves would be willing to cut field channels or market their produce through state cooperatives. Where these voices were not heard, projects often failed.

Careful structuring of participatory planning can ameliorate the common distributional problem that the relatively well-to-do tend to be better organized and more influential even in the village settings where central planners might consider everyone to be disadvantaged. Instead of simply relying on a few local notables to establish the definition of the project's objectives by monopolizing contact with the project planners, the planners can seek out a broader spectrum of input. Moreover, the presence of NGOs dedicated to serving the interests of the most disadvantaged populations can also help offset the typically skewed distribution of power on the local level. For example, the NGO Cultural Survival, originally started by Harvard anthropologists, has often been effective in bringing the urgent concerns of tribal peoples to national and world attention.

Market Mechanisms

In several ways, markets constitute another means of securing information and allocating resources for natural resource exploitation. Market mechanisms do not necessarily imply the operation of a private sector or the further privatization of publicly operated projects or programs. Broadly speaking, a market is a mechanism for the exchange of goods and services that permits prices to respond to the laws of supply and demand. The most significant implication is that the price (in money or an equivalent like labor) reflects the purchasers' actual valuations of the goods and services they are receiving as well as the costs of production. Thus the rationale for using market signals in the allocation of access to natural resource exploitation opportunities, and in the sale of natural resource outputs, is that prices are more likely to reflect scarcity and to avoid overuse for little gain in societal welfare. By depending on myriad individual decisions to make exchanges, markets are less vulnerable to errors of centralized ignorance or weaknesses in administrative capability. They simultaneously transmit information about relative scarcity and give suppliers and demanders incentives to act on that knowledge.

Market pricing for access to natural resource exploitation. It has become commonplace for institutions like the World Bank to insist that the consumers of irrigation water and hydroelectric power pay appropriate "user charges." The same logic holds for timber concessions, for which a price that comes closer to the value of the timber (less extraction costs) would discourage distressingly high current rates of deforestation (Repetto and Gillis 1988). The issue is not so much fairness or even budgetary solvency as it is to make the costs of natural resource exploitation explicit and to allow for a willingness-to-pay comparison of the costs and benefits of the project's outputs. Without user charges or realistic exploitation concessions, the beneficiary of the water, electricity, harvesting concession, or other output does not have to decide whether the benefits outweigh the costs because the costs are borne by others. The willingness of people to pay at least the price that corresponds with the actual costs of resource exploitation is a test of whether the benefits outweigh these costs.

Market pricing of natural resource outputs. In its broadest sense, the logic of user charges can be extended to the pricing of natural resource outputs. Like other goods and services, these should be allowed to find their market levels in order to be used according to their true valuation by consumers. Although many natural resources can be made available for the often modest costs of extracting them, efficient allocation requires that they be priced at their highest and best use, including the possibility of retaining them for use by a subsequent generation. The usual practice is that the prices of energy or other resource outputs are kept artificially low, but then they will be overused relative to the level that is optimal for the overall welfare of the citizenry. Similarly, when products based on natural resources—such as food—are kept at artificially low prices, they will be used in wasteful ways, and so too will be the resources going into them. The classic case is the price of bread in Egypt, kept so low that farmers feed it to their livestock.

Of course, the pricing of any good entails obvious issues of equity; raising the prices of food and energy would clearly hurt the poor *if* no other adjustments were made. There are, however, more efficient and more equitable ways of providing the poor access to these goods. It is more efficient for the government to provide cash transfers to the poor to purchase market-priced food than to distort the price of food for rich and poor alike. Direct transfers of this sort also have the virtue of making the subsidy more visible, so that its merit can be more openly assessed.

While it is common to think of markets as apart from and even a substitute for collective action, in some respects the effective operation of the market is highly dependent on both effective administration and participation. For one thing, the price system does not address the side effects of resource use (externalities) and distributional issues. Unless the government manages satisfactory resolutions of these issues while allowing for adequate sensitivity to market forces, the pressures for ignoring the discipline of price signals and market forces may be insurmountable. The danger of an unqualified infatuation with the market is that efficiency will dominate over the other legitimate objectives of natural resource exploitation, such as equity and environmental protection. Yet the next danger is that ignoring these objectives will lead to a heavy-handed interventionist backlash that could disregard price discipline altogether. Ironically, weak governments are often under greater pressure to distort the operations of the market than are strong governments.

Second, to the extent that presently uncorrectable market distortions make actual market prices unreflective of true costs (including opportunity costs), the government must have the capacity to make the necessary adjustments in assessing the true societal rates of return of projects and programs (Chenery 1975). For example, planning models ought to pay attention to replacement costs of resources in order to force consideration of whether current consumption of the resource justifies its cost to unrepresented future generations. The government's analytic strength is therefore essential for market forces to operate as well as possible under less than ideal conditions.

Finally, the key to effective markets is information. Therefore in using a "market test" as to whether target groups have sufficient incentive to participate productively in natural resource projects, whether cutting field channels for irrigation or investing in high-yield grains, the people must be involved enough to be sufficiently informed of the proposed benefits of the projects. Farmers' reluctance to cut field channels is a graphic example of the breakdown in information flows both ways—farmers excluded from planning are left unaware of benefits that planners presume are evident, and the planners are often unaware that the incentives go unappreciated. For the farmers to make the market decision to exchange their labor, or their cash to cover user charges, requires at least enough participation to generate adequate awareness.

In summary, each of the mechanisms for gathering information and allocating resources related to natural resource exploitation has its strengths and weaknesses, and the channels are surprisingly intertwined. Therefore the policymaking challenge is to be thoughtful and undogmatic not only in ordinary policymaking over specific projects and policies, but also at the highest level of selecting systems of authority and control. Only with the vigorous use of such mechanisms can we create positive connections among growth, equity, environmental protection, and participation.

1 Introduction

1 For a useful overview of Third World resource and environmental problems, see Eckholm (1986) and World Resources Institute (1988).

2 For example, in the case of the Himalayas, Ives and Messerli (1989) point out that forest clearance has a long history, in many cases extending over hundreds of years; that the links between upstream land use and downstream sedimentation have not been clearly demonstrated; and that spatial variation in rates of land use change and a general lack of quantitative information make generalization difficult. Nevertheless, we believe that the preponderance of studies cited by Ives and Messerli seems to indicate that a process of land degradation and environmental damage is occurring in the Himalayas, although we accept their contention that the linkages are more complex and geographically varied than those offered in many overviews of the region's environmental problems. It is clear that the specific experience of other areas, as with the Himalayas, deserves detailed study.

3 For an introduction to the "policy sciences" approach, see Brewer and deLeon (1983) and Ascher (1987).

4 Among the studies of political and institutional factors in U.S. resource and environmental policy are Robinson's analysis of the U.S. Forest Service (1975); Stroup and Baden's application of public choice theory to U.S. resource management agencies (1983); Petulla's study of U.S. environmental policy (1987); and a series of essays on U.S. energy policy published in a special issue of *Policy Sciences* (e.g., Sabatier, 1988). Among international examples are the study of the political economy of soil erosion by Blaikie (1985) and the study of the Amazon by Bunker (1985). Of these works, only Sabatier uses a formal model of the policy process.

5 For retrospectives on early thinking about development, see Meier and Seers (1984) and Arndt (1987).

6 Caldwell (1984) credits as well the "political skill of Secretary-General Maurice F. Strong, who had formerly headed the international development program of the government of Canada" and "the thorough preparatory meetings in which conflicting perspectives on environment and development had been clarified and, in some instances, reconciled."

2 Vicious Circles

1 Furthermore, resources are generally more susceptible than environmental systems to being owned and alienated. But natural resources can include those privately owned (most farmland); those managed as communal commons (some village forests and grazing lands); government-owned resources (most mineral deposits); and unmanaged commons to which open access is allowed. We prefer to distinguish "resources" from "environment" in order to emphasize the importance of complex, service-providing natural systems. Biologically complex, rarely susceptible to ownership and alienation, and very difficult to manage, environmental systems have sustained very serious damage as developing countries have sought economic growth.

2 This occurs even when education is nominally free, because the poor family must rely on the income brought in by working children.

3 For detail on this particular situation, see Williams (1986, 13–73).

4 Clapham (1985) provides an illuminating discussion of how groups and individuals seek favors from the Third World state.

3 Agricultural Modernization

1 There are interesting parallels here with the "big push" theories of industrial development and with the idea of concentrating resources in particular geographic areas that lay behind the Model Cities urban development program in the U.S. during the 1960s.

2 Scott notes "it is not clear exactly what happened to these ex-tenants. Some have undoubtedly become landless laborers in the village, while others, particularly if young, have emigrated temporarily or permanently to urban areas for work. A small proportion have perhaps been tenants who have retired from active farming and who have then not been replaced" (Scott 1985, 71).

3 Sometimes plantation forests replace natural forests that had been destroyed by past timber harvest or agricultural clearing. The decision to eliminate the natural forest is made in many cases independent of the decision to create a plantation, which may occur several years in the future.

4 Moving the People to the Resources

1 Less dramatic initiatives include providing access to forests or other resource sites near the populations but previously off-limits to the poor, and the replenishment of these adjacent forests or other resource sites.

2 At 6.5 rupees per dollar.

3   The *Eastern Economist* (1965) notes that "only 55 percent [of cultivators] were able to
     obtain over 30 mds. [1 maund = 82.28 lbs.] of paddy from an area of 4 acres each which
     would just support a family (p. 880). S. K. Gupta (1965, 17, 23), who estimated that an
     average family of 4.5 persons requires 36 mds. for food alone and an additional 7 mds.
     for seed and 18 mds. for cash expenses, found that in one zone less than 15 percent of the
     families received above 40 mds.; in the second zone less than half; in the third zone just
     over half and in the fourth zone less than 30 percent.

4    $160 million of the $600 million in loans was later withdrawn with the scaling back of
     Indonesia's targets for 1986–87.

5   See also the Mahaweli case in chapter 6.

6   The unassisted migrants can also get land from the *transmigrasi* program.

7   The descriptions of the policymaking apparatus are based on Bunker 1985, particularly
     100–150.

8   Soils were of "low input" quality (requiring mainly manual labor for successful annual
     cropping), "medium input" quality (requiring animal labor and "reasonable amounts of
     fertilizer and lime"), or "high input" quality (requiring a fundamental transformation
     of the soil through applications of complex fertilizers). "High input" soils are rarely
     viable, especially for poor settlers, and even "medium input" soils may require more
     fertilization than the settlers would be willing to provide in practice. (Fearnside 1986,
     233).

5   Grandiose Designs

1   The administration announced it would take up five of the major reservoir projects
     outlined in the Master Plan, namely the Victoria, Kotmale, Maduru Oya, Randenigala
     and Moragahakanda reservoirs, and the smaller Rotalawala project, constituting 83
     percent of the estimated costs, and then at various times launched efforts to secure the
     funding for the smaller Taldena, Kalu Ganga, Pallewela, Malwatu Oya and Yan Oya
     complexes. Proportions are based on figures given in Iriyagolle 1981, 19.

2   In 1979, a team from the International Fund for Agricultural Development noted that
     "Water management is not only a major cause of the country's high food imports but hits
     hardest the small farmer who has little margin to fall back on if his crop is a partial
     failure" (Wijesinghe 1981, 108).

3   *The United Kingdom* funded the Victoria Dam through a grant of 100 million pounds;
     Canada funded the Maduru Oya Project through an interest-free loan of Canadian $76
     million and a technical assistance grant of Canadian $7 million; *Sweden* funded the
     Kotmale Project through a loan of Sw. Kroner 330 million repayable in 6 half-yearly
     installments; *West Germany* funded the Randenigala Project through a grant of DM
     6,600,000 for downstream development and feasibility studies. In addition the Federal
     Republic of Germany provided a long-term interest-free loan of DM 400 million for the
     entire project; *Japan and Kuwait* funded the irrigation network labeled System C (lands
     on the right bank of the New Minipe Diversion in Badulla and Ampara); the *European
     Economic Community* funded various irrigation and downstream development compo-
     nents.

4 Regarding individual project cost increases:

Project	Original Estimate	Revised Estimate (1980)
Kotmale	1800 (Rs. million)	8000
Victoria	960	6000
Maduru Oya	680	2200
Housing	2200	6400

5 The Mahaweli master plan assumed an average water use of 6 acre feet/acre for double-cropped areas—even though the actual water usage rates in the project area were 12 acre feet/acre and above!

6 The outcomes of such an emphasis on quantity over quality became evident in studies of sample villages. One sample settlement village in system H_1, Midellawa, showed that settlers were facing great hardships, based upon the analysis that their expenditures showed a very high percentage spent on food and clothing. The majority of settlers, who had received 2.5 acres of irrigable land during 1975–76, had cultivated ten seasons up to 1981, but did not appear to have any improvement in standard of living. Some settlers had pawned jewelry and parted with personal belongings such as radios and bicycles which had been put up as collateral. Many families subsisted only on rations of milk, sugar, flour, and *dhal* provided under the World Food Program (Wijesinghe 1981, 56). In fact, the Ministry of Plan Implementation found that Area H of the Mahaweli irrigation project recorded the highest levels of chronic malnutrition in all of Sri Lanka (Siriwardhana 1981, 55).

7 In 1979–80, 54 percent of the Midellawa village settlers leased out their land to someone else. The average size of the land leased was greater than 2 acres, implying that a large part or even entire allotments of village settlers were cultivated by outsiders. The worsening plight of the tenant was exemplified by his decreasing share in total production under the land-lease system. The share agreement giving the settler only 25 percent of the total harvest virtually replaced the 50-50 share agreement because settlers could not contribute even half the costs of production. Land use data also illustrate the villagers' loss of control and share in production. During the 1978–79 season, only 68 percent of the land area in the village was used to obtain the actual total production of settler households. By the 1979–80 season, this share of land area had dropped to 53 percent (Siriwardhana 1981,17). Out of the settlers giving out cultivation on share, 64.9 percent did it due to lack of finance and 46 percent did it due to the poor quality of the soil (Siriwardhana 1981, 21).

8 The installed capacity of power stations under the jurisdiction of the Madhya Pradesh Electricity Board is presently about 2,700 MW., but of this, the hydroelectric component is only 193 MW. Hydroelectric power constitutes only 7 percent of the total installed capacity. The Madhya Pradesh Electricity Board has proposed to add another 630 MW of thermal capacity in the Seventh Plan period. In addition, the National Thermal Power Corporation would install two large thermal power stations in Madhya Pradesh during the Seventh Plan, resulting in a total capacity of 3360 MW.

9 The generation cost would be approximately 45 paise per KWH.

10 These groups argued that some invaluable forest would be lost in perpetuity. The prospects of its replacement, it was argued, were bleak because land earmarked for

compensatory forestation has long been under cultivation, some portions are unsuitable for plantation, and others are village forest to which the tribals have customary rights. The disjointed patches could not constitute a national forest. They expressed skepticism about the competence of the field staff involved in reforestation, the prospects for maintaining the ecological balance, and the problem of the *sal* trees. They estimated the cost of replacement forest is a mind-boggling sum of over Rs 2,000,000,000, and asked whether the cost would be commensurate with the gain.

11 The 9,500 hectares of land identified for afforestation consists of about 100 plots in chunks of 50 hectares and more, reflecting special effort to maintain contiguity with the existing forest land.

6 Irrigation

1 Calculated from International Institute for Environment and Development 1987, 269, 280.

2 Some analysts also distinguish medium-scale irrigation, but this seems to cover irrigation systems of dams and canals that divert water from one location to another, but do so on a more restricted scale than large-scale or "major" irrigation, whereas small-scale or "minor" irrigation involves the use of groundwater or wells atthe site. See Satpathy 1984, ch. 4.

3 These assessments, taking the results five to seven years after disbursements, do not take into account the longer-term environmental problems such as siltation and salinization, which would typically reduce the calculated rates of return even further.

4 The Jamuna River is a perennial tributary of the Kapili River and in turn is fed by its own tributaries of Dimoru Nala on the left bank and the Dikhari Nala on the right as it flows largely westward for about 131 km., covering an area of 3,960 sq. km. in its basin. The entire command area of the project lies in the revenue district of Nagaon and is bounded by the river Jamuna on the north and the Kapili on the south and southwest. The Dimoru Nala passes through the command area which encompasses a number of fairly large villages but no urban habitats.

5 Though the average annual rainfall in Assam is high, it varies from about 1300 mm in some years to about 2200 mm in others. The district of Nagaon has much lower average annual rainfall than the state as a whole, and in the command area of the project it ranges from about 1,000 mm to 1,150 mm.

6 Of these, the main canal was 47.20 km. in length and could discharge 700 cusecs. The distributaries were designed to be 25.73 km. (475 cusecs.); 85.55 km. (180 cusecs.); and 41.29 km. (225 cusecs.). The total gross command area to be fed by these canals came to 23,443 hectares.

7 It was estimated in the project report that with the introduction of multiple cropping following the provision of irrigation facilities, it would be possible to raise the total gross area under different crops from 25,708 hectares to 38,761 hectares with traditional varieties of crops. This would also mean additional production of paddy crop alone of 27,165 M.T. per year. For rabi (spring) crops (wheat, pulses, oilseeds, etc.) and jute, the corresponding figures would be 1,927 M.T. and 2,100 M.T. respectively. In money terms, at prices at which the project cost was estimated, the value of this additional

production would have been Rs 19.33 million annually. The project also envisaged that with the change over to high yielding varieties of crops with provision of full irrigation facilities in the command area, about 39,251 hectares of gross land area would come under multiple cropping annually for production of different crops. The additional production of the paddy crop would then be 91,890 M.T. as against 27,165 M.T. with traditional varieties. The coverage of land under wheat, which would be a possible new crop in the command area after utilization of irrigation capacity created under the project, would be 8,502 hectares yielding 31,500 M.T. of wheat annually. The value of this additional production was estimated at Rs 77.95 million annually.

8   Conducted by Arunoday Bhattacharjya, CIDR Fellow and coauthor of this volume, as Director of Evaluation and Monitoring, Government of Assam. The Irrigation Department and the State Evaluation Committee by and large agreed with the suggestions made in the evaluation report.

9   Assuming a 10 percent discount rate (or interest rate) for each year into the future, each year's income has only two-thirds the present value that it would have had if it had come four years sooner.$(R/(1.1)^4)$.

References

Ali, Syed Hashim. 1984. "Planning and Implementation of Measures to Ensure Productivity and Equity under Irrigation Systems." In N. Pant, ed., *Productivity and Equity in Irrigation Systems*. New Delhi: Ashish Publishing House.

Anderson, Robert S., and Walter Huber. 1988. *The Hour of the Fox: Tropical Forests, the World Bank, and Indigenous People in Central India*. Seattle: University of Washington Press.

Annis, Sheldon. 1987. "Costa Rica's Dual Debt: A Story About a Little Country That Did Things Right." Unpublished paper. Overseas Development Council.

Anonymous. 1989. "An Appeal to the People of the World Bank and the International Monetary Fund by Non-Governmental and Citizens Organizations on the Occasion of the 1989 World Bank/IMF Annual Meeting." September 27–28.

Arndt, H. W. 1987. *Economic Development: The History of an Idea*. Chicago: University of Chicago Press.

Ascher, William. 1987. "Policy Sciences and the Economic Approach in a 'Post-positivist' Era." *Policy Sciences* 20: 3–9.

Attanayake, Abhaya, et al. 1985. *Mahaweli Saga—Challenges and Response*. Colombo: Mahaweli Authority of Sri Lanka.

Austin, James E., and Gustavo Esteva, eds. 1987. *Food Policy in Mexico: The Search for Self-Sufficiency*. Ithaca: Cornell University Press.

Australia, Government of. 1984. *A National Conservation Strategy for Australia*. Canberra: Australian Government Publishing Service.

Barkin, David. 1987. "SAM and Seeds." In Austin and Esteva, *Food Policy in Mexico*. 111–32.

Barkin, David, and Blanca Suarez. 1985. *El Fin de la Autosuficiencia Alimentaria*. Mexico City: Centro de Ecodesarrollo.

Bass, Stephen M. J. 1987. "The National Conservation Strategy for Zambia: A Case Study." Gland, Switzerland. Conservation for Development Centre, IUCN. Unpublished paper.

Batie, Sandra S. 1989. "Sustainable Development: Challenges to the Profession of Agricultural Economics.'' Presidential Address to American Agricultural Economics Association. Baton Rouge. July 30–August 2.

Blaikie, Piers. 1985. *The Political Economy of Soil Erosion in Developing Countries.* London: Longman.

Bock, Edwin A. 1967. ''The Last Colonialism: Governmental Problems Arising from the Use and Abuse of the Future.'' CAG occasional paper. Bloomington, Ind.: American Society for Public Administration.

Botafogo, José. 1985. ''Development and Environment: Reply to *The Ecologist*,'' *The Ecologist* 1, 6: 207–19.

Brewer, Garry D., and Peter deLeon. 1983. *Foundations of Policy Analysis.* Homewood, Ill.: Dorsey Press.

Brockett, Charles D. 1988. *Land, Power, and Poverty: Agrarian Transformation and Political Conflict in Central America.* Boston: Unwin Hyman.

Bromley, Daniel W., and Devendra P. Chapagain. 1984. ''The Village Against the Center: Resource Depletion in South Asia.'' *American Journal of Agricultural Economics* 66, 5 (December): 869–73.

Budiardjo, Carmel. 1986. ''Politics of Transmigration.'' *The Ecologist* 16, 2/3: 112–16.

Bull, David. 1982. *A Growing Problem: Pesticides and the Third World Poor.* Oxford: OXFAM.

Bunker, Steven. 1985. *Underdeveloping the Amazon: Extraction, Unequal Exchange, and the Failure of the Modern State.* Urbana: University of Illinois.

Burns, David. 1986. *Runway and Treadmill Deforestation: Reflections on the Economics of Forest Development in the Tropics.* London: International Institute for Environment and Development.

Caldwell, Lynton Keith. 1984. *International Environmental Policy.* Durham, N.C.: Duke University Press.

Caufield, Catherine. 1984. ''Pioneers of the Outer Islands,'' *Natural History* 93 (March): 22–32.

———. 1985. *In the Rainforest.* New York: Knopf.

Central Bank of Sri Lanka. 1984. *Review of the Economy 1984.* Colombo: Dept. of Economic Research, Central Bank of Sri Lanka.

———. 1985. *Review of the Economy 1985.* Colombo: Dept. of Economic Research, Central Bank of Sri Lanka.

Centre for Science and Environment. 1984. *State of India's Environment 1984-1985.* New Delhi: Centre for Science and Environment.

CGIAR. 1980. *Consultative Group on International Agricultural Research.* Washington: CGIAR Secretariat.

Chambers, R. 1984. ''Irrigation Management: Ends, Means and Opportunities.'' In N. Pant, ed., *Productivity and Equity in Irrigation Systems.* New Delhi: Ashish Publishing House.

Chavan, S. B. 1983. ''Development of Narmada Valley.'' *Indian and Foreign Review* (New Delhi) 20 (January 15): 19–20.

Chenery, Hollis B., ed. 1974. *Redistribution with Growth.* London: Oxford University Press.

———. 1975. ''The Structuralist Approach to Development Policy.'' *American Economic Review* 65, 2: 310–16.

Clapham, Christopher. 1985. *Third World Politics.* Madison: University of Wisconsin Press.

Cleaves, Peter. 1974. *Bureaucratic Politics and Administration in Chile*. Berkeley: University of California Press.

Colchester, Marcus. 1986. "Unity and Diversity: Indonesia's Policy toward Tribal Peoples." *The Ecologist* 16, 2/3: 99–110.

Comte, Christine. 1978. "Balancing Regional Development." *Ceres* 11, 4 (July/August): 30–35.

Conable, Barber B. 1989. "Address to the Board of Governors of the World Bank Group." Washington, D.C.: World Bank. September 26.

Dahlberg, Kenneth A. 1979. *Beyond the Green Revolution*. New York: Plenum.

Dalrymple, Dana G. 1985. "The Development and Adoption of High-Yielding Varieties of Wheat and Rice in Developing Countries." *American Journal of Agricultural Economics* 67, 5 (December): 1067–73.

de Onis, Juan. 1987. "Tightening Up on Third World Loans." *U.S. News & World Report*. October 5: 41.

de Silva, Chandra Richard. 1987. *Sri Lanka: A History*. New Delhi: Vikas.

Dhawan, B. D. 1985. "Questionable Conceptions and Simplistic Views about Irrigated Agriculture of India." *Indian Journal of Agricultural Economics* 40, 1 (January-March): 1–13.

———. 1988. *Irrigation in India's Agricultural Development*. New Delhi: Sage Publications.

Donner, Wolf. 1987. *Land Use and Environment in Indonesia*. Honolulu: University of Hawaii Press.

Dror, Yehezkel. 1968. *The Policy Sciences Re-examined*. New York: Elsevier.

Dube, S.C. 1987. "Tribes and Development: Human Aspects of Bodhghat." *Times of India* (New Delhi). May 11:7.

Eastern Economist. 1965. "Development in Dandakaranya." November 5, 1965: 879–81.

Eckholm, Erik. 1986. *Down to Earth: Environment and Human Needs*. New York: Norton.

The Ecologist. 1985. "Indonesian Transmigration: The World Bank's Most Irresponsible Project." 15, 5/6: 300–301.

Economic and Scientific Research Foundation. 1986. *Agricultural Exports Strategy: Problems and Prospects*. New Delhi: Radiant Publishers.

Evans, Julian. 1982. *Plantation Forestry in the Tropics*. Oxford: Clarendon Press.

Fachurrozie, S. A., and C. MacAndrews. 1978. "Buying Time: Forty Years of Transmigration in Belintang." *Bulletin of Indonesian Economic Studies* 14, 3: 94–103.

Farmer, B. H. 1974. *Agricultural Colonization in India Since Independence*. London: Oxford University Press.

Fearnside, Philip. 1985. "Deforestation and Decisionmaking in the Development of the Brazilian Amazonia." *Interciencia* 10, 5: 243–47.

———. 1986. "Settlement in Rôndonia and the Token Role of Science and Technology in Brazil's Amazonian Development Planning." *Interciencia* 11, 5: 229–36.

Freeman, Orville. 1989. "Reaping the Benefits: Cash Crops in the Development Process." *International Health and Development* 1, 1 (March–April): 20–23.

Friedmann, John. 1964. *Regional Development and Planning: A Reader*. Cambridge, Mass.: MIT Press.

Gardner, Roy, Elinor Ostrom, and James M. Walker. 1989. "The Nature of Common-Pool

Resource Problems." Paper presented at the Public Choice Society Meetings, Orlando, Fla., March 17–19. W87–25.

George, Susan. 1977. *How the Other Half Dies: The Real Reasons for World Hunger.* Hammondsworth, U.K.: Penguin.

Glaeser, Bernhard. 1987. *The Green Revolution Revisited.* London: Allen and Unwin.

Goldsmith, Edward, and Nicholas Hildyard. 1985. *The Social and Environmental Effects of Large Dams.* San Francisco: Sierra Club.

Goodland, Robert. 1986. "Environmental Aspects of Amazonian Development Projects in Brazil." *Interciencia* 11, 1: 16–24.

Gupta, S. K. 1965. "Dandakaranya: A Survey of Rehabilitation." *Economic Weekly* (India): January 2: 15–26; January 9: 59–65; January 16: 89–96.

Hansen, Roger. 1971. *The Politics of Mexican Development.* Baltimore: Johns Hopkins University Press.

Hanson, Arthur J. 1981. "Transmigration and Marginal Land Development." In Gary E. Hansen, ed., *Agricultural and Rural Development in Indonesia.* Boulder, Colo.: Westview Press.

Hardin, Garrett. 1968. "The Tragedy of the Commons." *Science* 162, 1: 243–48.

Hewitt de Alcantara, Cynthia. 1976. *Modernizing Mexican Agriculture.* Geneva: United Nations Research Institute for Social Development.

Hossain, Mahbub. 1988. "Nature and Impact of the Green Revolution in Bangladesh." International Food Policy Research Institute. Research Report No. 67. Washington: IFPRI.

Hyman, E. L. 1983. "Smallholder Tree Farming in the Philippines." *Unasylva* 35, 139: 25–31.

Iliffe, John. 1987. *The African Poor.* Cambridge: Cambridge University Press.

India, Department of Rehabilitation. 1967. *Report 1966–67.* New Delhi: Ministry of Labour, Employment, and Rehabilitation.

International Institute for Environment and Development, and World Resources Institute. 1987. *World Resources 1987.* New York: Basic Books.

International Union for the Conservation of Nature and Natural Resources. 1980. *World Conservation Strategy: Living Resource Conservation for Sustainable Development.* Gland, Switzerland: IUCN.

Iriyagolle, Gamini. 1978. *The Truth about Mahaweli.* Nugegoda: Gamini Iriyagolle.

Ives, Jack D., and Bruno Messerli. 1989. *Himalayan Dilemma: Reconciling Development and Conservation.* London: Rutledge.

Jackson, Karl D. 1978. "Bureaucratic Polity: A Theoretical Framework for the Analysis of Power and Communications in Indonesia." In Karl D. Jackson and Lucian W. Pye, eds., *Political Power and Communications in Indonesia,* Berkeley: University of California.

Johnson, Brian D. G. 1983. *The Conservation and Development Programme for the U.K.* London: Kogan Page.

Johnson, Stanley. 1972. *The Green Revolution.* New York: Harper and Row.

Joseph, C. J. 1986. "Irrigation Water Management in Kerala—A Case Study." [abstract] *Indian Journal of Agricultural Economics* 41, 4 (October-December): 541–42.

Joshi, P. K. 1987. "Effect of Surface Irrigation on Land Degradation—Problems and Strategies." *Indian Journal of Agricultural Economics* 42, 3 (July-September): 416–23.

Kamble, N., A. Aziz, C. Nelson, and N. M. Rao. 1979. "Economics of Well Irrigation (A Case Study of Kolar District, Karnataka)." In Institute for Social and Economic Change (Bangalore), *Impact of Irrigation*. Bombay: Himalaya Publishing House.

Kendall, Jonathan. 1984. *Passage Through El Dorado*. New York: Avon Books.

Kent, T. J. 1964. *The Urban General Plan*. San Francisco: Chandler.

Kothari, Ashish, and Rajiv Bhartari. 1984. "Narmada Valley Project: Development or Destruction?" *Economic and Political Weekly* (Bombay) 19 (June 2-9): 907–20.

Lachica, Eduardo. 1986. "Indonesia Curbing Relocation Plan: World Bank Will Cut Loans As a Result." *The Wall Street Journal* December 23: 12E.

Ladejinsky, Wolf. 1969. "The Green Revolution in the Punjab: A Field Trip." *Economic and Political Weekly* 4 (June 28, 1969): A73–A83. Cited in Ruttan (1977).

Lasswell, Harold D. 1971. *A Preview of Policy Sciences*. New York: American Elsevier.

Lindblom, Charles E. 1976. *Politics, Economics, and Welfare*. Chicago: University of Chicago Press.

McCord, William. 1986. *Paths to Progress: Bread and Freedom in Developing Societies*. New York: Norton.

McHarg, Ian L. 1969. *Design With Nature*. Garden City, N.Y.: Natural History Press.

McLean, Iain. *Public Choice: An Introduction*. Oxford: Basil Blackwell.

MacNamara, Robert S. 1973. "Address for the Board of Governors of the World Bank." Nairobi. September 24.

Mahalanobis, P. C. 1965. *Essays on Econometrics and Planning*. Oxford and New York: Pergammon.

Maharashtra State. 1970. *Nalganga Project*. Poona: Maharashtra Department of Agriculture.

Mahaweli Development Board. 1977. *Summary Reports on Projects*. Colombo: Mahaweli Authority of Sri Lanka.

Maheshwari, S. 1985. *Rural Development in India: A Public Policy Approach*. New Delhi: Sage Publications.

Malhotra, S. P., and S. K. Raheja and D. Seckler. 1984. "Performance Monitoring in the Warabandi System of Irrigation Management." In N. Pant, ed., *Productivity and Equity in Irrigation Systems*. New Delhi: Ashish Publishing House.

Meier, Gerald, and Dudley Seers. 1984. *Pioneers in Development*. New York: Oxford University Press for the World Bank.

Modern Review. 1967. "Bengalese Refugees in Dandakaranya." 122: 242–43.

Murdoch, William W. 1980. *The Poverty of Nations: The Political Economy of Hunger and Population*. Baltimore: Johns Hopkins University Press.

Nadkarni, M. V. 1979. "Irrigation Development in Karnataka." In Institute for Social and Economic Change (Bangalore), *Impact of Irrigation*. Bombay: Himalaya Publishing House.

Navaratne, Gamini. 1981. "Lanka to Go Ahead with its Biggest-Ever Project," *Times of India* (Delhi) March 5: 6g–h.

Nobelstiftelsen. *Les Prix Nobel en 1970*. 1971. Stockholm: Imprimerieal Royal P.A. Norstedt and Soner.

Norgaard, Richard. 1981. "Sociosystem and Ecosystem Co-evolution in the Amazon." *Journal of Environmental Economics and Management* 8: 238–54.

Nurkse, Ragnar. 1953. *Problems of Capital Formation in Underdeveloped Countries*. New York: Oxford University Press.

Oasa, Edmund K. 1987. "The Political Economy of International Agricultural Research: A Review of CGIAR's Response to Criticisms of the 'Green Revolution.'" In Bernhard Glaeser, ed., *The Green Revolution*. London: Allen and Unwin. 13–55.

Oberai, A. S. 1983. *State Policies and Internal Immigration*. London: Croom Helm.

Ostrom, Elinor. 1988. "Institutional Arrangements and the Commons Dilemma." In Vincent Ostrom, David Feeny, and Hartmut Picht, eds., *Rethinking Institutional Analysis and Development: Issues, Alternatives, and Choices*. San Francisco: ICS Press. 103–39.

Otten, Mariel. 1986. "*Transmigrasi*: From Poverty to Bare Subsistence," *The Ecologist* 16, 2/3: 77–88.

Paley Commission (U.S. President's Materials Policy Commission). 1952. *Resources for Freedom*. Washington, D.C.: U.S. Government Printing Office.

Panda, R. 1986. "Anomaly in the Use of Water in a Canal Irrigation System—A Case Study." *Indian Journal of Agricultural Economics* 41, 4 (October-December): 529–33.

Pant, N. 1984. "Introduction." In N. Pant, ed., *Productivity and Equity in Irrigation Systems*. New Delhi: Ashish Publishing House.

Pearse, Andrew. 1977. "Technology and Peasant Production: Reflections on a Global Study." *Development and Change* 8: 125–59.

———. 1980. *Seeds of Plenty, Seeds of Want: Social and Economic Aspects of the Green Revolution*. Oxford: Clarendon Press.

Petulla, Joseph. 1987. *Environmental Protection in the United States*. San Francisco: San Francisco Study Center.

Pujari, A. G. 1986. "A Note on the Problem of Irrigation to the Flat Impermeable Clayey Black Soil in Mangalwedhe Tahsil under Ujjani Right Bank Canal." [abstract] *Indian Journal of Agricultural Economics* 41, 4 (October-December): 549.

Punalekar, S. P. 1984. "Voluntary Action and Rehabilitation: A Case of Narmada Dam Oustees in Gujarat State." *Indian Journal of Social Work* 19, 4 (January): 353–64.

Rao, V. M. 1979. "Linking Irrigation with Development—Policy Issues." In Institute for Social and Economic Change (Bangalore), *Impact of Irrigation*. Bombay: Himalaya Publishing House.

Repetto, Robert, and Malcolm Gillis, eds. 1988. *Public Policies and the Misuse of Forest Resources*. Cambridge: Cambridge University Press.

Richards, Peter, and Wilbert Gooneratne. 1980. *Basic Needs, Poverty, and Government Policies in Sri Lanka*. Geneva: International Labour Organization.

Robinson, Glen O. 1975. *The Forest Service: A Study in Public Land Management*. Baltimore: Johns Hopkins University Press.

Rose, Adam, Brandt Stevens, and Gregg Davis. 1988. *Natural Resource Policy and Income Distribution*. Baltimore: Johns Hopkins University Press.

Roy, S. K. 1979. "Irrigation Development under India's New Plan (1978–83): An Appraisal." In India, Ministry of Agriculture and Irrigation, *Agricultural Situation in India*. New Delhi: Manager of Publications, Civil Lines.

———. 1986. "Social Forestry—For Whom?" In Desh Bandhu and R. K. Garg, *Social Forestry and Tribal Development*. New Delhi: Indian Environmental Society. 1–6.

Ruttan, Vernon W. 1977. "The Green Revolution: Seven Generalizations." *International Development Review* 19, 4 (December): 16–22.

Sabatier, Paul. 1988. "An Advocacy Coalition Framework of Policy Change and the Role of Policy-Oriented Learning Therein." *Policy Sciences* 21: 129–68.

Sanderson, Steven E. 1986. *The Transformation of Mexican Agriculture*. Princeton: Princeton University Press.

Satpathy, T. 1984. *Irrigation and Economic Development*. New Delhi: Ashish Publishing House.

Schultz, Theodore W. 1964. *Transforming Traditional Agriculture*. New Haven, Conn.: Yale University Press.

Scott, James C. 1985. *Weapons of the Weak: Everyday Forms of Peasant Resistance*. New Haven: Yale University Press.

Secrett, Charles. 1986. "The Environmental Impact of Transmigration." *The Ecologist* 16, 2/3: 77–88.

Selznick, Philip. 1949. *TVA and the Grass Roots*. Berkeley: University of California Press.

Sewell, John W. 1989. "No Longer a Tradeoff." *Foundation News* September/October: 56–8.

Shane, Douglas R. 1986. *Hoofprints in the Forest: Cattle Ranching and the Destruction of Latin America's Tropical Forests*. Philadelphia: Institute for the Study of Human Issues.

Sharma, K. K. 1987. "Modest Tree Farming in Haryana." Unpublished paper prepared for the Program in International Development Policy, Duke University. November.

Shingi, Prakash M., M. S. Patel and Sanjay Wadwalkar. 1986. *Development of Social Forestry in India*. New Delhi: Oxford and IBH Publishing Company for Indian Institute of Management.

Shiva, Vandana, H. C. Sharatchandra, and J. Bandyopadhyay. 1982. "Social Forestry: No Solution Within the Market." *The Ecologist* 12, 4: 158–68.

Sinha, K. K. 1977. *Indian Water Resources and Power*. Calcutta: Jijnasa.

Siriwardhana, S. 1981. *Emerging Income Inequalities and Forms of Hidden Tenancy in the Mahaweli H Area*. Colombo: People's Bank Research Department.

Smith, Geoffrey A. J. 1987. "Campa Indian Agriculture in the Gran Pajonal of Peru," in Carl F. Jordan, ed., *Amazonian Rain Forests: Ecosystem Disturbance and Recovery*. New York. Springer-Verlag. 34–35.

Sri Lanka, Ministry of Finance and Planning. 1983. *Public Investment 1983–87*. Colombo: National Planning Division.

———. 1985. *Public Investment 1985–89*. Colombo: National Planning Division.

Sri Lanka, Ministry of Mahaweli Development. 1982. *Mahaweli Projects and Programme 1982*. Colombo: Information Service, Ministry of Lands and Land Development and the Ministry of Mahaweli Development.

Stakman, E. C., Richard Bradfield, and Paul C. Mangelsdorf. 1967. *Campaigns Against Hunger*. Cambridge: Belknap Press of Harvard University.

Streeten, Paul. 1987. *What Price Food: Agricultural Price Policies in Developing Countries*. New York: St. Martin's Press.

Stroup, Richard L., and John A. Baden. 1983. *Natural Resources: Bureaucratic Myths and Environmental Management*. Cambridge: Ballinger.

Suratman, and P. Guiness. 1977. "The Changing Focus of Transmigration." *Bulletin of Indonesian Economic Studies* 13, 2: 78–101.

Suryawanshi, S. D. 1986. "Policies and Problems in the Use of Irrigation Water under

Maharashtra Water Utilisation Projects." [abstract] *Indian Journal of Agricultural Economics* 41, 4 (October-December): 540–41.

Teece, David. 1987. "Brazil's Greater Carajas Programme." *The Ecologist* 17, 2/3: 75.

Thakurta, P. G. 1989. "Funding Fracas." *India Today* (May 31): 90–91.

UNESCO. 1983. *Swidden Cultivation in Asia.* Bangkok: UNESCO. 3 vols.

United Nations Industrial Development Organization. 1986. *Sri Lanka.* Vienna: UNIDO.

U.S. National Research Council. 1986. *Proceedings of the Conference on Common-Property Resource Management.* Washington, D.C.: National Academy Press.

Van der Wijst, Ton. 1985. "Transmigration: An Evaluation of a Population Redistribution Policy." *Population and Policy Review* 4: 1–30.

Ward, Barbara, and Rene Dubos. 1972. *Only One Earth.* New York: Norton.

Weir, David. 1981. *Circle of Poison: Pesticides and People in a Hungry World.* San Francisco: Institute for Food and Development Policy.

Whitmore, J. L. 1981. "Plantations vs. Other Land Use Options in Latin America." In *Proceedings of XVIII IUFRO World Congress, Japan.* Vienna. IUFRO Secretariat. 448–62.

Wijesinghe, Mallory E. 1981. *Sri Lanka's Development Thrust.* Colombo: Aitken Spence and Company.

Williams, Robert G. 1986. *Export Agriculture and the Crisis in Central America.* Chapel Hill: University of North Carolina Press.

World Bank. 1978. *Development in Sri Lanka: Issues and Prospects.* Washington, D.C.: World Bank.

———. 1983. *Focus on Poverty.* Washington, D.C.: World Bank. 4–8.

———. 1988. *Environment and Development: Implementing the World Bank's New Policies.* Washington, D.C.: World Bank.

World Commission on Environment and Development. 1987. *Our Common Future.* Oxford: Oxford University Press.

World Resources Institute and International Institute for Environment and Development. 1988. *World Resources 1988–89.* New York: Basic Books.

Yates, P. Lamartine. 1981. *Mexico's Agricultural Dilemma.* Tucson: University of Arizona Press.

Yudelman, M. 1989. "The World Bank Turns to Rural Development." Ms. in preparation.

Zobel, Bruce. 1987. *Growing Exotic Forests.* New York: Wiley.

About the Authors

William Ascher is Professor of Public Policy Studies and Political Science at Duke University, where he directs the Program in International Development Policy. He has written two books on political-economic forecasting and planning, and another book on income redistribution in Latin America. Professor Ascher has also served as the project director for the International Commission for Central American Recovery and Development. He holds a Ph.D. in Political Science from Yale University.

Robert Healy is a Professor in the Duke University School of Forestry and Environmental Studies specializing in natural resources and environmental policy. He is also a Senior Fellow at the Conservation Foundation/World Wildlife Fund, Washington, D.C. He is the author or co-author of six previous books on natural resource topics.

Library of Congress Cataloging-in-Publication Data
Ascher, William.
Natural resource policymaking in developing countries: environment, economic growth, and
income distribution / William Ascher & Robert Healy.
Includes bibliographical references (p.
ISBN 0–8223–1034–1. — ISBN 0–8223–1049–X (pbk.)
1. Natural resources—Government policy—Developing countries.   2. Developing
countries—Economic policy.   I. Healy, Robert G.   II. Title.
HC59.7.A834   1990
333.7'09172'4—dc20   90–2743   CIP